ABOUT THIS PUBLICATION

FOR SERVICE ASSISTANCE

Customer Service
1.704.898.0770

North Carolina General Statues is published by The Muliti-Media Group of Greater Charlotte in Charlotte, North Carolina. Copyright 2015 by the Multi-Media Group of Greater Charlotte. This book or parts thereof may not be reproduced in any form, stored in a retrieval system, or transmitted in any form by any means—electronic, mechanical, photocopy, recording or otherwise—without prior written permission of the publisher, except as provided by United States of America copyright law.

The records required by U.S. Code 2257(a) through (c) and the pertinent regulations 28 C.F.R. Cli. 1, Part 75 with respect to this publication and all materials associated with such records are maintained by The Multi-Media Group of Greater Charlotte, Publisher and available for review by Attorney General.

www.visionbooks.org

Copyright © 2015 by MMGGC
All rights reserved!

TID: 5107876
ISBN (10) digit: 1503244229
ISBN (13) digit: 978-1503244221

123-4-56789-01239-Paperback
123-4-56789-01239-Hardback

First Edition

090520140547

Printed in the United States of America

2015 EDITION

North Carolina Criminal Law And Procedure-Pamphlet # 82

Printed In conjunction with the Administration of the Courts

North Carolina Criminal Law and Procedure
Pamphlet Reference Guide

Chapters	Pamphlet
Chapter 1 Civil Procedure	1
Chapter 1 Civil Procedure (Continue)	2
Chapter 1A Rules of Civil Procedure	2
Chapter 1B Contribution.	2
Chapter 1C Enforcement of Judgments.	2
Chapter 1D Punitive Damages.	2
Chapter 1E Eastern Band of Cherokee Indians.	2
Chapter 1F North Carolina Uniform Interstate Depositions and Discovery Act.	2
Chapter 2 - Clerk of Superior Court [Repealed and Transferred.]	3
Chapter 3 - Commissioners of Affidavits and Deeds [Repealed.]	3
Chapter 4 - Common Law	3
Chapter 5 - Contempt [Repealed.]	3
Chapter 5A - Contempt	3
Chapter 6 - Liability for Court Costs	3
Chapter 7 - Courts [Repealed and Transferred.]	3
Chapter 7A – Judicial Department	3
Chapter 7A – Continuation (Judicial Department)	4
Chapter 7A – Continuation (Judicial Department)	5
Chapter 7B - Juvenile Code	5
Chapter 8 - Evidence	6
Chapter 8A - Interpreters for Deaf Persons [Recodified.]	6
Chapter 8B - Interpreters for Deaf Persons	6
Chapter 8C - Evidence Code	6
Chapter 9 - Jurors	6
Chapter 10 - Notaries [Repealed.]	6
Chapter 10A - Notaries [Recodified.]	6
Chapter 10B - Notaries	6
Chapter 11 - Oaths	6
Chapter 12 - Statutory Construction	6
Chapter 13 - Citizenship Restored	6
Chapter 14 - Criminal Law	7
Chapter 14 –Criminal Law (Continuation)	8
Chapter 15 - Criminal Procedure	9
Chapter 15A - Criminal Procedure Act (Continuation)	10
Chapter 15A - Criminal Procedure Act (Continuation)	11
Chapter 15B - Victims Compensation	11
Chapter 15C - Address Confidentiality Program	11
Chapter 16 - Gaming Contracts and Futures	11
Chapter 17 - Habeas Corpus	11

Chapter 17A - Law-Enforcement Officers [Recodified.]	11
Chapter 17B - North Carolina Criminal Justice Education and Training System [Recodified.] Chapter 17C - North Carolina Criminal Justice Education and Training Standards Commission	11 11
Chapter 17D - North Carolina Justice Academy	11
Chapter 17E - North Carolina Sheriffs' Education and Training Standards Commission	11
Chapter 18 - Regulation of Intoxicating Liquors [Repealed.]	12
Chapter 18A - Regulation of Intoxicating Liquors [Repealed.]	12
Chapter 18B - Regulation of Alcoholic Beverages	12
Chapter 18C - North Carolina State Lottery	12
Chapter 19 - Offenses against Public Morals	12
Chapter 19A - Protection of Animals	12
Chapter 20 - Motor Vehicles	13
Chapter 20 - Motor Vehicles (Continuation)	14
Chapter 20 - Motor Vehicles (Continuation)	15
Chapter 20 - Motor Vehicles (Continuation)	16
Chapter 21 - Bills of Lading	17
Chapter 22 - Contracts Requiring Writing	17
Chapter 22A - Signatures	17
Chapter 22B - Contracts Against Public Policy	17
Chapter 22C - Payments to Subcontractors	17
Chapter 23 - Debtor and Creditor	17
Chapter 24 – Interest	17
Chapter 25 – Uniform Commercial Code	18
Chapter 25 – Uniform Commercial Code (Continuation)	19
Chapter 25A – Retail Installment Sales Act	20
Chapter 25B - Credit	20
Chapter 25C - Sales of Artwork	20
Chapter 26 - Suretyship	20
Chapter 27 - Warehouse Receipts [Repealed.]	20
Chapter 28 - Administration [Repealed.]	20
Chapter 28A - Administration of Decedents' Estates	20
Chapter 28B - Estates of Absentees in Military Service	20
Chapter 28C - Estates of Missing Persons	20
Chapter 29 - Intestate Succession	21
Chapter 30 - Surviving Spouses	21
Chapter 31 - Wills	21
Chapter 31A - Acts Barring Property Rights	21
Chapter 31B - Renunciation of Property and Renunciation of Fiduciary Powers Act	21
Chapter 31C - Uniform Disposition of Community Property Rights at Death Act	21
Chapter 32 - Fiduciaries	21
Chapter 32A - Powers of Attorney	21
Chapter 33 - Guardian and Ward [Repealed and Recodified.]	21

Chapter 33A - North Carolina Uniform Transfers to Minors Act	21
Chapter 33B - North Carolina Uniform Custodial Trust Act	21
Chapter 34 - Veterans' Guardianship Act	22
Chapter 35 - Sterilization Procedures	22
Chapter 35A - Incompetency and Guardianship	22
Chapter 36 - Trusts and Trustees [Repealed.]	22
Chapter 36A - Trusts and Trustees	22
Chapter 36B - Uniform Management of Institutional Funds Act [Repealed.]	22
Chapter 36C - North Carolina Uniform Trust Code	22
Chapter 36D - North Carolina Community Third Party Trusts, Pooled Trusts	23
Chapter 36E - Uniform Prudent Management of Institutional Funds Act	23
Chapter 37 - Allocation of Principal and Income [Repealed.]	23
Chapter 37A - Uniform Principal and Income Act	23
Chapter 38 - Boundaries	23
Chapter 38A - Landowner Liability	23
Chapter 39 - Conveyances	23
Chapter 39A - Transfer Fee Covenants Prohibited	23
Chapter 40 - Eminent Domain [Repealed.]	23
Chapter 40A - Eminent Domain	23
Chapter 41 - Estates	23
Chapter 41A - State Fair Housing Act	23
Chapter 42 - Landlord and Tenant	23
Chapter 42A - Vacation Rental Act	23
Chapter 43 - Land Registration	23
Chapter 44 - Liens	24
Chapter 44A - Statutory Liens and Charges	24
Chapter 45 - Mortgages and Deeds of Trust	24
Chapter 45A - Good Funds Settlement Act	24
Chapter 46 - Partition	24
Chapter 47 - Probate and Registration	25
Chapter 47A - Unit Ownership	25
Chapter 47B - Real Property Marketable Title Act	25
Chapter 47C - North Carolina Condominium Act	25
Chapter 47D - Notice of Settlement Act [Expired.]	25
Chapter 47E - Residential Property Disclosure Act	25
Chapter 47F - North Carolina Planned Community Act	25
Chapter 47G - Option to Purchase Contracts	25
Chapter 47H - Contracts for Deed	25
Chapter 48 - Adoptions	26
Chapter 48A - Minors	26
Chapter 49 - Bastardy	26
Chapter 49A - Rights of Children	26
Chapter 50 - Divorce and Alimony	26
Chapter 50A - Uniform Child-Custody Jurisdiction and	

Enforcement Act	26
Chapter 50B - Domestic Violence	26
Chapter 50C - Civil No-Contact Orders	26
Chapter 51 - Marriage	26
Chapter 52 - Powers and Liabilities of Married Persons	27
Chapter 52A - Uniform Reciprocal Enforcement of Support Act [Repealed.]	27
Chapter 52B - Uniform Premarital Agreement Act	27
Chapter 52C - Uniform Interstate Family Support Act	27
Chapter 53 - Banks	27
Chapter 53A - Business Development Corporations and North Carolina Capital Resource Corporations	28
Chapter 53B - Financial Privacy Act	28
Chapter 54 - Cooperative Organizations	28
Chapter 54A - Capital Stock Savings and Loan Associations [Repealed.]	28
Chapter 54B - Savings and Loan Associations	29
Chapter 54C - Savings Banks	29
Chapter 55 - North Carolina Business Corporation Act	30
Chapter 55A - North Carolina Nonprofit Corporation Act	31
Chapter 55B - Professional Corporation Act	31
Chapter 55C - Foreign Trade Zones	31
Chapter 55D - Filings, Names, and Registered Agents for Corporations, Nonprofit Corporations, and Partnerships	31
Chapter 56 - Electric, Telegraph and Power Companies [Repealed.]	31
Chapter 57 - Hospital, Medical and Dental Service Corporations [Recodified.]	31
Chapter 57A - Health Maintenance Organization Act [Recodified.]	31
Chapter 57B - Health Maintenance Organization Act [Recodified.]	31
Chapter 57C - North Carolina Limited Liability Company Act.	31
Chapter 58 - Insurance.	32
Chapter 58 - Insurance (Continuation)	33
Chapter 58 - Insurance (Continuation)	34
Chapter 58 - Insurance (Continuation)	35
Chapter 58 - Insurance (Continuation)	36
Chapter 58 - Insurance (Continuation)	37
Chapter 58 - Insurance (Continuation)	38
Chapter 58A - North Carolina Health Insurance Trust Commission [Recodified.]	38
Chapter 59 - Partnership.	39
Chapter 59B - Uniform Unincorporated Nonprofit Association Act.	39
Chapter 60 - Railroads and Other Carriers [Repealed and Transferred.]	39
Chapter 61 - Religious Societies	39
Chapter 62 - Public Utilities	39

Chapter 62 - Public Utilities (Continuation)	40
Chapter 62A - Public Safety Telephone Service And Wireless Telephone Service	40
Chapter 63 - Aeronautics	40
Chapter 63A - North Carolina Global TransPark Authority	40
Chapter 64 - Aliens	40
Chapter 65 – Cemeteries	40
Chapter 66 - Commerce and Business	41
Chapter 67 - Dogs	41
Chapter 68 - Fences and Stock Law	41
Chapter 69 - Fire Protection	41
Chapter 70 - Indian Antiquities, Archaeological Resources and Unmarked Human Skeletal Remains Protection	42
Chapter 71 - Indians [Repealed.]	42
Chapter 71A - Indians	42
Chapter 72 - Inns, Hotels and Restaurants	42
Chapter 73 - Mills	42
Chapter 74 - Mines and Quarries	42
Chapter 74A - Company Police [Repealed.]	42
Chapter 74B - Private Protective Services Act [Repealed.]	42
Chapter 74C - Private Protective Services	42
Chapter 74D - Alarm Systems	42
Chapter 74E - Company Police Act	42
Chapter 74F - Locksmith Licensing Act	42
Chapter 74G - Campus Police Act	42
Chapter 75 - Monopolies, Trusts and Consumer Protection	42
Chapter 75A - Boating and Water Safety	43
Chapter 75B - Discrimination in Business	43
Chapter 75C - Motion Picture Fair Competition Act	43
Chapter 75D - Racketeer Influenced and Corrupt Organizations	43
Chapter 75E - Unlawful Activities in Connection With Certain Corporate Transactions	43
Chapter 76 - Navigation	43
Chapter 76A - Navigation and Pilotage Commissions	43
Chapter 77 - Rivers, Creeks, and Coastal Waters	43
Chapter 78 - Securities Law [Repealed.]	43
Chapter 78A - North Carolina Securities Act	43
Chapter 78B - Tender Offer Disclosure Act [Repealed.]	43
Chapter 78C - Investment Advisers	43
Chapter 78D - Commodities Act	43
Chapter 79 - Strays [Repealed.]	43
Chapter 80 - Trademarks, Brands, etc.	44
Chapter 81 - Weights and Measures [Recodified.]	44
Chapter 81A - Weights and Measures Act of 1975.	44
Chapter 82 - Wrecks [Repealed.]	44
Chapter 83 - Architects [Recodified.]	44

Chapter 83A - Architects	44
Chapter 84 - Attorneys-at-Law	44
Chapter 84A - Foreign Legal Consultants	44
Chapter 85 - Auctions and Auctioneers [Repealed.]	44
Chapter 85A - Bail Bondsmen and Runners [Recodified.]	44
Chapter 85B - Auctions and Auctioneers	44
Chapter 85C - Bail Bondsmen and Runners [Recodified.]	44
Chapter 86 - Barbers [Recodified.]	44
Chapter 86A - Barbers	44
Chapter 87 - Contractors	44
Chapter 88 - Cosmetic Art [Repealed.]	44
Chapter 88A - Electrolysis Practice Act	44
Chapter 88B - Cosmetic Art	45
Chapter 89 - Engineering and Land Surveying [Recodified.]	45
Chapter 89A - Landscape Architects	45
Chapter 89B - Foresters	45
Chapter 89C - Engineering and Land Surveying	45
Chapter 89D - Landscape Contractors	45
Chapter 89E - Geologists Licensing Act	45
Chapter 89F - North Carolina Soil Scientist Licensing Act	45
Chapter 89G - Irrigation Contractors	45
Chapter 90 - Medicine and Allied Occupations	45
Chapter 90 - Medicine and Allied Occupations (Continuation)	46
Chapter 90 - Medicine and Allied Occupations (Continuation)	47
Chapter 90 - Medicine and Allied Occupations (Continuation)	48
Chapter 90A - Sanitarians and Water and Wastewater Treatment Facility Operators	48
Chapter 90B - Social Worker Certification and Licensure Act	48
Chapter 90C - North Carolina Recreational Therapy Licensure Act	48
Chapter 90D - Interpreters and Transliterators	48
Chapter 91 - Pawnbrokers [Repealed.]	48
Chapter 91A - Pawnbrokers Modernization Act of 1989	48
Chapter 92 - Photographers [Deleted.]	48
Chapter 93 - Certified Public Accountants	48
Chapter 93A - Real Estate License Law	49
Chapter 93B - Occupational Licensing Boards	49
Chapter 93C - Watchmakers [Repealed.]	49
Chapter 93D - North Carolina State Hearing Aid Dealers and Fitters Board.	49
Chapter 93E - North Carolina Appraisers Act	49
Chapter 94 - Apprenticeship	49
Chapter 95 - Department of Labor and Labor Regulations	49
Chapter 95 - Department of Labor and Labor Regulations (Continuation)	50
Chapter 96 - Employment Security	50
Chapter 97 - Workers' Compensation Act	50
Chapter 97 - Workers' Compensation Act (Continuation)	51

Chapter 98 - Burnt and Lost Records	51
Chapter 99 - Libel and Slander	51
Chapter 99A - Civil Remedies for Criminal Actions	51
Chapter 99B - Products Liability	51
Chapter 99C - Actions Relating to Winter Sports Safety and Accidents	51
Chapter 99D - Civil Rights	51
Chapter 99E - Special Liability Provisions	51
Chapter 100 - Monuments, Memorials and Parks	51
Chapter 101 - Names of Persons	51
Chapter 102 - Official Survey Base	51
Chapter 103 - Sundays, Holidays and Special Days	51
Chapter 104 - United States Lands	51
Chapter 104A - Degrees of Kinship	51
Chapter 104B - Hurricanes or Other Acts of Nature	51
Chapter 104C - Atomic Energy, Radioactivity and Ionizing Radiation [Repealed and Recodified.]	51
Chapter 104D - Southern States Energy Compact	51
Chapter 104E - North Carolina Radiation Protection Act	51
Chapter 104F - Southeast Interstate Low-Level Radioactive Waste Management Compact [Repealed]	51
Chapter 104G - North Carolina Low-Level Radioactive Waste Management Authority Act of 1987 [Repealed]	51
Chapter 105 - Taxation	51
Chapter 105 - Taxation (Continuation)	52
Chapter 105 - Taxation (Continuation)	53
Chapter 105 - Taxation (Continuation)	54
Chapter 105A - Setoff Debt Collection Act	55
Chapter 105B - Defaulted Student Loan Recovery Act	55
Chapter 106 - Agriculture	55
Chapter 106 - Agriculture (Continue)	56
Chapter 106 - Agriculture (Continue)	57
Chapter 107 - Agricultural Development Districts [Repealed.]	57
Chapter 108 - Social Services [Repealed and Recodified.]	57
Chapter 108A - Social Services	57
Chapter 108B - Community Action Programs	58
Chapter 108C Medicaid and Health Choice Provider Requirements.	58
Chapter 108D Medicaid Managed Care for Behavioral Health Services.	58
Chapter 109 - Bonds [Recodified.]	58
Chapter 110 - Child Welfare	58
Chapter 111 - Aid to the Blind	58
Chapter 112 - Confederate Homes and Pensions [Repealed.]	58
Chapter 113 - Conservation and Development	58
Chapter 113 - Conservation and Development (Continuation)	59

Chapter 113A - Pollution Control and Environment	59
Chapter 113A - Pollution Control and Environment (Continuation)	60
Chapter 113B - North Carolina Energy Policy Act of 1975	60
Chapter 114 - Department of Justice	60
Chapter 115 - Elementary and Secondary Education [Repealed.]	60
Chapter 115A - Community Colleges, Technical Institutes, and Industrial Education Centers [Repealed.]	60
Chapter 115B - Tuition and Fee Waivers	60
Chapter 115C - Elementary and Secondary Education	60
Chapter 115C - Elementary and Secondary Education (Continuation)	61
Chapter 115C - Elementary and Secondary Education (Continuation)	62
Chapter 115C - Elementary and Secondary Education (Continuation)	63
Chapter 115D - Community Colleges	63
Chapter 115E - Private Educational Facilities Finance Act [Recodified]	63
Chapter 116 - Higher Education	63
Chapter 116 - Higher Education (Continuation)	63
Chapter 116A - Escheats and Abandoned Property [Repealed.]	64
Chapter 116B - Escheats and Abandoned Property	64
Chapter 116C - Continuum of Education Programs	64
Chapter 116D - Higher Education Bonds	64
Chapter 116E -Education Longitudinal Data System	64
Chapter 117 - Electrification	64
Chapter 118 - Firemen's and Rescue Squad Workers' Relief and Pension Funds [Recodified.]	64
Chapter 118A - Firemen's Death Benefit Act [Repealed.]	64
Chapter 118B - Members of a Rescue Squad Death Benefit Act [Repealed.]	64
Chapter 119 - Gasoline and Oil Inspection and Regulation	64
Chapter 120 - General Assembly	65
Chapter 120 - General Assembly (Continuation)	66
Chapter 120 - General Assembly (Continuation)	67
Chapter 120C - Lobbying	67
Chapter 121 - Archives and History	67
Chapter 122 - Hospitals for the Mentally Disordered [Repealed.]	67
Chapter 122A - North Carolina Housing Finance Agency	67
Chapter 122B - North Carolina Agricultural Facilities Finance Act [Repealed.]	67
Chapter 122C - Mental Health, Developmental Disabilities, and Substance Abuse Act of 1985	67
Chapter 122C - Mental Health, Developmental Disabilities, and Substance Abuse Act of 1985 (Continuation)	68

Chapter 122D - North Carolina Agricultural Finance Act	68
Chapter 122E - North Carolina Housing Trust and Oil Overcharge Act	68
Chapter 123 - Impeachment	69
Chapter 123A - Industrial Development [Repealed.]	69
Chapter 124 - Internal Improvements	69
Chapter 125 - Libraries	69
Chapter 126 - State Personnel System	69
Chapter 127 - Militia [Repealed.]	69
Chapter 127A - Militia	69
Chapter 127B - Military Affairs	69
Chapter 127C - Advisory Commission on Military Affairs	69
Chapter 128 - Offices and Public Officers	69
Chapter 128 - Offices and Public Officers (Continuation)	70
Chapter 129 - Public Buildings and Grounds	70
Chapter 130 - Public Health [Repealed.]	70
Chapter 130A - Public Health	70
Chapter 130A - Public Health (Continuation)	71
Chapter 130A - Public Health (Continuation)	72
Chapter 130B - Hazardous Waste Management Commission [Repealed.]	72
Chapter 131 - Public Hospitals [Repealed.]	72
Chapter 131A - Health Care Facilities Finance Act	72
Chapter 131B - Licensing of Ambulatory Surgical Facilities [Repealed.]	72
Chapter 131C - Charitable Solicitation Licensure Act [Repealed.]	72
Chapter 131D - Inspection and Licensing of Facilities	72
Chapter 131E - Health Care Facilities and Services	72
Chapter 131E - Health Care Facilities and Services (Continuation)	73
Chapter 131F - Solicitation of Contributions	73
Chapter 132 - Public Records	73
Chapter 133 - Public Works	74
Chapter 134 - Youth Development [Recodified.]	74
Chapter 134A - Youth Services [Repealed.]	74
Chapter 135 - Retirement System for Teachers and State Employees; Social Security; Health Insurance Program for Children	74
Chapter 135 - Retirement System for Teachers and State Employees; Social Security; Health Insurance Program for Children	75
Chapter 136 - Transportation	75
Chapter 136 - Transportation (Continuation)	76
Chapter 137 - Rural Rehabilitation [Repealed.]	76
Chapter 138 - Salaries, Fees and Allowances	76
Chapter 138A - State Government Ethics Act	76

Chapter 139 - Soil and Water Conservation Districts	76
Chapter 140 - State Art Museum; Symphony and Art Societies	76
Chapter 140A - State Awards System	76
Chapter 141 - State Boundaries	76
Chapter 142 - State Debt	76
Chapter 143 - State Departments, Institutions, and Commissions	77
Chapter 143 - State Departments, Institutions, and Commissions (Continuation)	78
Chapter 143 - State Departments, Institutions, and Commissions (Continuation)	79
Chapter 143 - State Departments, Institutions, and Commissions (Continuation)	80
Chapter 143A - State Government Reorganization	80
Chapter 143B - Executive Organization Act of 1973	80
Chapter 143B - Executive Organization Act of 1973 (Continuation)	81
Chapter 143B - Executive Organization Act of 1973 (Continuation)	82
Chapter 143C - State Budget Act	83
Chapter 143D - The State Governmental Accountability and Internal Control Act	83
Chapter 144 - State Flag, Official Governmental Flags, Motto, and Colors	83
Chapter 145 - State Symbols and Other Official Adoptions.	83
Chapter 146 - State Lands	83
Chapter 147 - State Officers	83
Chapter 148 - State Prison System	84
Chapter 149 - State Song and Toast	84
Chapter 150 - Uniform Revocation of Licenses [Repealed.]	84
Chapter 150A - Administrative Procedure Act [Recodified.]	84
Chapter 150B - Administrative Procedure Act	84
Chapter 151 - Constables [Repealed.]	84
Chapter 152 - Coroners	84
Chapter 152A - County Medical Examiner [Repealed.]	84
Chapter 152A - County Medical Examiner [Repealed.] (Continuation)	84
Chapter 153 - Counties and County Commissioners [Repealed.]	84
Chapter 153A - Counties	84
Chapter 153A – Counties (Continue)	85
Chapter 153B - Mountain Resources Planning Act	85
Chapter 153C - Uwharrie Regional Resources Act	85
Chapter 154 - County Surveyor [Repealed.]	85
Chapter 155 - County Treasurer [Repealed.]	85

Chapter 156 - Drainage	85
Chapter 156 – Drainage (Continuation)	86
Chapter 157 - Housing Authorities and Projects	86
Chapter 157A - Historic Properties Commissions [Transferred.]	86
Chapter 158 - Local Development	86
Chapter 159 - Local Government Finance	86
Chapter 159 - Local Government Finance (Continuation)	87
Chapter 159A - Pollution Abatement and Industrial Facilities Financing Act [Unconstitutional.]	87
Chapter 159B - Joint Municipal Electric Power and Energy Act	87
Chapter 159C - Industrial and Pollution Control Facilities Financing Act	87
Chapter 159D - The North Carolina Capital Facilities Financing Act	87
Chapter 159E - Registered Public Obligations Act	87
Chapter 159F - North Carolina Energy Development Authority [Repealed.]	87
Chapter 159G - Water Infrastructure	87
Chapter 159H - [Reserved.]	87
Chapter 159I - Solid Waste Management Loan Program and Local Government Special Obligation Bonds	87
Chapter 160 - Municipal Corporations [Repealed And Transferred.]	87
Chapter 160A - Cities and Towns	88
Chapter 160A - Cities and Towns (Continuation)	89
Chapter 160B - Consolidated City-County Act	89
Chapter 160C - Baseball Park Districts [Repealed.]	90
Chapter 161 - Register of Deeds	90
Chapter 162 - Sheriff	90
Chapter 162A - Water and Sewer Systems	90
Chapter 162B Continuity of Local Government in Emergency.	90
Chapter 163 Elections and Election Laws.	90
Chapter 163 Elections and Election Laws. (Continuation)	91
Chapter 164 Concerning the General Statutes of North Carolina.	92
Chapter 165 Veterans.	92
Chapter 166 Civil Preparedness Agencies [Repealed.]	92
Chapter 166A North Carolina Emergency Management Act.	92
Chapter 167 State Civil Air Patrol [Repealed.]	92
Chapter 168 Persons with Disabilities.	92
Chapter 168A Persons With Disabilities Protection Act.	92

Part 11. North Carolina Manpower Council.

§§ 143B-395 through 143B-396: Repealed by Session Laws 1977, c. 771, s. 14.

Part 12. Standardization Committee.

§§ 143B-397 through 143B-398: Repealed by Session Laws 1983, c. 717, s. 81.

Part 13. Veterans' Affairs Commission.

§ 143B-399. Veterans' Affairs Commission - creation, powers and duties.

There is hereby created the Veterans' Affairs Commission of the Department of Administration. The Veterans' Affairs Commission shall have the following functions and duties:

(1)   To advise the Governor on matters relating to the affairs of veterans in North Carolina;

(2)   To maintain a continuing review of the operation and budgeting of existing programs for veterans and their dependents in the State and to make any recommendations to the Governor for improvements and additions to such matters to which the Governor shall give due consideration;

(3)   To serve collectively as a liaison between the Division of Veterans Affairs and the veterans organizations represented on the Commission;

(4)   To promulgate rules and regulations concerning the awarding of scholarships for children of North Carolina veterans as provided by Article 4 of Chapter 165 of the General Statutes of North Carolina. The Commission shall make rules and regulations consistent with the provisions of this Chapter. All rules and regulations not inconsistent with the provisions of this Chapter heretofore adopted by the State Board of Veterans' Affairs shall remain in full force and effect unless and until repealed or superseded by action of the Veterans Affairs Commission. All rules and regulations adopted by the Commission shall be enforced by the Division of Veterans' Affairs;

(4a)   To promulgate rules concerning the awarding of the North Carolina Services Medal to all veterans who have served in any period of war as defined in 38 U.S.C. § 101. The award shall be self-financing; those who wish to be awarded the medal shall pay a fee to cover the expenses of producing the medal and awarding the medal. All rules adopted by the Commission with respect to the North Carolina Services Medal shall be implemented and enforced by the Division of Veterans' Affairs; and

(5)   To advise the Governor on any matter the Governor may refer to it. (1973, c. 620, s. 7; 1977, c. 70, ss. 24, 25, 27; c. 622; 1991 (Reg. Sess., 1992), c. 998, s. 1; 1993, c. 553, s. 47.)

§ 143B-400. Veterans' Affairs Commission - members; selection; quorum; compensation.

The Veterans' Affairs Commission of the Department of Administration shall consist of one voting member from each congressional district, all of whom shall be veterans, appointed by the Governor for four-year terms. In making these appointments, the Governor shall insure that both major political parties will be continuously represented on the Veterans' Affairs Commission.

The initial members of the Commission shall be the appointed members of the current Veterans' Affairs Commission who shall serve for the remainder of their current terms and six additional members appointed by the Governor for terms expiring June 30, 1981. Thereafter, all members shall be appointed for terms of four years. Any appointment to fill a vacancy on the Commission created by the resignation, dismissal, death or disability of a member shall be for the balance of the unexpired term. The Governor shall have the power to remove any member of the Commission in accordance with provisions of G.S. 143B-13.

In the event that more than 11 congressional districts are established in the State, the Governor shall on July 1 following the establishment of such additional congressional districts appoint a member of the Commission from that congressional district. If on July 1, 1977, or at any time thereafter due to congressional redistricting, two or more members of the Veterans' Affairs Commission shall reside in the same congressional district then such members shall continue to serve as members of the Commission for a period equal to the remainder of their current terms on the Commission provided that upon the expiration of said term or terms the Governor shall fill such vacancy or vacancies in such a manner as to insure that as expeditiously as possible there is one member of the Veterans' Affairs Commission who is a resident of each congressional district in the State.

The Governor shall designate from the membership of the Commission a chairman and vice-chairman of the Commission who shall serve at the pleasure of the Governor. The Secretary of the Department of Administration or his designee shall serve as secretary of the Commission.

Members of the Commission shall receive per diem and necessary travel and subsistence expenses in accordance with provisions of G.S. 138-5.

A majority of the Commission shall constitute a quorum for the transaction of business.

The Veterans' Affairs Commission shall meet at least twice a year and may hold special meetings at any time or place within the State at the call of the chairman, at the call of the Secretary of the Department of Administration or upon the written request of at least six members.

All clerical and other services required by the Commission shall be provided by the Secretary of the Department of Administration. (1973, c. 620, s. 8; 1977, c. 70, ss. 24, 25, 27; c. 637, s. 1.)

§ 143B-401. Veterans' Affairs Commission Advisory Committee - members; compensation.

The department commander or official head of each veterans' organization which has been chartered by an act of the United States Congress and which is legally constituted and operating in this State pursuant to said charter shall constitute an Advisory Committee to the Veterans' Affairs Commission. Members of the Veterans' Affairs Commission Advisory Committee shall receive per diem and necessary travel and subsistence expenses in accordance with the provisions of G.S. 138-5. (1977, c. 637, s. 3.)

Part 14. Advocacy Council for the Handicapped.

§§ 143B-402, 143B-403: Repealed by Session Laws 1979, c. 575, s. 1.

Part 14A. Governor's Advocacy Council for Persons with Disabilities.

§ 143B-403.1: Repealed by Session Laws 2007-323, s. 19.1(a), effective July 1, 2007.

§ 143B-403.2: Repealed by Session Laws 2007-323, s. 19.1(a), effective July 1, 2007.

Part 15. North Carolina State Commission of Indian Affairs.

§ 143B-404. North Carolina State Commission of Indian Affairs - creation; name.

There is hereby created and established the North Carolina State Commission of Indian Affairs. The Commission shall be administered under the direction and supervision of the Department of Administration pursuant to G.S. 143A-6(b) and (c). (1977, c. 849, s. 1; 1977, 2nd Sess., c. 1189.)

§ 143B-405. North Carolina State Commission of Indian Affairs - purposes for creation.

The purposes of the Commission shall be as follows:

(1) To deal fairly and effectively with Indian affairs.

(2) To bring local, State, and federal resources into focus for the implementation or continuation of meaningful programs for Indian citizens of the State of North Carolina.

(3) To provide aid and protection for Indians as needs are demonstrated; to prevent undue hardships.

(4) To hold land in trust for the benefit of State-recognized Indian tribes. This subdivision shall not apply to federally recognized Indian tribes.

(5)   To assist Indian communities in social and economic development.

(6)   To promote recognition of and the right of Indians to pursue cultural and religious traditions considered by them to be sacred and meaningful to Native Americans. (1977, c. 849, s. 1; 1977, 2nd Sess., c. 1189; 2001-344, s. 1; 2006-264, s. 15.)

§ 143B-406. North Carolina State Commission of Indian Affairs - duties; use of funds.

(a)   The Commission shall have the following duties:

(1)   To study, consider, accumulate, compile, assemble and disseminate information on any aspect of Indian affairs.

(2)   To investigate relief needs of Indians of North Carolina and to provide technical assistance in the preparation of plans for the alleviation of such needs.

(3)   To confer with appropriate officials of local, State and federal governments and agencies of these governments, and with such congressional committees that may be concerned with Indian affairs to encourage and implement coordination of applicable resources to meet the needs of Indians in North Carolina.

(4)   To cooperate with and secure the assistance of the local, State and federal governments or any agencies thereof in formulating any such programs, and to coordinate such programs with any programs regarding Indian affairs adopted or planned by the federal government to the end that the State Commission of Indian Affairs secure the full benefit of such programs.

(5)   To act as trustee for any interest in real property that may be transferred to the Commission for the benefit of State-recognized Indian tribes in accordance with a trust agreement approved by the Commission. The Commission shall not hold any interest in real property for the benefit of federally recognized Indian tribes.

(6)   To review all proposed or pending State legislation and amendments to existing State legislation affecting Indians in North Carolina.

(7) To conduct public hearings on matters relating to Indian affairs and to subpoena any information or documents deemed necessary by the Commission.

(8) To study the existing status of recognition of all Indian groups, tribes and communities presently existing in the State of North Carolina.

(9) To establish appropriate procedures to provide for legal recognition by the State of presently unrecognized groups.

(10) To provide for official State recognition by the Commission of such groups.

(11) To initiate procedures for their recognition by the federal government.

(b) The Commission may adopt rules to implement the provisions of subdivision (a)(5) of this section. (1977, c. 849, s. 1; 1977, 2nd Sess., c. 1189; 001-344, s. 2.)

§ 143B-407. North Carolina State Commission of Indian Affairs - membership; term of office; chairman; compensation.

(a) The State Commission of Indian Affairs shall consist of two persons appointed by the General Assembly, the Secretary of Health and Human Services, the Assistant Secretary of Commerce in charge of the Division of Employment Security, the Secretary of Administration, the Secretary of Environment and Natural Resources, the Commissioner of Labor or their designees and 21 representatives of the Indian community. These Indian members shall be selected by tribal or community consent from the Indian groups that are recognized by the State of North Carolina and are principally geographically located as follows: the Coharie of Sampson and Harnett Counties; the Eastern Band of Cherokees; the Haliwa Saponi of Halifax, Warren, and adjoining counties; the Lumbees of Robeson, Hoke and Scotland Counties; the Meherrin of Hertford County; the Waccamaw-Siouan from Columbus and Bladen Counties; the Sappony; the Occaneechi Band of the Saponi Nation of Alamance and Orange Counties, and the Native Americans located in Cumberland, Guilford, Johnston, Mecklenburg, Orange, and Wake Counties. The Coharie shall have two members; the Eastern Band of Cherokees, two; the Haliwa Saponi, two; the Lumbees, three; the Meherrin, one;

the Waccamaw-Siouan, two; the Sappony, one; the Cumberland County Association for Indian People, two; the Guilford Native Americans, two; the Metrolina Native Americans, two; the Occaneechi Band of the Saponi Nation, one, the Triangle Native American Society, one. Of the two appointments made by the General Assembly, one shall be made upon the recommendation of the Speaker, and one shall be made upon recommendation of the President Pro Tempore of the Senate. Appointments by the General Assembly shall be made in accordance with G.S. 120-121 and vacancies shall be filled in accordance with G.S. 120-122.

(b) Members serving by virtue of their office within State government shall serve so long as they hold that office. Members representing Indian tribes and groups shall be elected by the tribe or group concerned and shall serve for three-year terms except that at the first election of Commission members by tribes and groups one member from each tribe or group shall be elected to a one-year term, one member from each tribe or group to a two-year term, and one member from the Lumbees to a three-year term. The initial appointment from the Indians of Person County shall expire on June 30, 1999. The initial appointment from the Triangle Native American Society shall expire June 30, 2003. The initial appointment of the Occaneechi Band of the Saponi Nation shall expire June 30, 2005. Thereafter, all Commission members will be elected to three-year terms. All members shall hold their offices until their successors are appointed and qualified. Vacancies occurring on the Commission shall be filled by the tribal council or governing body concerned. Any member appointed to fill a vacancy shall be appointed for the remainder of the term of the member causing the vacancy. The Governor shall appoint a chairman of the Commission from among the Indian members of the Commission, subject to ratification by the full Commission. The initial appointments by the General Assembly shall expire on June 30, 1983. Thereafter, successors shall serve for terms of two years.

In the event that a vacancy occurs among the membership representing Indian tribes and groups and the vacancy temporarily cannot be filled by the tribe or group for any reason, the Commission membership may designate a tribal or group member to serve on the Commission on an interim basis until the tribe or group is able to select a permanent member to fill the vacancy. The service of the interim member shall terminate immediately upon appointment by the tribe or group of a member to fill the vacancy in its membership.

(c) Commission members who are seated by virtue of their office within the State government shall be compensated at the rate specified in G.S. 138-6.

Commission members who are members of the General Assembly shall be compensated at the rate specified in G.S. 120-3.1. Indian members of the commission shall be compensated at the rate specified in G.S. 138-5. (1977, c. 771, s. 4; c. 849, s. 1; 1977, 2nd Sess., c. 1189; 1981, c. 47, s. 5; 1981 (Reg. Sess., 1982), c. 1191, ss. 74, 76; 1989, c. 727, s. 218(149); 1991, c. 467, s. 1; 1995, c. 490, s. 27; 1997-147, s. 2; 1997-293, s. 2; 1997-443, ss. 11A.118(a), 11A.119(a); 2001-318, s. 1; 2002-126, s. 19.1A(a); 2003-87, s. 2; 2009-39, s. 1; 2011-401, s. 3.20.)

§ 143B-408. North Carolina State Commission of Indian Affairs - meetings; quorum; proxy vote.

(a)   The Commission shall meet quarterly, and at any other such time that it shall deem necessary. Meetings may be called by the chairman or by a petition signed by a majority of the members of the Commission. Ten days' notice shall be given in writing prior to the meeting date.

(b)   Simple majority of the Indian members of the Commission must be present to constitute a quorum.

(c)   Proxy vote shall not be permitted. (1977, c. 849, s. 1; 1977, 2nd Sess., c. 1189.)

§ 143B-409. North Carolina State Commission of Indian Affairs - reports.

The Commission shall prepare a written annual report giving an account of its proceedings, transactions, findings, and recommendations. This report shall be submitted to the Governor and the legislature. The report will become a matter of public record and will be maintained in the State Historical Archives. It may also be furnished to such other persons or agencies as the Commission may deem proper. (1977, c. 849, s. 1; 1977, 2nd Sess., c. 1189.)

§ 143B-410. North Carolina State Commission of Indian Affairs - fiscal records; clerical staff.

Fiscal records shall be kept by the Secretary of Administration. The audit report will become a part of the annual report and will be submitted in accordance with the regulations governing preparation and submission of the annual report. (1977, c. 849, s. 1; 1977, 2nd Sess., c. 1189; 1983, c. 913, s. 41.)

§ 143B-411. North Carolina State Commission of Indian Affairs - executive director; employees.

The Commission may, subject to legislative or other funds that would accrue to the Commission, employ an executive director to carry out the day-to-day responsibilities and business of the Commission. The executive director shall serve at the pleasure of the Commission. The executive director, also subject to legislative or other funds that would accrue to the Commission, may hire additional staff and consultants to assist in the discharge of his responsibilities, as determined by the Commission. The executive director shall not be a member of the Commission, and shall be of Indian descent. (1977, c. 849, s. 1; 1977, 2nd Sess., c. 1189; 1991, c. 88.)

Part 15A. North Carolina Advisory Council on the Eastern Band of the Cherokee.

§ 143B-411.1. North Carolina Advisory Council on the Eastern Band of the Cherokee - creation; membership; terms of office.

The North Carolina Advisory Council on the Eastern Band of the Cherokee is created in the Department of Administration. The Council shall consist of 16 members and shall include the following members: eight members shall be appointed by the Chief with the consent of the Tribal Council of the Eastern Band of the Cherokee; the Superintendent of Public Instruction or his designee; the Secretary of Administration or his designee; the Secretary of Health and Human Services or his designee; the Secretary of Environment and Natural Resources or his designee; the Attorney General or his designee; one member appointed by the Governor who shall be a representative of local government in Swain, Jackson, or Cherokee Counties; one legislator appointed by the Speaker of the House; and one legislator appointed by the President Pro Tempore of the Senate. Members serving by virtue of their office within State Government shall serve so long as they hold that office, except that the members appointed by the

Speaker of the House and the President Pro Tempore of the Senate shall serve for two-year terms. Members appointed by the Chief shall serve at the pleasure of the Chief. Members appointed by the Governor shall serve a term of four years at the pleasure of the Governor. (1983 (Reg. Sess., 1984), c. 1085, s. 1; 1989, c. 727, s. 218(150); 1997-443, ss. 11A.118(a), 11A.119(a).)

§ 143B-411.2. North Carolina Advisory Council on the Eastern Band of the Cherokee - purpose or creation; powers and duties.

The purpose of the Council is to study on a continuing basis the relationship between the Eastern Band of the Cherokee and the State of North Carolina in order to resolve any matters of concern to the State or the Tribe. It shall be the duty of the Council:

(1)   Identify existing and potential conflicts between the State of North Carolina and the Eastern Band of Cherokee Indians;

(2)   Propose State and federal legislation and agreements between the State of North Carolina and the Cherokee Tribe to resolve existing and potential conflicts;

(3)   To study and make recommendations concerning any issue referred to the Council by any official of the Eastern Band of the Cherokee, the State of North Carolina, or the government of Haywood, Jackson, Swain, Graham, or Cherokee Counties.

(4)   Study other issues of mutual concern to the Eastern Band of the Cherokee;

(5)   Make a report with recommendations as needed, but not less often than biannually to the Governor, the Chief of the Eastern Band of the Cherokee, the General Assembly, and the Tribal Council of the Eastern Band of the Cherokee. (1983 (Reg. Sess., 1984), c. 1085, s. 1.)

§ 143B-411.3. North Carolina Advisory Council of the Eastern Band of the Cherokee - meetings; quorum; compensation; chairman.

The Council shall meet at least quarterly or at the call of the chairman or a majority of the Council. A quorum shall consist of a majority of the Council. Designees of Council members serving by virtue of office shall be entitled to vote. The Chairman of the Council shall be elected from the membership. The selection of a member as chairman shall have no effect on the member's voting privileges. Council members who are seated by virtue of their office within State government shall be compensated at the rate specified in G.S. 138-6. Council members who are members of the General Assembly shall be compensated at the rate specified in G.S. 120-31. Other Council members shall be compensated at the rate specified in G.S. 138-5. (1983 (Reg. Sess., 1984), c. 1085, s. 1.)

§ 143B-411.4. North Carolina Advisory Council on the Eastern Band of the Cherokee - clerical and administrative support.

All clerical and other services required by the Council shall be supplied by the Secretary of Administration. (1983 (Reg. Sess., 1984), c. 1085, s. 1.)

Part 16. Governor's Council on Employment of the Handicapped.

§§ 143B-412 through 143B-413. Repealed by Session Laws 1979, c. 575, s. 1.

Part 17. Governor's Advocacy Council on Children and Youth.

§ 143B-414: Repealed by Session Laws 2011-266, s. 1.7, effective July 1, 2011.

§ 143B-415: Repealed by Session Laws 2011-266, s. 1.7, effective July 1, 2011.

§ 143B-416: Repealed by Session Laws 2011-266, s. 1.7, effective July 1, 2011.

Part 18. North Carolina Internship Council.

§ 143B-417. North Carolina Internship Council - creation; powers and duties.

There is hereby created the North Carolina Internship Council of the Department of Administration. The North Carolina Internship Council shall have the following functions and duties:

(1) To determine the number of student interns to be allocated to each of the following offices or departments:

a. Office of the Governor

b. Department of Administration

c. Repealed by Session Laws 2012-83, s. 49, effective June 26, 2012.

d. Department of Cultural Resources

e. Department of Revenue

f. Department of Transportation

g. Department of Environment and Natural Resources

h. Department of Commerce

i. Department of Public Safety

j. Department of Health and Human Services

k. Office of the Lieutenant Governor

l. Office of the Secretary of State

m. Office of the State Auditor

n. Office of the State Treasurer

o. Department of Public Instruction

p. Repealed by Session Laws 1985, c. 757, s. 162.

q. Department of Agriculture and Consumer Services

r. Department of Labor

s. Department of Insurance

t. Office of the Speaker of the House of Representatives

u. Justices of the Supreme Court and Judges of the Court of Appeals

v. Community Colleges System Office

w. Office of State Human Resources

x. Office of the Senate President Pro Tempore

y. Repealed by Session Laws 2012-83, s. 49, effective June 26, 2012.

z. Administrative Office of the Courts

aa. State Ethics Commission

bb. Division of Employment Security

cc. State Board of Elections

dd. Department of Justice

(2) To screen applications for student internships and select from these applications the recipients of student internships; and

(3) To determine the appropriateness of proposals for projects for student interns submitted by the offices and departments enumerated in subdivision (1) of this section. (1977, c. 771, s. 4; c. 967; 1979, c. 783; 1983, c. 710; 1985, c. 757, s. 162; 1989, c. 727, s. 218(151), c. 751, s. 7(21); 1989 (Reg. Sess., 1990), c. 900, s. 1; 1991 (Reg. Sess., 1992), c. 959, s. 42; 1993, c. 522, s. 17; 1997-261, s. 104; 1997-443, ss. 11A.118(a), 11A.119(a); 1999-84, s. 25; 2000-137, s. 4(oo); 2007-121, s. 1; 2011-145, s. 19.1(g), (h), (l); 2011-401, s. 3.21; 2012-83, s. 49; 2013-382, s. 9.1(c).)

§ 143B-418. North Carolina Internship Council - members; selection; quorum; compensation; clerical, etc., services.

The North Carolina Internship Council shall consist of 17 members, including the Secretary of Administration or his designee, one member to be designated by and to serve at the pleasure of the President Pro Tempore of the Senate, one member to be designated by and to serve at the pleasure of the Speaker of the House of Representatives and the following 14 members to be appointed by the Governor to a two-year term commencing on July 1 of odd-numbered years: two representatives of community colleges; four representatives of The University of North Carolina system; two representatives of private colleges or universities; three representatives of colleges or universities with an enrollment of less than 5,000 students; and three former interns.

At the end of the respective terms of office of the 14 members of the Council appointed by the Governor, the appointment of their successors shall be for terms of two years and until their successors are appointed and qualify. The Governor may remove any member appointed by the Governor.

Any appointment to fill a vacancy on the Council created by the resignation, dismissal, death, or disability of a member shall be for the balance of the unexpired term.

The Council shall meet at the call of the chairman or upon written request of at least five members.

The Governor shall designate a member of the Council as chairman to serve at the pleasure of the Governor.

Members of the Council shall receive per diem and necessary travel and subsistence expenses in accordance with the provisions of G.S. 138-5.

A majority of the Council shall constitute a quorum for the transaction of business.

All clerical and other services required by the Council shall be supplied by the Secretary of Administration. (1977, c. 967; 1987, c. 564, s. 9; 1995, c. 490, s. 28.)

§ 143B-419. North Carolina Internship Council - committees for screening applications.

The North Carolina Internship Council may designate one representative from each office or department enumerated in G.S. 143B-417 to serve on a committee to assist pursuant to guidelines adopted by the Council, in the screening and selection of applicants for student internships. (1977, c. 967.)

Part 19. Jobs for Veterans Committee.

§ 143B-420. Governor's Jobs for Veterans Committee - creation; appointment, organization, etc.; duties.

(a) There is hereby created and established in the North Carolina Department of Administration, Division of Veterans Affairs, a committee to be known as the Governor's Jobs for Veterans Committee, with one member from each Congressional district, appointed by the Governor. Members of the Committee shall serve at the pleasure of the Governor. The Secretary of Administration, with the concurrence of the Governor, shall appoint a chairman to administer this Committee who shall be subject to the direction and supervision of the Secretary. The chairman shall serve at the pleasure of the Secretary. The chairman shall devote full time to his duties of office.

(b) Subject to the general supervision of the Secretary, the duties of the chairman shall include but not be limited to the following:

(1) Serving as a liaison between the Office of the Governor and all State agencies to insure that veterans receive the employment preference to which they are legally entitled and that such State agencies list available jobs with appropriate public employment services;

(2) Evaluating existing programs designed to benefit veterans and submitting reports and recommendations to the Governor and Secretary;

(3) Developing and furthering favorable employer attitudes toward the employment of veterans by appropriate promulgation of information concerning veterans and the functions of the Committee;

(4) Serving as a liaison between the Committee and communities throughout the State to the end that civic committees and volunteer groups are formed and utilized to promote the objectives of the Committee;

(5) Assisting employers in properly designing affirmative action plans as they relate to handicapped and Vietnam-era veterans;

(6) Serving as a liaison between veterans and State agencies on questions regarding the employment practices of such State agencies. (1977, c. 1032; 1985, c. 479, s. 166.)

§ 143B-421. Governor's Jobs for Veterans Committee - authority to receive grants-in-aid.

The Committee is hereby authorized to receive grants-in-aid from the federal government and charitable organizations for carrying out its duties. (1977, c. 1032.)

Part 19A. Selective Service Registration.

§ 143B-421.1. Selective Service registration.

(a) A person who is required under 50 United States Code Appx. § 453 (Military Selective Service Act) to present himself for and submit to registration and fails to do so in accordance with any proclamation or any rule or regulation issued under this section, shall be ineligible for:

(1) Employment by or service for the State, or a political subdivision of the State, including all boards and commissions, departments, agencies, institutions, and instrumentalities.

(2) State-supported scholarships, programs for financial assistance for postsecondary education, or loans insured by any State agency, including educational assistance authorized under Article 23 of Chapter 116 of the General Statutes.

(b) It shall be the duty of all persons or officials having charge of and authority over either the hiring of employees or granting of educational assistance, as described in this section, to adopt rules and regulations which shall require applicants to indicate on a form whether they are in compliance with the registration requirements described in subsection (a). Rules and regulations issued under the authority of this section shall provide that an applicant be given not less than 30 days after notification of a proposed finding of ineligibility for employment or benefits to provide the issuing official with information that he is in compliance with the registration requirements described in subsection (a). The issuing official may afford such person an opportunity for a hearing to establish his compliance or for any other purpose.

(c)   A person may not be denied a right, privilege, or benefit under State law by reason of failure to present himself for and submit to registration under 50 U.S.C.S. Appx. § 453 if:

(1)   The requirement for the person to so register has terminated or become inapplicable to the person; and

(2)   The person shows by a preponderance of the evidence that the failure of the person to register was not a knowing and willful failure to register. (1989, c. 618.)

§ 143B-421.2. Reserved for future codification purposes.

§ 143B-421.3. Consultation required for welcome and visitor centers.

The Department of Commerce and the Department of Transportation shall consult with the Joint Legislative Commission on Governmental Operations and the House and Senate Appropriations Subcommittees on Natural and Economic Resources before beginning the design or construction of any new welcome center or visitor center buildings. (2007-356, s. 1.)

Part 20. Public Officers and Employees Liability Insurance Commission.

§§ 143B-422 through 143B-426.1: Recodified as §§ 58-27.20 through 58-27.26 (now 58-32-1 through 58-32-30) by Session Laws 1985, c. 666, s. 79.

Part 21. Child and Family Services Interagency Committees.

§§ 143B-426.2 through 143B-426.7A. Repealed by Session Laws 1985 (Reg. Sess., 1986), c. 1028, s. 31.

Part 22. North Carolina Agency for Public Telecommunications.

§ 143B-426.8. Definitions.

As used in this Part, except where the context clearly requires otherwise:

(1)   "Agency" means the North Carolina Agency for Public Telecommunications.

(2)   "Board" means the Board of Public Telecommunications Commissioners.

(3)   "Telecommunications" means any origination, creation, transmission, emission, storage-retrieval, or reception of signs, signals, writing, images and sounds, or intelligence of any nature, by wire, radio, television, optical or other electromagnetic systems. (1979, c. 900, s. 1.)

§ 143B-426.9. North Carolina Agency for Public Telecommunications - Creation; membership; appointments, terms and vacancies; officers; meetings and quorum; compensation.

The North Carolina Agency for Public Telecommunications is created. It is governed by the Board of Public Telecommunications Commissioners, composed of 26 members as follows:

(1)   A Chairman appointed by, and serving at the pleasure of, the Governor;

(2)   Ten at-large members, appointed by the Governor from the general public;

(3)   Two members appointed by the General Assembly upon the recommendation of the Speaker of the House of Representatives in accordance with G.S. 120-121;

(4)   Two members appointed by the General Assembly upon the recommendation of the President Pro Tempore of the Senate in accordance with G.S. 120-121;

(5)   The Secretary of Administration, ex officio;

(6) The Chairman of the Board of Trustees of The University of North Carolina Center for Public Television (if and when established), ex officio;

(7) The Chairman of the State Board of Education, ex officio;

(8) The Chairman of the OPEN/net Committee, ex officio, so long as such person is not a State employee;

(9) The Chairman of the North Carolina Utilities Commission, ex officio;

(10) The Director of the Public Staff of the North Carolina Utilities Commission, ex officio;

(11) Repealed by Session Laws 2011-266, s. 1.13(b), effective July 1, 2011.

(12) The Superintendent of Public Instruction, ex officio;

(13) The President of the University of North Carolina, ex officio;

(14) The President of the Community Colleges System, ex officio; and

(15) Two members ex officio who shall rotate from among the remaining heads of departments enumerated in G.S. 143A-11 or G.S. 143B-6, appointed by the Governor.

The 10 at-large members shall serve for terms staggered as follows: four terms shall expire on June 30, 1980; and three terms shall expire on June 30, 1982; and three terms shall expire on June 30, 1984. Thereafter, the members at large shall be appointed for full four-year terms and until their successors are appointed and qualified. In making appointments of members at large, the Governor shall seek to appoint persons from the various geographic areas of the State including both urban and rural areas; persons from various classifications as to sex, race, age, and handicapped persons; and persons who are representatives of the public broadcast, commercial broadcast, nonbroadcast distributive systems and private education communities of the State.

The terms of the ex officio members are coterminous with their respective terms of office. In the event that any of the offices represented on the Board ceases to exist, the successor officer to the designated member shall become an ex officio member of the Board; if there shall be no successor, then the position on the

Board shall be filled by a member to be appointed by the Governor from the general public. The ex officio members shall have the right to vote.

The initial members appointed to the Board by the General Assembly shall serve for terms expiring June 30, 1983. Thereafter, their successors shall serve for two-year terms beginning July 1 of odd-numbered years.

The terms of the rotating ex officio members shall be of one-year duration, and the schedule of rotation is determined by the Governor.

Each State official who serves on the Board may designate a representative of his department, agency or institution to sit in his place on the Board and to exercise fully the official's privileges of membership.

The Secretary of Administration or his designee serves as secretary of the Board.

Vacancies in appointments made by the General Assembly shall be filled in accordance with G.S. 120-122. Other vacancies shall be filled in the same manner as the original appointment.

The Governor may remove any member of the Board from office in accordance with the provisions of G.S. 143B-16.

The Board meets quarterly and at other times at the call of the chairman or upon written request of at least six members.

A majority of the Board members shall constitute a quorum for the transaction of business. (1979, c. 900, s. 1; 1981 (Reg. Sess., 1982), c. 1191, ss. 6-8; 1983 (Reg. Sess., 1984), c. 1116, s. 92; 1995, c. 490, s. 42; 1999-84, s. 26; 2011-266, s. 1.13(b).)

§ 143B-426.10. Purpose of Agency.

The North Carolina Agency for Public Telecommunications shall serve as an instrumentality of the State of North Carolina for the accomplishment of the following general purposes:

(1) To advise the Governor, the Council of State, the principal State departments, the University of North Carolina, the General Assembly and all other State agencies and institutions on all matters of telecommunications policy as may affect the State of North Carolina and its citizens;

(2) To foster and stimulate the use of telecommunications programming, services and systems for noncommercial educational and cultural purposes by public agencies for the improvement of the performance of governmental services and functions;

(3) To serve State government, local governments and other public agencies and councils in the following ways:

a. To provide a clearinghouse of information about innovative projects, programs or demonstrations in telecommunications;

b. To provide advice on the acquisition, location and operation of telecommunications systems, equipment, and facilities and to provide particularly such advice as may foster compatibility of systems, equipment and facilities and as may reduce or eliminate duplication or mismatching of systems and facilities;

c. To provide advice on the disposition of excess or unused telecommunications equipment;

d. To provide information and advice on new telecommunications developments and emerging technologies;

e. To provide advice on procurement matters on all purchases and contracts for telecommunications systems, programming and services;

f. To provide information and advice on the most cost-effective means of using telecommunications for management, operations and service delivery;

g. To provide advice and assistance in the evaluation of alternative media programming so that the most efficient and effective products may be developed and used;

h. To provide advice and assistance in the identification of various methods of distributing programs and materials;

(4) To study the utilization of the frequency spectrum and to advise appropriate authorities as to effective frequency management;

(5) To assist in the development of a State plan or plans for the best development of telecommunications systems, both public and private, to insure that all citizens of North Carolina will enjoy the benefits which such systems may deliver;

(6) In addition to and not in place of the programs, projects, and services of The University of North Carolina Center for Public Television (or its functional predecessor), to develop and provide media programs and programming materials and services of a noncommercial educational, informational, cultural or scientific nature;

(7) To undertake innovative projects in interactive telecommunications and teleconferencing whenever such projects might serve to improve services, expand opportunities for citizen participation in government and reduce the costs of delivering a service;

(8) To serve as a means of acquiring governmental and private funds for use in the development of services through telecommunications;

(9) To serve as a means of distributing State funds and awarding grants for any purpose determined to be in furtherance of the purposes of this Part;

(10) To operate such telecommunications facilities or systems as may fall within the purview of this Part or as may be assigned to the Agency by the Governor, by the General Assembly, or by the Secretary of Administration consistent with the provisions of G.S. 143-340(14);

(11) To review, assess and report to the Governor on an annual basis on the telecommunications needs and services of State and local government and on the production capabilities and services, the nonproduction services, and the research and development services offered by the Agency and by all other agencies of State government;

(12) To review, assess and report to the Governor, after a period of not less than two years and not more than three years after the enactment of this Part, on the telecommunications statutes, plans and operations in State government, including those resulting from the enactment of this Part and from revision of statutes pertaining to telecommunications in the Department of Administration;

(13) To serve as liaison between State government and local governments, regional organizations, the federal government, foundations and other states and nations on common telecommunications concerns;

(14) To study and evaluate all existing or proposed statutes, rules or regulations at all levels of government touching upon or affecting telecommunications policy, services, systems, programming, rates or funds and to advise the appropriate officials, agencies and councils;

(15) To acquire, construct, equip, maintain, develop and improve such facilities as may be necessary to the fulfillment of the purpose of the Part;

(16) To provide information and advice on any related matter which may be referred to it by any agency or council of State or local government;

(17) And in general to do and perform any act or function which may tend to be useful toward the development and improvement of telecommunications services within State government and which may increase the delivery of services through telecommunications programs or systems.

The enumeration of the above purposes shall not limit or circumscribe the broad objective of developing to the utmost the possibilities of telecommunications programming, services and systems in the State of North Carolina. (1979, c. 900, s. 1.)

§ 143B-426.11. Powers of Agency.

In order to enable it to carry out the purposes of this Part, the Agency:

(1) Has the powers of a body corporate, including the power to sue and be sued, to make contracts, to hold and own copyrights and to adopt and use a common seal and to alter the same as may be deemed expedient;

(2) May make all necessary contracts and arrangements with any parties which will serve the purposes and facilitate the business of the North Carolina Agency for Public Telecommunications; except that, the Agency may not contract or enter into any agreement for the production by the Agency of programs or programming materials with any person, group, or organization

other than government agencies; principal State departments; public and noncommercial broadcast licensees;

(3)   May rent, lease, buy, own, acquire, mortgage, or otherwise encumber and dispose of such property, real or personal; and construct, maintain, equip and operate any facilities, buildings, studios, equipment, materials, supplies and systems as said Board may deem proper to carry out the purposes and provisions of this Part;

(4)   May establish an office for the transaction of its business at such place or places as the Board deems advisable or necessary in carrying out the purposes of this Part;

(5)   May apply for and accept loans and grants of money from any federal agency or the State of North Carolina or any political subdivision thereof or from any public or private sources for any and all of the purposes authorized in this Part; may extend or distribute the funds in accordance with directions and requirements attached thereto or imposed thereon by the federal agency, the State of North Carolina or any political subdivision thereof, or any public or private lender or donor; and may give such evidences of indebtedness as shall be required, but no indebtedness of any kind incurred or created by the Agency shall constitute an indebtedness of the State of North Carolina or any political subdivision thereof, and no such indebtedness shall involve or be secured by the faith, credit or taxing power of the State of North Carolina or any political subdivision thereof. At no time may the total outstanding indebtedness of the Agency, excluding bond indebtedness, exceed five hundred thousand dollars ($500,000) unless the Agency has consulted with the Director of the Budget;

(6)   May pay all necessary costs and expenses involved in and incident to the formation and organization of the Agency and incident to the administration and operation thereof, and may pay all other costs and expenses reasonably necessary or expedient in carrying out and accomplishing the purposes of this Part;

(7)   Under such conditions as the Board may deem appropriate to the accomplishment of the purposes of this Part, may distribute in the form of grants, gifts, or loans any of the revenues and earnings received by the Agency from its operations;

(8)   May adopt, alter or repeal its own bylaws, rules and regulations governing the manner in which its business may be transacted and in which the

power granted to it may be exercised, and may provide for the creation of such divisions and for the appointment of such committees, and the functions thereof, as the Board deems necessary or expedient in facilitating the business and purposes of the Agency;

(9)   The Board shall be responsible for all management functions of the Agency. The chairman shall serve as the chief executive officer, and shall have the responsibility of executing the policies of the Board. The Executive Director shall be the chief operating and administrative officer and shall be responsible for carrying out the decisions made by the Board and its chairman. The Executive Director shall be appointed by the Governor upon the recommendation of the Board and shall serve at the pleasure of the Governor. The salary of the Executive Director shall be fixed by the General Assembly in the Current Operations Appropriations Act. Subject to the provisions of the North Carolina Human Resources Act and with the approval of the Board, the Executive Director may appoint, employ, dismiss and fix the compensation of such professional, administrative, clerical and other employees as the Board deems necessary to carry out the purposes of this Part; but any employee who serves as the director of any division of the Agency which may be established by the Board shall be appointed with the additional approval of the Secretary of Administration. There shall be an executive committee consisting of three of the appointed members and three of the ex officio members elected by the Board and the chairman of the Board, who shall serve as chairman of the executive committee. The executive committee may do all acts which are authorized by the bylaws of the Agency. Members of the executive committee shall serve until their successors are elected;

(10)   May do any and all other acts and things in this Part authorized or required to be done, whether or not included in the general powers in this section; and

(11)   May do any and all things necessary to accomplish the purposes of this Part.

Nothing herein authorizes the Agency to exercise any control over any public noncommercial broadcast licensee, its staff or facilities or over any community antenna television system (Cable TV; CATV), its staff, employees or facilities operating in North Carolina, or the Police Information Network (PIN), its staff, employees or facilities or the Judicial Department.

The property of the Agency shall not be subject to any taxes or assessments. (1979, c. 900, s. 1; 1983, c. 666; c. 717, s. 82; 1983 (Reg. Sess., 1984), c. 1034, s. 164; 1985, c. 122, ss. 3, 4; 1985 (Reg. Sess., 1986), c. 955, ss. 99-101; 2006-203, s. 107; 2013-382, s. 9.1(c).)

§ 143B-426.11A. Use of Agency for Public Telecommunications required.

Notwithstanding any other provision of law, the Agency for Public Telecommunications shall be the primary party with whom all State agencies, departments, and institutions other than The University of North Carolina System and the Community College System may contract for media placement and the creation of the media to be placed. Agencies, departments, and institutions may use another party only if the Agency for Public Telecommunications determines that the Agency for Public Telecommunications cannot fulfill the agency's, department's, or institution's needs. Any contract entered into contrary to the provisions of this section is voidable at the discretion of the Governor and the Council of State. (2011-145, s. 20.1.)

§ 143B-426.12: Repealed by Session Laws 2011-266, s. 1.13(a), effective July 1, 2011.

§ 143B-426.13. Approval of acquisition and disposition of real property.

Any transaction relating to the acquisition or disposition of any estate or interest in real property by the North Carolina Agency for Public Telecommunications shall be subject to prior review by the Governor and Council of State, and shall become effective only after the transaction has been approved by the Governor and Council of State. Upon the acquisition of an estate in real property by the North Carolina Agency for Public Telecommunications, the fee title or other estate shall vest in and the instrument of conveyance shall name "North Carolina Agency for Public Telecommunications" as grantee, lessee, or transferee. Upon the disposition of an interest or estate in real property, the instrument of lease conveyance or transfer shall be executed by the North Carolina Agency for Public Telecommunications. The approval of any transaction by the Governor or Council of State shall be evidenced by a duly certified copy of excerpt of minutes of the meeting of the Governor and the Council of State, attested by the Governor or by the private secretary to the

Governor, reciting the approval, affixed to the instrument of acquisition or transfer; the certificate may be recorded as a part of the instrument, and shall be conclusive evidence of review and approval of the subject transaction by the Governor and Council of State. The Governor, acting with the approval of the Council of State, may delegate the review and approval of such classes of lease, rental, easement or right-of-way transactions as he deems advisable, and he may likewise delegate the review and approval of the severance of buildings and timber from the land. (1979, c. 900, s. 1.)

§ 143B-426.14. Issuance of bonds.

As a means of raising the funds needed from time to time in the acquisition, construction, equipment, maintenance and operation of any facility, building, structure, telecommunications equipment or systems or any other matter or thing which the Agency is herein authorized to acquire, construct, equip, maintain, or operate, the Agency may at one time or from time to time issue negotiable revenue bonds of the Agency. The principal and interest of the revenue bonds shall be payable solely from the revenues to be derived from the operation of all or any part of the Agency's properties and facilities. A pledge of the net revenues derived from the operation of specified properties and facilities of the Agency may be made to secure the payment of the bonds as they mature. Revenue bonds issued under the provisions of this Part shall not be deemed to constitute a debt of the State of North Carolina or a pledge of the faith and credit of the State. The issuance of revenue bonds shall not directly or indirectly or contingently obligate the State to levy or to pledge any form of taxation whatever therefor or to make any appropriation for their payment. The bonds and the income therefrom shall be exempt from all taxation within the State. (1979, c. 900, s. 1; 2006-203, s. 108.)

§ 143B-426.15. Exchange of property; removal of building, etc.

The Agency may exchange any property or properties acquired under the authority of this Chapter for other property or properties usable in carrying out the powers hereby conferred, and also may remove from lands needed for its purposes and reconstruct on other locations, buildings, facilities, equipment, telecommunications systems or other structures, upon the payment of just compensation. (1979, c. 900, s. 1.)

§ 143B-426.16. Treasurer of the Agency.

The Board shall select its own treasurer from among the at-large members. The Board shall require a corporate surety bond of the treasurer in an amount fixed by the Board, and the premium or premiums thereon shall be paid by the Board as a necessary expense of the Agency. (1979, c. 900, s. 1.)

§ 143B-426.17. Deposit and disbursement of funds.

All Agency funds shall be handled in accordance with the Executive Budget Act. (1979, c. 900, s. 1.)

§ 143B-426.18. Audit.

The operations of the North Carolina Agency for Public Telecommunications shall be subject to the oversight of the State Auditor pursuant to Article 5A of Chapter 147 of the General Statutes. (1979, c. 900, s. 1; 1983, c. 913, s. 42.)

§ 143B-426.19. Purchase of supplies, material and equipment.

All the provisions of Article 3 of Chapter 143 of the General Statutes relating to the purchase of supplies, material and equipment by the State government are applicable to the North Carolina Agency for Public Telecommunications. (1979, c. 900, s. 1.)

§ 143B-426.20. Liberal construction of Part.

It is intended that the provisions of this Part shall be liberally construed to accomplish the purposes provided for herein. (1979, c. 900, s. 1.)

Part 23. Information Technology [Resource Management] Commission.

§ 143B-426.21: Recodified as § 143B-472.41 by Session Laws 1997-148, s. 2.

Part 24. Governor's Management Committee.

§ 143B-426.22. Governor's Management Council.

(a) Creation; Membership. - The Governor's Management Council is created in the Department of Administration. The Council shall contain the following members: The Secretary of Administration, who shall serve as chairman, a senior staff officer responsible for productivity and management programs from the Departments of Commerce, Revenue, Environment and Natural Resources, Transportation, Public Safety, Cultural Resources, Health and Human Services, and Administration; and an equivalent officer from the Offices of State Personnel, State Budget and Management, and the Governor's Program for Executive and Organizational Development. The following persons may also serve on the Council if the entity represented chooses to participate: a senior staff officer responsible for productivity and management programs from any State department not previously specified in this section, and a representative from The University of North Carolina.

(b) Powers. - The Council may:

(1) Coordinate efforts to make State government more efficient and productive;

(2) Review plans and policies submitted by participating agencies to improve agency management and productivity;

(3) Recommend to the Governor the issuance of specific Management Directive and Executive Orders that will establish management policies and procedures to be implemented by the agencies to improve agency management and productivity;

(4) Provide a clearinghouse for productivity initiatives and communicate these initiatives to all agencies;

(5) Authorize special projects on specific management and productivity improvement issues;

(6) Review plans and policies of statewide management programs such as the Incentive Pay Program, the North Carolina Employee Suggestion System, the Work Options Program, and similar productivity improvement programs; and

(7) Develop criteria for annual recognition for outstanding Government Executives. (1983, c. 540, s. 1; c. 907, s. 3; 1989, c. 727, s. 218(152); c. 751, s. 9(c); 1991 (Reg. Sess., 1992), c. 959, s. 43; 1997-443, ss. 11A.109, 11A.119(a); 2000-137, s. 4(pp); 2011-145, s. 19.1(g); 2012-83, s. 50.)

§ 143B-426.23. Meetings; clerical services report.

The Council shall meet monthly or at the call of the chairman. The Department of Administration is responsible for providing clerical and other services required by the Council. The Council shall make an annual report of its work to the Governor and to the Joint Appropriations Committee of the General Assembly. (1983, c. 540, s. 1.)

Part 25. Board of Trustees of the North Carolina Public Employee Deferred Compensation Plan.

§ 143B-426.24. North Carolina Public Employee Deferred Compensation Plan.

(a) The Governor may, by Executive Order, establish a Board of Trustees of the North Carolina Public Employee Deferred Compensation Plan, which when established shall be constituted an agency of the State of North Carolina within the Department of State Treasurer. The Board shall create, establish, implement, coordinate and administer a Deferred Compensation Plan for employees of the State, any county or municipality, the North Carolina Community College System, and any political subdivision of the State. Until so established, the Board heretofore established pursuant to Executive Order XII dated November 12, 1974, shall continue in effect. Likewise, the Plan heretofore established shall continue until a new plan is established. Effective July 1, 2008, the Plan shall be administered by the Supplemental Retirement Board of Trustees established under G.S. 135-96.

(b)-(f) Repealed by Session Laws 2008-132, s. 3, effective July 1, 2009.

(g) It shall be the duty of the Supplemental Retirement Board to review all contracts, agreements or arrangements then in force relating to G.S. 147-9.2 and Executive Order XII to include, but not be limited to, such contracts, agreements or arrangements pertaining to the administrative services and the investment of deferred funds under the Plan for the purpose of recommending continuation of or changes to such contracts, agreements or arrangements.

(h) It shall be the duty of the Supplemental Retirement Board to devise a uniform Deferred Compensation Plan for teachers and employees, which shall include a reasonable number of options to the teacher or employee, for the investment of deferred funds, among which may be life insurance, fixed or variable annuities and retirement income contracts, regulated investment trusts, pooled investment funds managed by the Board or its designee, or other forms of investment approved by the Board, always in such form as will assure the desired tax treatment of such funds. The Board may alter, revise and modify the Plan from time to time to improve the Plan or to conform to and comply with requirements of State and federal laws and regulations relating to the deferral of compensation of teachers and public employees generally.

(h1) Notwithstanding any other law, an employee of any county or municipality, an employee of the North Carolina Community College System, or an employee of any political subdivision of the State may participate in any 457 Plan adopted by the State, with the consent of the Supplemental Retirement Board and with the consent of the proper governing authority of such county, municipality, community college, or political subdivision of the State where such employee is employed.

(i) The Supplemental Retirement Board is authorized to delegate the performance of such of its administrative duties as it deems appropriate including coordination, administration, and marketing of the Plan to teachers and employees. Prior to entering into any contract with respect to such administrative duties, it shall seek bids, hold public hearings and in general take such steps as are calculated by the Board to obtain competent, efficient and worthy services for the performance of such administrative duties.

(j) The Supplemental Retirement Board may acquire investment vehicles from any company duly authorized to conduct such business in this State or may establish, alter, amend and modify, to the extent it deems necessary or desirable, a trust for the purpose of facilitating the administration, investment and maintenance of assets acquired by the investment of deferred funds. All assets of the Plan, including all deferred amounts, property and rights purchased with deferred amounts, and all income attributed thereto shall be held in trust for the exclusive benefit of the Plan participants and their beneficiaries.

(k),(l) Repealed by Session Laws 2008-132, s. 3, effective July 1 2009.

(m) Investment of deferred funds shall not be unreasonably delayed, and in no case shall the investment of deferred funds be delayed more than 30 days. The Supplemental Retirement Board may accumulate such funds pending investment, and the interest earned on such funds pending investment shall be available to and may be spent in the discretion of the Board only for the reasonable and necessary expenses of the Board. The State Treasurer is authorized to prescribe guidelines for the expenditure of such funds by the Board. From time to time as the Board may direct, funds not required for such expenses may be used to defray administrative expenses and fees which would otherwise be required to be borne by teachers and employees who are then participating in the Plan.

(n) Repealed by Session Laws 2008-132, s. 3, effective July 1 2009.

(o) It is intended that the provisions of this Part shall be liberally construed to accomplish the purposes provided for herein. (1983, c. 559, s. 1; 1991, c. 389, s. 2; 1995, c. 490, s. 40; 1999-456, s. 42; 2004-137, s. 1; 2006-66, s. 20.1; 2008-132, s. 3.)

Part 26. North Carolina Farmworker Council.

§ 143B-426.25. North Carolina Farmworker Council - creation; membership; meetings.

(a) There is established within the Department of Administration the North Carolina Farmworker Council.

(b) The North Carolina Farmworker Council shall consist of 13 members as follows:

(1) Four shall be appointed by the Governor.

(2) Two shall be appointed by the Speaker of the House of Representatives.

(3) Two shall be appointed by the President Pro Tempore of the Senate.

(4) The Secretary of the Department of Health and Human Services or the Deputy Secretary of the Department if designated by the Secretary shall serve ex officio.

(5) The Commissioner of Labor or the Deputy Commissioner of the Department if designated by the Commissioner shall serve ex officio.

(6) The Commissioner of Agriculture or the Deputy Commissioner of the Department if designated by the Commissioner shall serve ex officio.

(7) The Assistant Secretary of Commerce in charge of the Division of Employment Security or that officer's designee shall serve ex officio.

(8) The Secretary of Environment and Natural Resources or his designee shall serve ex officio.

(c) Vacancies in membership of the Council shall be filled by the original appointing authority for the remainder of the unexpired term.

(d) The Governor shall appoint the chairman of the Council. At its first meeting the Council shall select a vice-chairman from its membership and a secretary. The chairman shall preside at all meetings and in his absence the vice-chairman shall act as chairman.

(e) A majority of the membership shall constitute a quorum.

(f) The initial meeting of the Council shall be called by the Governor. Subsequent meetings shall be held upon the call of the chairman or upon the written request of four members. The Council shall meet at least four times per year.

(g) Council members who are members of the General Assembly shall receive subsistence and travel allowances at the rate set forth in G.S. 120-3.1. Council members and ex officio members who are employees of the State of North Carolina shall receive travel allowances at the rate set forth in G.S. 138-6. All other Council members shall receive per diem, subsistence and travel expenses at the rate set forth in G.S. 138-5.

(h) The Department of Administration shall provide necessary clerical equipment and administrative services to the Council, provided the Council may hire and discharge its own staff if it so desires. (1983, c. 923, s. 205; 1987, c.

876, s. 29.1; 1991, c. 130, s. 1; 1995, c. 490, s. 19; 1997-443, ss. 11A.118(a), 11A.119(a); 2011-401, s. 3.22.)

§ 143B-426.26. North Carolina Farmworker Council - duties; annual report.

(a) The Council shall have the following duties:

(1) Study and evaluate the existing system of delivery of services to farmworkers.

(2) Seek effective methods for the improvement of living, working, and related problems affecting farmworkers.

(3) Recommend a mechanism for coordinating all farmworkers' activities in the State.

(4) Identify and make recommendations to alleviate gaps and duplication of services or programs.

(5) Propose and review legislation relating to farmworkers.

(b) By February 1 of each year, the Council shall make a report describing its activities for the preceding calendar year to the Governor and General Assembly. (1983, c. 923, s. 205.)

§ 143B-426.27. Reserved for future codification purposes.

§ 143B-426.28. Reserved for future codification purposes.

§ 143B-426.29. Reserved for future codification purposes.

Part 27. North Carolina Board of Science and Technology.

§§ 143B-426.30, 143B-426.31: Recodified as §§ 143B-472.80, 143B-472.81 by Session Laws 2001-424, s. 7.6.

§ 143B-426.32. Reserved for future codification purposes.

§ 143B-426.33. Reserved for future codification purposes.

§ 143B-426.34. Reserved for future codification purposes.

Part 27A. Martin Luther King, Jr. Commission.

§ 143B-426.34A. Martin Luther King, Jr. Commission - creation; powers and duties.

There is hereby created the Martin Luther King, Jr. Commission of the Department of Administration. The Martin Luther King, Jr. Commission shall have the following functions and duties:

(1)   To encourage appropriate ceremonies and activities throughout the State relating to the observance of the legal holiday honoring Martin Luther King, Jr.'s birthday;

(2)   To provide advice and assistance to local governments and private organizations across the State with respect to the observance of such holiday; and

(3)   To promote among the people of North Carolina an awareness and appreciation of the life and work of Martin Luther King, Jr. (1993, c. 502.)

§ 143B-426.34B. Martin Luther King, Jr. Commission - members; selection; quorum; compensation.

(a)   The Martin Luther King, Jr. Commission of the Department of Administration shall consist of 16 members. The Governor shall appoint 12 members, one of whom he shall designate as the chair of the Commission. The Governor shall make reasonable efforts to assure that his appointees are equally distributed geographically throughout the State. The President Pro Tempore of the Senate shall appoint two members and the Speaker of the House of Representatives shall appoint two members. The terms of four of the members appointed by the Governor shall expire June 30, 1997. The terms of four of the members appointed by the Governor shall expire June 30, 1996.

The terms of four of the members appointed by the Governor shall expire June 30, 1994. The terms of the members appointed by the President Pro Tempore of the Senate and the Speaker of the House of Representatives shall expire June 30, 1995. At the end of the respective terms of office of the initial members of the Commission, the appointment of their successors shall be for terms of four years. No member of the Commission shall serve more than two consecutive terms. A member having served two consecutive terms shall be eligible for reappointment one year after the expiration of the second term. A member who fails to attend any three meetings of the Commission shall be dismissed automatically from the Commission upon failure to attend the third such meeting. Provided, however, that the Commission may, by majority vote, reinstate any such dismissed member for the remainder of the unexpired term for good cause shown for failing to attend the meetings. Vacancies shall be filled by the appointing officer for the unexpired term.

(b)   A majority of the Commission shall constitute a quorum for the transaction of business.

(c)   Members of the Commission shall be compensated for their services as authorized by G.S. 138-5. Members of the Commission who are State officials or employees shall be reimbursed as authorized by G.S. 138-6.

(d)   The Department of Administration shall provide necessary clerical and administrative support services to the Commission. (1993, c. 502.)

Part 28. Office of the State Controller.

§ 143B-426.35. Definitions.

As used in this Part, unless the context clearly indicates otherwise:

(1)   "Accounting system" means the total structure of records and procedures which discover, record, classify, and report information on the financial position and operating results of a governmental unit or any of its funds, balanced account groups, and organizational components.

(2)   "Office" means the Office of the State Controller.

(3)   "State agency" means any State agency as defined in G.S. 147-64.4(4).

(4) "State funds" means any moneys appropriated by the General Assembly, or moneys collected by or for the State, or any agency of the State, pursuant to the authority granted in any State laws. (1985 (Reg. Sess., 1986), c. 1024, s. 1; 1991, c. 542, s. 13.)

§ 143B-426.36. Office of the State Controller; creation.

There is created the Office of the State Controller. This office shall be located administratively within the Department of Administration but shall exercise all of its prescribed statutory powers independently of the Secretary of Administration. (1985 (Reg. Sess., 1986), c. 1024, s. 1.)

§ 143B-426.37. State Controller.

(a) The Office of the State Controller shall be headed by the State Controller who shall maintain the State accounting system and shall administer the State disbursing system.

(b) The State Controller shall be a person qualified by education and experience for the office and shall be appointed by the Governor subject to confirmation by the General Assembly. The term of office of the State Controller shall be for seven years; the first full term shall begin July 1, 1987.

The Governor shall submit the name of the person to be appointed, for confirmation by the General Assembly, to the President of the Senate and the Speaker of the House of Representatives by May 1 of the year in which the State Controller is to be appointed. If the Governor does not submit the name by that date, the President of the Senate and the Speaker of the House of Representatives shall submit a name to the General Assembly for confirmation.

In case of death, incapacity, resignation, removal by the Governor for cause, or vacancy for any other reason in the Office of State Controller prior to the expiration of the term of office while the General Assembly is in session, the Governor shall submit the name of a successor to the President of the Senate and the Speaker of the House of Representatives within four weeks after the vacancy occurs. If the Governor does not do so, the President of the Senate and the Speaker of the House of Representatives shall submit a name to the General Assembly for confirmation.

In case of death, incapacity, resignation, removal by the Governor for cause, or vacancy for any other reason in the Office of State Controller prior to the expiration of the term of office while the General Assembly is not in session, the Governor shall appoint a State Controller to serve on an interim basis pending confirmation by the General Assembly.

(c)   The salary of the State Controller shall be set by the General Assembly in the Current Operations Appropriations Act. (1985 (Reg. Sess., 1986), c. 1024, s. 1; 1991 (Reg. Sess., 1992), c. 1039, s. 27.)

§ 143B-426.38. Organization and operation of office.

(a)   The State Controller may appoint a Chief Deputy State Controller. The salary of the Chief Deputy State Controller shall be set by the State Controller.

(b)   The State Controller may appoint all employees necessary to carry out his powers and duties. These employees shall be subject to the North Carolina Human Resources Act.

(c)   All employees of the office shall be under the supervision, direction, and control of the State Controller. Except as otherwise provided by this Part, the State Controller may assign any function vested in him or his office to any subordinate officer or employee of the office.

(d)   The State Controller may, subject to the provisions of G.S. 147-64.7(b)(2), obtain the services of independent public accountants, qualified management consultants, and other professional persons or experts to carry out his powers and duties.

(e)   The State Controller shall have legal custody of all books, papers, documents, and other records of the office.

(f)   The State Controller shall be responsible for the preparation of and the presentation of the office budget request, including all funds requested and all receipts expected for all elements of the budget.

(g) The State Controller may adopt regulations for the administration of the office, the conduct of employees of the office, the distribution and performance of business, the performance of the functions assigned to the State Controller and the office of the State Controller, and the custody, use, and preservation of the records, documents, and property pertaining to the business of the office. (1985 (Reg. Sess., 1986), c. 1024, s. 1; 2013-382, s. 9.1(c).)

§ 143B-426.38A. Government Data Analytics Center; State data-sharing requirements.

(a) State Government Data Analytics. - The State shall initiate across State agencies, departments, and institutions a data integration and data-sharing initiative that is not intended to replace transactional systems but is instead intended to leverage the data from those systems for enterprise-level State business intelligence.

(1) Creation of initiative. - In carrying out the purposes of this section, the Office of the State Controller shall conduct an ongoing, comprehensive evaluation of State data analytics projects and plans in order to identify data integration and business intelligence opportunities that will generate greater efficiencies in, and improved service delivery by, State agencies, departments, and institutions. The State Controller and State CIO shall continue to utilize public-private partnerships and existing data integration and analytics contracts and licenses as appropriate to continue the implementation of the initiative.

(2) Application to State government. - The initiative shall include all State agencies, departments, and institutions, including The University of North Carolina.

(3) Governance. - The State Controller shall lead the initiative established pursuant to this section. The Chief Justice of the North Carolina Supreme Court and the Legislative Services Commission each shall designate an officer or agency to advise and assist the State Controller with respect to implementation of the initiative in their respective branches of government. The judicial and legislative branches shall fully cooperate in the initiative mandated by this section in the same manner as is required of State agencies.

(b) Government Data Analytics Center. -

(1) GDAC established. - There is established in the Office of the State Controller the Government Data Analytics Center (GDAC). GDAC shall assume the work, purpose, and resources of the current data integration effort in the Office of the State Controller and shall otherwise advise and assist the State Controller in the management of the initiative. The State Controller shall make any organizational changes necessary to maximize the effectiveness and efficiency of GDAC.

(2) Powers and duties of the GDAC. - The State Controller shall, through the GDAC, do all of the following:

a. Continue and coordinate ongoing enterprise data integration efforts, including:

1. The deployment, support, technology improvements, and expansion for the Criminal Justice Law Enforcement Automated Data System (CJLEADS).

2. The pilot and subsequent phase initiative for the North Carolina Financial Accountability and Compliance Technology System (NCFACTS).

3. Individual-level student data and workforce data from all levels of education and the State workforce.

4. Other capabilities developed as part of the initiative.

b. Identify technologies currently used in North Carolina that have the capability to support the initiative.

c. Identify other technologies, especially those with unique capabilities, that could support the State's business intelligence effort.

d. Compare capabilities and costs across State agencies.

e. Ensure implementation is properly supported across State agencies.

f. Ensure that data integration and sharing is performed in a manner that preserves data privacy and security in transferring, storing, and accessing data, as appropriate.

g. Immediately seek any waivers and enter into any written agreements that may be required by State or federal law to effectuate data sharing and to carry out the purposes of this section.

h. Coordinate data requirements and usage for State business intelligence applications in a manner that (i) limits impacts on participating State agencies as those agencies provide data and business knowledge expertise and (ii) assists in defining business rules so the data can be properly used.

i. Recommend the most cost-effective and reliable long-term hosting solution for enterprise-level State business intelligence as well as data integration, notwithstanding Section 6A.2(f) of S.L. 2011-145.

(c) Implementation of the Enterprise-Level Business Intelligence Initiative. -

(1) Phases of the initiative. - The initiative shall cycle through these phases on an ongoing basis:

a. Phase I requirements. - In the first phase, the State Controller through GDAC shall:

1. Inventory existing State agency business intelligence projects, both completed and under development.

2. Develop a plan of action that does all of the following:

I. Defines the program requirements, objectives, and end state of the initiative.

II. Prioritizes projects and stages of implementation in a detailed plan and benchmarked time line.

III. Includes the effective coordination of all of the State's current data integration initiatives.

IV. Utilizes a common approach that establishes standards for business intelligence initiatives for all State agencies and prevents the development of projects that do not meet the established standards.

V. Determines costs associated with the development efforts and identifies potential sources of funding.

VI. Includes a privacy framework for business intelligence consisting of adequate access controls and end user security requirements.

VII. Estimates expected savings.

3. Inventory existing external data sources that are purchased by State agencies to determine whether consolidation of licenses is appropriate for the enterprise.

4. Determine whether current, ongoing projects support the enterprise-level objectives.

5. Determine whether current applications are scalable or are applicable for multiple State agencies or both.

b. Phase II requirements. - In the second phase, the State Controller through the GDAC shall:

1. Identify redundancies and recommend to the State CIO any projects that should be discontinued.

2. Determine where gaps exist in current or potential capabilities.

c. Phase III requirements. - In the third phase:

1. The State Controller through GDAC shall incorporate or consolidate existing projects, as appropriate.

2. The State Controller shall, notwithstanding G.S. 147-33.76 or any rules adopted pursuant thereto, eliminate redundant business intelligence projects, applications, software, and licensing.

3. The State Controller through GDAC shall complete all necessary steps to ensure data integration in a manner that adequately protects privacy.

(2) Project management. - The State CIO shall ensure that all current and new business intelligence/data analytics projects are in compliance with all State laws, policies, and rules pertaining to information technology procurement, project management, and project funding and that they include quantifiable and verifiable savings to the State. The State CIO shall report to the Joint Legislative Oversight Committee on Information Technology on projects that are not

achieving projected savings. The report shall include a proposed corrective action plan for the project.

The Office of the State CIO, with the assistance of the Office of State Budget and Management, shall identify potential funding sources for expansion of existing projects or development of new projects. No GDAC project shall be initiated, extended, or expanded:

a. Without the specific approval of the General Assembly unless the project can be implemented within funds appropriated for GDAC projects.

b. Without prior consultation to the Joint Legislative Commission on Governmental Operations and a report to the Joint Legislative Oversight Committee on Information Technology if the project can be implemented within funds appropriated for GDAC projects.

(d) Funding. - The Office of the State Controller, with the support of the Office of State Budget and Management, shall identify and make all efforts to secure any matching funds or other resources to assist in funding this initiative. Savings resulting from the cancellation of projects, software, and licensing, as well as any other savings from the initiative, shall be returned to the General Fund and shall remain unexpended and unencumbered until appropriated by the General Assembly in a subsequent fiscal year. It is the intent of the General Assembly that expansion of the initiative in subsequent fiscal years be funded with these savings and that the General Assembly appropriate funds for projects in accordance with the priorities identified by the Office of the State Controller in Phase I of the initiative.

(d1) Appropriations. - Of the funds appropriated to the Information Technology Fund, the sum of three million dollars ($3,000,000) for the 2013-2014 fiscal year and the sum of four million four hundred seventeen thousand five hundred fifteen dollars ($4,417,515) for the 2014-2015 fiscal year shall be used to support the GDAC and NCFACTS. Of these funds, the sum of one million four hundred seventeen thousand five hundred fifteen dollars ($1,417,515) shall be used in each fiscal year of the 2013-2015 biennium for OSC internal costs. For fiscal year 2014-2015, of the funds generated by GDAC and NCFACTS projects and returned to the General Fund, the sum of up to five million dollars ($5,000,000) is appropriated to fund GDAC and NCFACTS, to include vendor payments. Prioritization for the expenditure of these funds shall be for State costs associated with GDAC first, then vendor costs second. Funds in the 2013-2015 fiscal year budgets for GDAC and NCFACTS shall be used solely to support the continuation for these priority project areas.

(e) Reporting. - The Office of the State Controller shall:

(1) Submit and present quarterly reports on the implementation of Phase I of the initiative and the plan developed as part of that phase to the Chairs of the House of Representatives Appropriations and Senate Base Budget/Appropriations Committees, to the Joint Legislative Oversight Committee on Information Technology, and to the Fiscal Research Division of the General Assembly. The State Controller shall submit a report prior to implementing any improvements, expending funding for expansion of existing business intelligence efforts, or establishing other projects as a result of its evaluations, and quarterly thereafter, a written report detailing progress on, and identifying any issues associated with, State business intelligence efforts.

(2) Report the following information as needed:

a. Any failure of a State agency to provide information requested pursuant to this section. The failure shall be reported to the Joint Legislative Oversight Committee on Information Technology and to the Chairs of the House of Representatives Appropriations and Senate Base Budget/Appropriations Committees.

b. Any additional information to the Joint Legislative Commission on Governmental Operations and the Joint Legislative Oversight Committee on Information Technology that is requested by those entities.

(f) Data Sharing. -

(1) General duties of all State agencies. - Except as limited or prohibited by federal law, the head of each State agency, department, and institution shall do all of the following:

a. Grant the Office of the State Controller access to all information required to develop and support State business intelligence applications pursuant to this section. The State Controller and the GDAC shall take all necessary actions and precautions, including training, certifications, background checks, and governance policy and procedure, to ensure the security, integrity, and privacy of the data in accordance with State and federal law and as may be required by contract.

b. Provide complete information on the State agency's information technology, operational, and security requirements.

c. Provide information on all of the State agency's information technology activities relevant to the State business intelligence effort.

d. Forecast the State agency's projected future business intelligence information technology needs and capabilities.

e. Ensure that the State agency's future information technology initiatives coordinate efforts with the GDAC to include planning and development of data interfaces to incorporate data into the initiative and to ensure the ability to leverage analytics capabilities.

f. Provide technical and business resources to participate in the initiative by providing, upon request and in a timely and responsive manner, complete and accurate data, business rules and policies, and support.

g. Identify potential resources for deploying business intelligence in their respective State agencies and as part of the enterprise-level effort.

h. Immediately seek any waivers and enter into any written agreements that may be required by State or federal law to effectuate data sharing and to carry out the purposes of this section, as appropriate.

(2) Specific requirements. - The State Controller and the GDAC shall enhance the State's business intelligence through the collection and analysis of data relating to workers' compensation claims for the purpose of preventing and detecting fraud, as follows:

a. The North Carolina Industrial Commission shall release to GDAC, or otherwise provide electronic access to, all data requested by GDAC relating to workers' compensation insurance coverage, claims, appeals, compliance, and enforcement under Chapter 97 of the General Statutes.

b. The North Carolina Rate Bureau (Bureau) shall release to GDAC, or otherwise provide electronic access to, all data requested by GDAC relating to workers' compensation insurance coverage, claims, business ratings, and premiums under Chapter 58 of the General Statutes. The Bureau shall be immune from civil liability for releasing information pursuant to this subsection, even if the information is erroneous, provided the Bureau acted in good faith and without malicious or willful intent to harm in releasing the information.

c. The Department of Commerce, Division of Employment Security (DES), shall release to GDAC, or otherwise provide access to, all data requested by GDAC relating to unemployment insurance coverage, claims, and business reporting under Chapter 96 of the General Statutes.

d. The Department of Labor shall release to GDAC, or otherwise provide access to, all data requested by GDAC relating to safety inspections, wage and hour complaints, and enforcement activities under Chapter 95 of the General Statutes.

e. The Department of Revenue shall release to GDAC, or otherwise provide access to, all data requested by GDAC relating to the registration and address information of active businesses, business tax reporting, and aggregate federal tax Form 1099 data for comparison with information from DES, the Rate Bureau, and the Department of the Secretary of State for the evaluation of business reporting. Additionally, the Department of Revenue shall furnish to the GDAC, upon request, other tax information, provided that the information furnished does not impair or violate any information-sharing agreements between the Department and the United States Internal Revenue Service. Notwithstanding any other provision of law, a determination of whether furnishing the information requested by GDAC would impair or violate any information-sharing agreements between the Department of Revenue and the United States Internal Revenue Service shall be within the sole discretion of the State Chief Information Officer. The Department of Revenue and the Office of the State Controller shall work jointly to assure that the evaluation of tax information pursuant to this subdivision is performed in accordance with applicable federal law.

(3) All information shared with GDAC and the State Controller under this subdivision is protected from release and disclosure in the same manner as any other information is protected under this section.

(g) Provisions on Privacy and Confidentiality of Information.

(1) Status with respect to certain information. - The State Controller and the GDAC shall be deemed to be all of the following for the purposes of this section:

a. With respect to criminal information, and to the extent allowed by federal law, a criminal justice agency (CJA), as defined under Criminal Justice Information Services (CJIS) Security Policy. The State CJIS Systems Agency (CSA) shall ensure that CJLEADS receives access to federal criminal information deemed to be essential in managing CJLEADS to support criminal justice professionals.

b. With respect to health information covered under the Health Insurance Portability and Accountability Act of 1996 (HIPAA), as amended, and to the extent allowed by federal law:

1. A business associate with access to protected health information acting on behalf of the State's covered entities in support of data integration, analysis, and business intelligence.

2. Authorized to access and view individually identifiable health information, provided that the access is essential to the enterprise fraud, waste, and improper payment detection program or required for future initiatives having specific definable need for the data.

c. Authorized to access all State and federal data, including revenue and labor information, deemed to be essential to the enterprise fraud, waste, and improper payment detection program or future initiatives having specific definable need for the data.

d. Authorized to develop agreements with the federal government to access data deemed to be essential to the enterprise fraud, waste, and improper payment detection program or future initiatives having specific definable need for such data.

(2) Release of information. - The following limitations apply to (i) the release of information compiled as part of the initiative, (ii) data from State agencies that is incorporated into the initiative, and (iii) data released as part of the implementation of the initiative:

a. Information compiled as part of the initiative. - Notwithstanding the provisions of Chapter 132 of the General Statutes, information compiled by the State Controller and the GDAC related to the initiative may be released as a public record only if the State Controller, in that officer's sole discretion, finds that the release of information is in the best interest of the general public and is not in violation of law or contract.

b. Data from State agencies. - Any data that is not classified as a public record under G.S. 132-1 shall not be deemed a public record when incorporated into the data resources comprising the initiative. To maintain confidentiality requirements attached to the information provided to the State Controller and GDAC, each source agency providing data shall be the sole custodian of the data for the purpose of any request for inspection or copies of the data under Chapter 132 of the General Statutes.

c. Data released as part of implementation. - Information released to persons engaged in implementing the State's business intelligence strategy under this section that is used for purposes other than official State business is not a public record pursuant to Chapter 132 of the General Statutes.

d. Data from North Carolina Rate Bureau. - Notwithstanding any other provision of this section, any data released by or obtained from the North Carolina Rate Bureau under this initiative relating to workers' compensation insurance claims, business ratings, or premiums are not public records and public disclosure of such data, in whole or in part, by the GDAC or State Controller, or by any State agency, is prohibited. (2013-360, s. 7.10(d); 2013-363, s. 2.4(a).)

§ 143B-426.39. Powers and duties of the State Controller.

The State Controller shall:

(1) Prescribe, develop, operate, and maintain in accordance with generally accepted principles of governmental accounting, a uniform state accounting system for all state agencies. The system shall be designed to assure compliance with all legal and constitutional requirements including those associated with the receipt and expenditure of, and the accountability for public funds. The State Controller may elect to review a State agency's compliance with prescribed uniform State accounting system standards, as well as applicable legal and constitutional requirements related to compliance with such standards.

(2) On the recommendation of the State Auditor, prescribe and supervise the installation of any changes in the accounting systems of an agency that, in the judgment of the State Controller, are necessary to secure and maintain internal control and facilitate the recording of accounting data for the purpose of preparing reliable and meaningful statements and reports. The State Controller

shall be responsible for seeing that a new system is designed to accumulate information required for the preparation of budget reports and other financial reports.

(3) Maintain complete, accurate and current financial records that set out all revenues, charges against funds, fund and appropriation balances, interfund transfers, outstanding vouchers, and encumbrances for all State funds and other public funds including trust funds and institutional funds available to, encumbered, or expended by each State agency, in a manner consistent with the uniform State accounting system.

(4) Prescribe the uniform classifications of accounts to be used by all State agencies including receipts, expenditures, assets, liabilities, fund types, organization codes, and purposes. The State Controller shall also, after consultation with the Office of State Budget and Management, prescribe a form for the periodic reporting of financial accounts, transactions, and other matters that is compatible with systems and reports required by the State Controller under this section. Additional records, accounts, and accounting systems may be maintained by agencies when required for reporting to funding sources provided prior approval is obtained from the State Controller.

(4a) Prescribe that, unless exempted by the State Controller, newly created or acquired component units of the State are required to have the same fiscal year as the State.

(5) Prescribe the manner in which disbursements of the State agencies shall be made and may require that warrants, vouchers, electronic payments, or checks, except those drawn by the State Auditor, State Treasurer, and Administrative Officer of the Courts, shall bear two signatures of officers as designated by the State Controller.

(6) Prescribe, develop, operate, and maintain a uniform payroll system, in accordance with G.S. 143B-426.40G and G.S. 143C-6-6 for all State agencies. This uniform payroll system shall be designed to assure compliance with all legal and constitutional requirements. When the State Controller finds it expedient to do so because of a State agency's size and location, the State Controller may authorize a State agency to operate its own payroll system. Any State agency authorized by the State Controller to operate its own payroll system shall comply with the requirements adopted by the State Controller.

(7) Keep a record of the appropriations, allotments, expenditures, and revenues of each State agency.

(8) Make appropriate reconciliations with the balances and accounts kept by the State Treasurer.

(9) Develop, implement, and amend as necessary a uniform statewide cash management plan for all State agencies in accordance with G.S. 147-86.11.

(9a) Implement a statewide accounts receivable program in accordance with Article 6B of Chapter 147 of the General Statutes.

(10) Prepare and submit to the Governor, the State Auditor, the State Treasurer, and the Office of State Budget and Management each month, a report summarizing by State agency and appropriation or other fund source, the results of financial transactions. This report shall be in the form that will most clearly and accurately set out the current fiscal condition of the State. The State Controller shall also furnish each State agency a report of its transactions by appropriation or other fund source in a form that will clearly and accurately present the fiscal activities and condition of the appropriation or fund source.

(11) Prepare and submit to the Governor, the State Auditor, the State Treasurer, and the Office of State Budget and Management, at the end of each quarter, a report on the financial condition and results of operations of the State entity for the period ended. This report shall clearly and accurately present the condition of all State funds and appropriation balances and shall include comments, recommendations, and concerns regarding the fiscal affairs and condition of the State.

(12) Prepare on or before October 31 of each year, a Comprehensive Annual Financial Report in accordance with generally accepted accounting principles of the preceding fiscal year, in accordance with G.S. 143B-426.40H. The report shall include State agencies and component units of the State, as defined by generally accepted accounting principles.

(13) Perform additional functions and duties assigned to the State Controller, within the scope and context of the State Budget Act, Chapter 143C of the General Statutes.

(14) through (16) Recodified as G.S. 143B-472.42 (1), (2), and (3) by Session Laws 1997-148, s. 3.

(17) Coordinate data integration and data sharing pursuant to G.S. 143B-426.38A across State agencies, departments, and institutions to support the State's enterprise-level business intelligence initiative. (1985 (Reg. Sess., 1986), c. 1024, s. 1; 1987, c. 738, s. 59(a)(2); 1989, c. 239, s. 4; 1989 (Reg. Sess., 1990), c. 1024, s. 37; 1991, c. 542, s. 14; 1993, c. 512, s. 2; 1993 (Reg. Sess., 1994), c. 777, s. 1(a); 1997-148, s. 3; 2000-67, s. 7(b); 2000-140, s. 93.1(a); 2001-424, s. 12.2(b); 2005-65, s. 1; 2005-276, s. 6.19; 2006-66, s. 6.19(a), (c); 2006-203, s. 8; 2006-221, s. 3A; 2006-259, s. 40(a), (c); 2013-360, s. 7.10(e).)

§ 143B-426.39A: Recodified as § 143B-472.43 by Session Laws 1997-148, s. 4.

§ 143B-426.39B. Compliance review work papers not public records.

Work papers and other supportive material created as a result of a compliance review conducted under G.S. 143B-426.39(1) are not public records under Chapter 132 of the General Statutes. The State Controller shall make all work papers and other supportive materials available to the State Auditor. The State Controller may, unless otherwise prohibited by law, make work papers available for inspection by duly authorized representatives of the State and federal governments in connection with matters officially before them. Any report resulting from a compliance review is a public record under Chapter 132 of the General Statutes. (2005-65, s. 2.)

Part 28A. State Information Processing Services.

§ 143B-426.40: Recodified as § 143B-472.44 by Session Laws 1997-148, s. 5.

Part 28B. Assignment of Claims Against State.

§ 143B-426.40A. Assignments of claims against State.

(a) Definitions. - The following definitions apply in this section:

(1) Assignment. An assignment or transfer of a claim, or a power of attorney, an order, or another authority for receiving payment of a claim.

(2) Claim. A claim, a part or a share of a claim, or an interest in a claim, whether absolute or conditional.

(3) Qualified charitable organization. A charitable organization that is exempt from federal income tax pursuant to section 501(c)(3) of the Internal Revenue Code.

(4) State employee credit union. A credit union organized under Chapter 54 of the General Statutes whose membership is at least one-half employees of the State.

(5) The State. The State of North Carolina and any department, bureau, or institution of the State of North Carolina.

(b) Assignments Prohibited. - Except as otherwise provided in this section, any assignment of a claim against the State is void, regardless of the consideration given for the assignment, unless the claim has been duly audited and allowed by the State and the State has issued a warrant for payment of the claim. Except as otherwise provided in this section, the State shall not issue a warrant to an assignee of a claim against the State.

(c) Assignments in Favor of Certain Entities Allowed. - This section does not apply to an assignment in favor of:

(1) A hospital.

(2) A building and loan association.

(3) A uniform rental firm in order to allow an employee of the Department of Transportation to rent uniforms that include Day-Glo orange shirts or vests as required by federal and State law.

(4) An insurance company for medical, hospital, disability, or life insurance.

(d) Assignments to Meet Child Support Obligations Allowed. - This section does not apply to assignments made to meet child support obligations pursuant to G.S. 110-136.1.

(e) Assignments for Prepaid Legal Services Allowed. - This section does not apply to an assignment for payment for prepaid legal services.

(f) Payroll Deduction for State Employees' Credit Union Accounts Allowed. - An employee of the State who is a member of a State employee credit union may authorize, in writing, the periodic deduction from the employee's salary or wages paid for employment by the State of a designated lump sum for deposit to any credit union accounts, purchase of any credit union shares, or payment of any credit union obligations agreed to by the employee and the State Employees' Credit Union.

(f1) Payroll Deduction for Contributions to the Parental Savings Fund Allowed. - An employee of the State may authorize, in writing, the periodic deduction from the employee's salary or wages paid for employment by the State of a designated lump sum for deposit in the Parental Savings Trust Fund administered by the State Education Assistance Authority.

(g) Payroll Deduction for Payments to Certain Employees' Associations Allowed. - An employee of the State or any of its political subdivisions other than local boards of education, institutions, departments, bureaus, agencies or commissions, or any of its community colleges, who is a member of a domiciled employees' association that has at least 2,000 members, 500 of whom are employees of the State or a political subdivision of the State other than a local board of education, may authorize, in writing, the periodic deduction each payroll period from the employee's salary or wages a designated lump sum to be paid to the employees' association. A political subdivision may also allow periodic deductions for a domiciled employees' association that does not otherwise meet the minimum membership requirements set forth in this paragraph.

An authorization under this subsection shall remain in effect until revoked by the employee. A plan of payroll deductions pursuant to this subsection for employees of the State and other association members shall become void if the employees' association engages in collective bargaining with the State, any political subdivision of the State, or any local school administrative unit. This subsection does not apply to county or municipal governments or any local governmental unit.

(h) Payroll Deduction for State Employees Combined Campaign Allowed. - Subject to rules adopted by the State Controller, an employee of the State may authorize, in writing, the periodic deduction from the employee's salary or wages paid for employment by the State of a designated lump sum to be paid to satisfy the employee's pledge to the State Employees Combined Campaign.

(i) Payroll Deduction for Public School and Community College Employees' Contributions to Charitable Organizations Allowed. - Subject to rules adopted by the State Controller, an employee of a local board of education or community college may authorize, in writing, the periodic deduction from the employee's salary or wages paid for employment by the board of education or community college of a designated lump sum to be contributed to a qualified charitable organization that has first been approved by the employee's board of education or community college board.

(j) Payroll Deduction for University of North Carolina System Employees' Contributions to Certain Charitable Organizations Allowed. - Subject to rules adopted by the State Controller, if a constituent institution of The University of North Carolina approves a payroll deduction plan under this subsection, an employee of the constituent institution may authorize, in writing, the periodic deduction from the employee's salary or wages paid for employment by the constituent institution of a designated lump sum to be contributed to a qualified charitable organization that exists to support athletic or charitable programs of the constituent institution and that has first been approved by the President of The University of North Carolina as existing to support athletic or charitable programs. If a payroll deduction plan under this subsection results in additional costs to a constituent institution, these costs shall be paid by the qualified charitable organizations receiving contributions under the plan.

(k) Payroll Deduction for University of North Carolina System Employees to Pay for Discretionary Privileges of University Service. - Subject to rules adopted by the State Controller, if a constituent institution of The University of North Carolina approves a payroll deduction plan under this subsection, an employee of the constituent institution may authorize, in writing, the periodic deduction from the employee's salary or wages paid for employment by the constituent institution, of one or more designated lump sums to be applied to the cost of corresponding discretionary privileges available at employee expense from the employing institution. Discretionary privileges from the employing institution that may be paid for through this subsection include parking privileges, athletic passes, use of recreational facilities, admission to campus concert series, and access to other institutionally hosted or provided entertainments, events, and facilities.

(l) Assignment of Payments From the Underground Storage Tank Cleanup Funds. - This section does not apply to an assignment of any claim for payment or reimbursement from the Commercial Leaking Petroleum Underground Storage Tank Cleanup Fund established by G.S. 143-215.94B or the

Noncommercial Leaking Petroleum Underground Storage Tank Cleanup Fund established by G.S. 143-215.94D.

(m) Assignment of Funds Allocated by the State Board of Education to Charter Schools. - This section does not apply to assignments by charter schools to obtain funds for facilities, equipment, or operations pursuant to G.S. 115C-238.29H. (2006-66, s. 6.19(a), (b); 2006-203, s. 9; 2006-221, s. 3A; 2006-259, s. 40(a), (b); 2006-264, s. 67(b); 2012-1, s. 1; 2013-355, s. 4.)

§ 143B-426.40B: Reserved for future codification purposes.

§ 143B-426.40C: Reserved for future codification purposes.

§ 143B-426.40D: Reserved for future codification purposes.

§ 143B-426.40E: Reserved for future codification purposes.

§ 143B-426.40F: Reserved for future codification purposes.

Part 28C. Accounting Systems.

§ 143B-426.40G. Issuance of warrants upon State Treasurer; delivery of warrants and disbursements for non-State entities.

(a) The State Controller shall have the exclusive responsibility for the issuance of all warrants for the payment of money upon the State Treasurer. All warrants upon the State Treasurer shall be signed by the State Controller, who before issuing them shall determine the legality of payment and the correctness of the accounts. All warrants issued for non-State entities shall be delivered by the appropriate agency to the entity's legally designated recipient by United States mail or its equivalent, including electronic funds transfer.

When the State Controller finds it expedient to do so because of a State agency's size and location, the State Controller may authorize a State agency to make expenditures through a disbursing account with the State Treasurer. The State Controller shall authorize the Judicial Department and the General Assembly to make expenditures through such disbursing accounts. All disbursements made to non-State entities shall be delivered by the appropriate agency to the entity's legally designated recipient by United States mail or its equivalent, including electronic funds transfer. All deposits in these disbursing accounts shall be by the State Controller's warrant. A copy of each voucher making withdrawals from these disbursing accounts and any supporting data required by the State Controller shall be forwarded to the Office of the State Controller monthly or as otherwise required by the State Controller. Supporting data for a voucher making a withdrawal from one of these disbursing accounts to meet a payroll shall include the amount of the payroll and the employees whose compensation is part of the payroll.

A central payroll unit operating under the Office of the State Controller may make deposits and withdrawals directly to and from a disbursing account. The disbursing account shall constitute a revolving fund for servicing payrolls passed through the central payroll unit.

The State Controller may use a facsimile signature machine in affixing his signature to warrants.

(b) The State Treasurer may impose on an agency a fee of fifteen dollars ($15.00) for each check drawn against the agency's disbursing account that causes the balance in the account to be in overdraft or while the account is in overdraft. The financial officer shall pay the fee from non-State or personal funds to the General Fund to the credit of the miscellaneous nontax revenue account by the agency. (2006-66, s. 6.19(a); 2006-203, s. 9; 2006-221, s. 3A; 2006-259, s. 40(a).)

§ 143B-426.40H. Annual financial information.

Every fiscal year, all State agencies and component units of the State, as defined by generally accepted accounting principles, shall prepare annual financial information on all funds administered by them no later than 60 days after the end of the State's fiscal year then ended in accordance with generally accepted accounting principles as described in authoritative pronouncements and interpreted or prescribed by the State Controller, and in the form and time frame required by the State Controller. The State Controller shall publish guidelines specifying the procedures to implement the necessary records, procedures, and accounting systems to reflect these statements on the proper basis of accounting.

Accordingly, the State Controller shall combine the financial information for the various agencies into a Comprehensive Annual Financial Report for the State of North Carolina in accordance with generally accepted accounting principles. These statements, along with the opinion of the State Auditor, shall be published as the official financial statements of the State and shall be distributed to the Governor, the Office of State Budget and Management, members of the General Assembly, heads of departments, agencies, and institutions of the State, and other interested parties. The State Controller shall notify the Director of the Budget of any State agencies and component units of the State, as defined by generally accepted accounting principles, that have not complied fully with the requirements of this section within the specified time, and the Director of the Budget shall employ whatever means necessary, including the withholding of allotments, to ensure immediate corrective actions. (2006-66, s. 6.19(a); 2006-203, s. 9; 2006-221, s. 3A; 2006-259, s. 40(a).)

Part 29. Board of Trustees of the North Carolina Public Employee Special Pay Plan.

§ 143B-426.41: Repealed by Session Laws 2011-266, s. 1.24, effective July 1, 2011.

§ 143B-426.42: Reserved for future codification purposes.

§ 143B-426.43: Reserved for future codification purposes.

§ 143B-426.44: Reserved for future codification purposes.

§ 143B-426.45: Reserved for future codification purposes.

§ 143B-426.46: Reserved for future codification purposes.

§ 143B-426.47: Reserved for future codification purposes.

§ 143B-426.48: Reserved for future codification purposes.

§ 143B-426.49: Reserved for future codification purposes.

Part 30. Eugenics Asexualization and Sterilization Compensation Program.

§ 143B-426.50. (For expiration date, see note) Definitions.

As used in this Part, the following definitions apply:

(1)   Claimant. - An individual on whose behalf a claim is made for compensation as a qualified recipient under this Part. An individual must be alive on June 30, 2013, in order to be a claimant.

(2)   Commission. - The North Carolina Industrial Commission.

(3)   Involuntarily. - In the case of:

a.   A minor child, either with or without the consent of the minor child's parent, guardian, or other person standing in loco parentis.

b.   An incompetent adult, with or without the consent of the incompetent adult's guardian or pursuant to a valid court order.

c.   A competent adult, without the adult's informed consent, with the presumption being that the adult gave informed consent.

(4)   Office. - The Office of Justice for Sterilization Victims.

(5)   Qualified recipient. - An individual who was asexualized involuntarily or sterilized involuntarily under the authority of the Eugenics Board of North Carolina in accordance with Chapter 224 of the Public Laws of 1933 or Chapter 221 of the Public Laws of 1937. (2013-360, s. 6.18(a).)

§ 143B-426.51. Compensation payments.

(a)   A claimant determined to be a qualified recipient under this Part shall receive lump-sum compensation in the amount determined by this subsection from funds appropriated to the Department of State Treasurer for these purposes. Except as provided by the succeeding sentence, the amount of compensation for each qualified recipient is the sum of ten million dollars ($10,000,000) divided by the total number of qualified recipients, and all such payments shall be made on June 30, 2015. The State Treasurer shall reduce the ten million dollars ($10,000,000) by holding out a pro-rata amount per claimant for any cases in which there has not been a final determination of the claim on June 30, 2015. Payments made to persons determined to be qualified claimants after that date shall be made upon such determination, and if after final adjudication of all claims there remains a balance from the funds held out, they shall be paid pro-rata to all qualified claimants.

(b) If any claimant shall die during the pendency of a claim, or after being determined to be a qualified recipient, any payment shall be made to the estate of the decedent.

(c) A qualified recipient may assign compensation received pursuant to subsection (a) of this section to a trust established for the benefit of the qualified recipient. (2013-360, s. 6.18(a).)

§ 143B-426.52. Claims for compensation for asexualization or sterilization.

(a) An individual shall be entitled to compensation as provided for in this Part if a claim is submitted on behalf of that individual in accordance with this Part on or before June 30, 2014, and that individual is subsequently determined by a preponderance of the evidence to be a qualified recipient, except that any competent adult who gave consent is not a qualified recipient unless that individual can show by a preponderance of the evidence that the consent was not informed.

(b) A claim under this section shall be submitted to the Office. The claim shall be in a form and supported by appropriate documentation and information, as required by the Commission. A claim may be submitted on behalf of a claimant by a person lawfully authorized to act on the individual's or the individual's estate's behalf.

(c) The Commission shall determine the eligibility of a claimant to receive the compensation authorized by this Part in accordance with G.S. 143B-426.53. The Commission shall notify the claimant in writing of the Commission's determination regarding the claimant's eligibility.

(d) The Commission shall adopt rules for the determination of eligibility and the processing of claims in accordance with G.S. 150B-21.1. Notwithstanding G.S. 150B-21.1(d), the rules adopted pursuant to this section shall expire on the earlier of the date all claims made under this section are finally adjudicated or June 30, 2018. (2013-360, s. 6.18(a); 2013-410, s. 40.)

§ 143B-426.53. Industrial Commission determination.

(a)   The Commission shall determine whether a claimant is eligible for compensation as a qualified recipient under this Part. The Commission shall have all powers and authority granted under Article 31 of Chapter 143 of the General Statutes with regard to claims filed pursuant to this Part.

(b)   A deputy commissioner shall be assigned by the Commission to make initial determinations of eligibility for compensation under this Part. The deputy commissioner shall review the claim and supporting documentation submitted on behalf of a claimant and shall make a determination of eligibility. In any case where the claimant was a competent adult when asexualized or sterilized, the burden is on the claimant to rebut the presumption that the claimant gave informed consent. If the claim is not approved, the deputy commissioner shall set forth in writing the reasons for the disapproval and notify the claimant.

(c)   A claimant whose claim is not approved under subsection (b) of this section may submit to the Commission additional documentation in support of the individual's claim and request a redetermination by the deputy commissioner.

(d)   A claimant whose claim is not approved under subsection (b) or (c) of this section shall have the right to request a hearing before the deputy commissioner. The hearing shall be conducted in accordance with rules of the Commission. For claimants who are residents of this State, at the request of the claimant, the hearing shall be held in the county of residence of the claimant. For claimants who are not residents of this State, the hearing shall be held in Wake County or at a location of mutual convenience as determined by the deputy commissioner. The claimant shall have the right to be represented, including the right to be represented by counsel, present evidence, and call witnesses. The deputy commissioner who hears the claim shall issue a written decision of eligibility which shall be sent to the claimant.

(e)   Upon the issuance of a decision by the deputy commissioner under subsection (d) of this section, the claimant may file notice of appeal with the Commission within 30 days of the date notice of the deputy commissioner's decision is given. Such appeal shall be heard by the Commission, sitting as the full Commission, on the basis of the record in the matter and upon oral argument. The full Commission may amend, set aside, or strike out the decision of the deputy commissioner and may issue its own findings of fact, conclusions of law, and decision. The Commission shall notify all parties concerned in writing of its decision.

(f)   A claimant may appeal the decision of the full Commission to the Court of Appeals within 30 days of the date notice of the decision of the full Commission is given. Appeals under this section shall be in accordance with the procedures set forth in G.S. 143-293 and G.S. 143-294.

(g)   If at any stage of the proceedings the claimant is determined to be a qualified recipient, the Commission shall give notice to the claimant and to the Office of the State Treasurer, and the State Treasurer shall make payment of compensation to the qualified recipient or a trust specified under G.S. 143B-426.51(b).

(h)   Decisions and determinations by the Commission favorable to the claimant shall be final and not subject to appeal by the State.

(i)   Costs under this section shall be taxed to the State. (2013-360, s. 6.18(a).)

§ 143B-426.54. Office of Justice for Sterilization Victims.

(a)   There is created in the Department of Administration the Office of Justice for Sterilization Victims.

(b)   At the request of a claimant or a claimant's legal representative, the Office shall assist an individual who may be a qualified recipient to determine whether the individual qualifies for compensation under this Part. The Office may assist an individual filing a claim under this Part and collect documentation in support of the claim. With the claimant's consent, the Office may represent and advocate for the claimant before the Commission and may assist the claimant with any good-faith further appeal of an adverse decision on a claim.

(c)   The Office shall plan and implement an outreach program to attempt to notify individuals who may be possible qualified recipients. (2013-360, s. 6.18(a).)

§ 143B-426.55. Confidentiality.

Records of all inquiries of eligibility, claims, and payments under this Part shall be confidential and not public records under Chapter 132 of the General Statutes. (2013-360, s. 6.18(a).)

§ 143B-426.56. Compensation excluded as income, resources, or assets.

(a) Any payment made under this section shall not be considered income or assets for purposes of determining the eligibility for, or the amount of, any benefits or assistance under any State or local program financed in whole or in part with State funds.

(b) Pursuant to G.S. 108A-26.1, the Department of Health and Human Services shall do the following:

(1) Provide income, resource, and asset disregard to an applicant for, or recipient of, public assistance who receives compensation under this Part. The amount of the income, resource, and asset disregard shall be equal to the total compensation paid to the individual from the Eugenics Sterilization Compensation Fund.

(2) Provide resource protection by reducing any subsequent recovery by the State under G.S. 108A-70.5 from a deceased recipient's estate for payment of Medicaid-paid services by the amount of resource disregard given under subdivision (1) of this subsection.

(3) Adopt rules to implement the provisions of subdivisions (1) and (2) of this subsection. (2013-360, s. 6.18(a).)

§ 143B-426.57. Limitation of liability.

Nothing in this Part shall revive or extend any statute of limitations that may otherwise have expired prior to July 1, 2013. The State's liability arising from any cause of action related to any asexualization or sterilization performed pursuant to an order of the Eugenics Board of North Carolina shall be limited to the compensation authorized by this Part. (2013-360, s. 6.18(a).)

Article 10.

Department of Commerce.

Part 1. General Provisions.

§ 143B-427. Department of Commerce - creation.

There is hereby recreated and reconstituted a Department to be known as the "Department of Commerce," with the organization, powers, and duties defined in Article 1 of this Chapter, except as modified in this Article. (1977, c. 198, s. 1; 1989, c. 751, s. 7(23); 1991 (Reg. Sess., 1992), c. 959, ss. 44, 45.)

§ 143B-428. Department of Commerce - declaration of policy.

It is hereby declared to be the policy of the State of North Carolina to actively encourage the expansion of existing environmentally sound North Carolina industry; to actively encourage the recruitment of environmentally sound national and international industry into North Carolina through industrial recruitment efforts and through effective advertising, with an emphasis on high-wage-paying industry; to promote the development of North Carolina's labor force to meet the State's growing industrial needs; to promote the growth and development of our travel and tourist industries; to promote the development of our State ports; and to assure throughout State government, the coordination of North Carolina's economic development efforts. (1977, c. 198, s. 1; 1989, c. 751, s. 7(24); 1991 (Reg. Sess., 1992), c. 959, s. 46; 2003-340, s. 1.10.)

§ 143B-429. Department of Commerce - duties.

It shall be the duty of the Department of Commerce to provide for and promote the implementation of the declared policy of the State of North Carolina as provided in G.S. 143B-428, to promote and assist in the total economic development of North Carolina in accord with such declared policy and to perform such other duties and functions as are conferred by this Chapter, delegated or assigned by the Governor and conferred by the Constitution and laws of this State. (1977, c. 198, s. 1; 1989, c. 751, s. 7(25); 1991 (Reg. Sess., 1992), c. 959, s. 47.)

§ 143B-430. Secretary of Commerce - powers and duties.

(a) The head of the Department of Commerce is the Secretary of Commerce. The Secretary of Commerce shall have such powers and duties as are conferred on him by this Chapter, delegated to him by the Governor, and conferred on him by the Constitution and laws of this State. The Secretary of Commerce shall be responsible for effectively and efficiently organizing the Department of Commerce to promote the policy of the State of North Carolina as outlined in G.S. 143B-428 and to promote statewide economic development in accord with that policy. Except as otherwise specifically provided in this Article and in Article 1 of this Chapter, the functions, powers, duties and obligations of every agency or subunit in the Department of Commerce shall be prescribed by the Secretary of Commerce.

(b) The Secretary of Commerce shall have the power and duty to accept and administer federal funds provided to the State through the Job Training Partnership Act, Pub. L. No. 97-300, 96 Stat. 1322, 29 U.S.C. § 1501 et seq., as amended.

(c) The Secretary of Commerce may adopt rules to administer a program or fulfill a duty assigned to the Department of Commerce or the Secretary of Commerce. (1977, c. 198, s. 1; 1989, c. 727, s. 6, c. 751, ss. 7(26), 8(18); 1991 (Reg. Sess., 1992), c. 959, s. 48; 2003-284, s. 12.6A(c).)

§ 143B-431. Department of Commerce - functions.

(a) The functions of the Department of Commerce, except as otherwise expressly provided by Article 1 of this Chapter or by the Constitution of North Carolina, shall include:

(1) All of the executive functions of the State in relation to economic development and employment security, including by way of enumeration and not of limitation, the expansion and recruitment of environmentally sound industry, labor force development, the administration of unemployment insurance, the promotion of and assistance in the orderly development of North Carolina counties and communities, the promotion and growth of the travel and tourism industries, and energy resource management and energy policy development;

(2) All functions, powers, duties and obligations heretofore vested in an agency enumerated in Article 15 of Chapter 143A, to wit:

a. The State Board of Alcoholic Control,

b. The North Carolina Utilities Commission,

c. Repealed by Session Laws 2011-401, s. 1.4, effective November 1, 2011.

d. The North Carolina Industrial Commission,

e. State Banking Commission and the Commissioner of Banks,

f. Savings Institutions Division,

g. Repealed by Session Laws 2001-193, s. 10, effective July 1, 2001.

h. Credit Union Commission,

i. Repealed by Session Laws 2004-199, s. 27(c), effective August 17, 2004.

j. The North Carolina Mutual Burial Association Commission,

k. The North Carolina Rural Electrification Authority,

l. Repealed by Session Laws 2011-145, s. 14.6(f), effective July 1, 2011.

all of which enumerated agencies are hereby expressly transferred by a Type II transfer, as defined by G.S. 143A-6, to this recreated and reconstituted Department of Commerce; and

(3) All other functions, powers, duties and obligations as are conferred by this Chapter, delegated or assigned by the Governor and conferred by the Constitution and laws of this State. Any agency transferred to the Department of Commerce by a Type II transfer, as defined by G.S. 143A-6, shall have the authority to employ, direct and supervise professional and technical personnel, and such agencies shall not be accountable to the Secretary of Commerce in their exercise of quasi-judicial powers authorized by statute, notwithstanding any other provisions of this Chapter.

(b) The Department of Commerce is authorized to establish and provide for the operation of North Carolina nonprofit corporations for any of the following purposes:

(1) To aid the development of small businesses.

(2) To achieve the purposes of the United States Small Business Administration's 504 Certified Development Company Program.

(3) To acquire options and hold options for the purchase of land under G.S. 143B-437.02.

(b1) The Department of Commerce is authorized to contract for the preparation of proposals and reports in response to requests for proposals for location or expansion of major industrial projects.

(c) The Department of Commerce shall have the following powers and duties with respect to local planning assistance:

(1) To provide planning assistance to municipalities and counties and joint and regional planning boards established by two or more governmental units in the solution of their local planning problems. Planning assistance as used in this section shall consist of making population, economic, land use, traffic, and parking studies and developing plans based thereon to guide public and private development and other planning work of a similar nature. Planning assistance shall also include the preparation of proposed subdivision regulations, zoning ordinances, capital budgets, and similar measures that may be recommended for the implementation of such plans. The term planning assistance shall not be construed to include the providing of plans for specific public works.

(2) To receive and expend federal and other funds for planning assistance to municipalities and counties and to joint and regional planning boards, and to enter into contracts with the federal government, municipalities, counties, or joint and regional planning boards with reference thereto.

(3) To perform planning assistance, either through the staff of the Department or through acceptable contractual arrangements with other qualified State agencies or institutions, local planning agencies, or with private professional organizations or individuals.

(4) To assume full responsibility for the proper execution of a planning program for which a grant of State or federal funds has been made and for carrying out the terms of a federal grant contract.

(5) To cooperate with municipal, county, joint and regional planning boards, and federal agencies for the purpose of aiding and encouraging an orderly, coordinated development of the State.

(6) To establish and conduct, either with its own staff or through contractual arrangements with institutions of higher education, State agencies, or private agencies, training programs for those employed or to be employed in community development activities.

(d) The Department of Commerce, with the approval of the Governor, may apply for and accept grants from the federal government and its agencies and from any foundation, corporation, association, or individual and may comply with the terms, conditions, and limitations of such grants in order to accomplish the Department's purposes. Grant funds shall be expended pursuant to the Executive Budget Act. In addition, the Department shall have the following powers and duties with respect to its duties in administering federal programs:

(1) To negotiate, collect, and pay reasonable fees and charges regarding the making or servicing of grants, loans, or other evidences of indebtedness.

(2) To establish and revise by regulation, in accordance with Chapter 150B of the General Statutes, schedules of reasonable rates, fees, or charges for services rendered, including but not limited to, reasonable fees or charges for servicing applications. Schedules of rates, fees, or charges may vary according to classes of service, and different schedules may be adopted for public entities, nonprofit entities, private for-profit entities, and individuals.

(3) To pledge current and future federal fund appropriations to the State from the Community Development Block Grant (CDBG) program for use as loan guarantees in accordance with the provisions of the Section 108 Loan Guarantee program, Subpart M, 24 CFR 570.700, et seq., authorized by the Housing and Community Development Act of 1974 and amendments thereto. The Department may enter into loan guarantee agreements in support of projects sponsored by individual local governments or in support of pools of two or more projects supported by local governments with authorized State and federal agencies and other necessary parties in order to carry out its duties under this subdivision. In making loan guarantees and grants under this

subdivision the Department shall take into consideration project applications, geographic diversity and regional balance in the entire community development block grant program. In making loan guarantees authorized under this subdivision, the Department shall ensure that apportionment of the risks involved in pledging future federal funds in accordance with State policies and priorities for financial support of categories of assistance is made primarily against the category from which the loan guarantee originally derived. A pledge of future CDBG funds under this subdivision is not a debt or liability of the State or any political subdivision of the State or a pledge of the faith and credit of the State or any political subdivision of the State. The pledging of future CDBG funds under this subdivision does not directly, indirectly, or contingently obligate the State or any political subdivision of the State to levy or to pledge any taxes, nor may pledges exceed twice the amount of annual CDBG funds.

Prior to issuing a Section 108 Loan Guarantee agreement, the Department of Commerce must make the following findings:

a. The minimum size of the Section 108 Loan Guarantee is (i) seven hundred fifty thousand dollars ($750,000) for a project supported by an individual local government and (ii) two hundred fifty thousand dollars ($250,000) for a project supported as part of a loan pool; and the maximum size is five million dollars ($5,000,000) per project.

b. The Section 108 Loan Guarantee cannot constitute more than fifty percent (50%) of total project costs.

c. The project has ten percent (10%) equity from the corporation, partnership, or sponsoring party. "Equity" means cash, real estate, or other hard assets contributed to the project and loans that are subordinated in payment and collateral during the term of the Section 108 Loan Guarantee.

d. The project has the personal guarantee of any person owning ten percent (10%) or more of the corporation, partnership, or sponsoring entity, except for projects involving Low-Income Housing Tax Credits under section 42 of the Internal Revenue Code or Historic Tax Credits under section 47 of the Internal Revenue Code. Collateral on the loan must be sufficient to cover outstanding debt obligations.

e. The project has sufficient cash flow from operations for debt service to repay the Section 108 loan.

f. The project meets all underwriting and eligibility requirements of the North Carolina Section 108 Guarantee Program Guidelines and of the Department of Housing and Urban Development regulations, except that projects involving hotels, motels, private recreational facilities, private entertainment facilities, and convention centers are ineligible for Section 108 loan guarantees.

The Department shall create a loan loss reserve fund as additional security for loans guaranteed under this section and may deposit federal program income or other funds governed by this section into the loan loss reserve fund. The Department shall maintain a balance in the reserve fund of no less than ten percent (10%) of the outstanding indebtedness secured by Section 108 loan guarantees.

(e) The Department of Commerce may establish a clearinghouse for State business license information and shall perform the following duties:

(1) Establish a license information service detailing requirements for establishing and engaging in business in the State.

(2) Provide the most recent forms and information sheets for all State business licenses.

(3) Prepare, publish, and distribute a complete directory of all State licenses required to do business in North Carolina.

(4) Upon request, the Department shall assist a person as provided below:

a. Identify the type and source of licenses that may be required and the potential difficulties in obtaining the licenses based on an informal review of a potential applicant's business at an early stage in its planning. Information provided by the Department is for guidance purposes only and may not be asserted by an applicant as a waiver or release from any license requirement. However, an applicant who uses the services of the Department as provided in this subdivision, and who receives a written statement identifying required State business licenses relating to a specific business activity, shall not be assessed a penalty for failure to obtain any State business license which was not identified, provided that the applicant submits an application for each such license within 60 days after written notification by the Department or the agency responsible for issuing the license.

b. Arrange an informal conference between the person and the appropriate agency to clarify licensing requirements or standards, if necessary.

c. Assist in preparing the appropriate application and supplemental forms.

d. Monitor the license review process to determine the status of a particular license. If there is a delay in the review process, the Department may demand to know the reasons for the delay, the action required to end the delay, and shall provide this information to the applicant. The Department may assist the applicant in resolving a dispute with an agency during the application process. If a request for a license is refused, the Department may explain the recourse available to the person under the Administrative Procedure Act.

(5) Collaborate with the business license coordinator designated in State agencies in providing information on the licenses and regulatory requirements of the agency, and in coordinating conferences with applicants to clarify license and regulatory requirements.

Each agency shall designate a business license coordinator. The coordinator shall have the following responsibilities:

a. Provide to the Department the most recent application and supplemental forms required for each license issued by the agency, the most recent information available on existing and proposed agency rules, the most recent information on changes or proposed changes in license requirements or agency rules and how those changes will affect the business community, and agency publications that would be of aid or interest to the business community.

b. Work with the Department in scheduling conferences for applicants as provided under this subsection.

c. Determine, upon request of an applicant or the Department, the status of a license application or renewal, the reason for any delay in the license review process, and the action needed to end the delay; and to notify the applicant or Department, as appropriate, of those findings.

d. Work with the Department or applicant, upon request, to resolve any dispute that may arise between the agency and the applicant during the review process.

e. Review agency regulatory and license requirements and to provide a written report to the Department that identifies the regulatory and licensing requirements that affect the business community; indicates which, if any, requirements should be eliminated, modified, or consolidated with other requirements; and explains the need for continuing those requirements not recommended for elimination.

f. Report, on an annual basis, to the Department on the number of licenses issued during the previous fiscal year on a form prescribed by the Department.

(f) Financial statements submitted to the Department by a private company or an individual seeking assistance from the Department are not public records as defined in G.S. 132-1. (1977, c. 198, s. 1; 1987, c. 214; 1989, c. 76, s. 25; c. 751, s. 2; 1991, c. 689, s. 153; 1991 (Reg. Sess., 1992), c. 959, s. 49; 1995, c. 310, s. 1; 1995 (Reg. Sess., 1996), c. 575, s. 1; 2001-193, s. 10; 2004-124, ss. 6.26(c), 6.26(d), 13.9A(c); 2004-199, s. 27(c); 2011-145, s. 14.6(f); 2011-297, s. 3; 2011-401, s. 1.4; 2012-187, s. 10.3.)

§ 143B-431.1. Toll-free number for information on housing assistance.

There shall be established in the Department of Commerce a toll-free telephone number to provide information on housing assistance to the citizens of the State. (1989, c. 751, s. 6; 1991 (Reg. Sess., 1992), c. 959, s. 50.)

§ 143B-431.2. Department of Commerce - limitation on grants and loans.

The Department of Commerce may not make a loan nor award a grant to any individual, organization, or governmental unit if that individual, organization, or governmental unit is currently in default on any loan made by the Department of Commerce. (2000-56, s. 4.)

§ 143B-432. Transfers to Department of Commerce.

(a) The Division of Economic Development of the Department of Natural and Economic Resources, the Science and Technology Committee of the Department of Natural and Economic Resources, and the Science and Technology Research Center of the Department of Natural and Economic

Resources are each hereby transferred to the Department of Commerce by a Type I transfer, as defined in G.S. 143A-6.

(b) All functions, powers, duties, and obligations heretofore vested in the following subunits of the Department of Natural Resources and Community Development are hereby transferred to and vested in the Department of Commerce by a Type I transfer as defined in G.S. 143A-6:

(1) Community Assistance Division.

(2) Employment and Training Division.

(c) All functions, powers, duties, and obligations heretofore vested in the following councils of the Department of Natural Resources and Community Development are hereby transferred to and vested in the Department of Commerce by a Type II transfer as defined in G.S. 143A-6:

(1) Community Development Council.

(2) Job Training Coordinating Council. (1977, c. 198, s. 1; 1989, c. 727, s. 7; c. 751, s. 7(27); 1989 (Reg. Sess., 1990), c. 1004, s. 32; 1991 (Reg. Sess., 1992), c. 959, s. 51; 2010-180, s. 7(e); 2012-201, s. 9.)

§ 143B-432.1. Department of Commerce - Small Business Ombudsman.

A Small Business Ombudsman is created in the Department of Commerce to work with small businesses to ensure they receive timely answers to questions and timely resolution of issues involving State government. The Small Business Ombudsman shall have the authority to make inquiry of State agencies on behalf of a business, to receive information concerning the status of a business's inquiry, and to convene representatives of various State agencies to discuss and resolve specific issues raised by a business. The Small Business Ombudsman shall also work with the small business community to identify problems in State government related to unnecessary delays, inconsistencies between regulatory agencies, and inefficient uses of State resources. (2004-124, s. 13.9A(e).)

§ 143B-433. Department of Commerce - organization.

The Department of Commerce shall be organized to include:

(1) The following agencies:

a. The North Carolina Alcoholic Beverage Control Commission.

b. The North Carolina Utilities Commission.

c. Repealed by Session Laws 2011-401, s. 1.5, effective November 1, 2011.

d. The North Carolina Industrial Commission.

e. State Banking Commission.

f. Savings Institutions Division.

g. Repealed by Session Laws 2001-193, s. 11, effective July 1, 2001.

h. Credit Union Commission.

i. Repealed by Session Laws 2004-199, s. 27(d), effective August 17, 2004.

j. The North Carolina Mutual Burial Association Commission.

k. Repealed by Session Laws 2012-120, s. 3(g), effective June 28, 2012.

l. The North Carolina Rural Electrification Authority.

m. Repealed by Session Laws 1985, c. 757, s. 179(d).

n. North Carolina Science and Technology Research Center.

o. Repealed by Session Laws 2011-145, s. 14.6(g), effective July 1, 2011.

p. Repealed by Session Laws 2010-180, s. 7(f), effective August 2, 2010.

q. Economic Development Board.

r. Labor Force Development Council.

s.,   t. Repealed by Session Laws 2000, c. 140, s. 76.(j), effective September 30, 2000.

u.   Navigation and Pilotage Commissions established by Chapter 76 of the General Statutes.

v.   Repealed by Session Laws 1993, c. 321, s. 313b.

w.   The Rural Economic Development Division.

x.   The Rural Infrastructure Authority.

(2)   Those agencies which are transferred to the Department of Commerce including the:

a.   Community Assistance Division.

b.   Community Development Council.

c.   Employment and Training Division.

d.   Job Training Coordinating Council.

(3)   The Division of Employment Security.

(4)   Such divisions as may be established pursuant to Article 1 of this Chapter. (1977, c. 198, s. 1; 1979, c. 668, s. 2; 1981, c. 412, ss. 4, 5; 1983, c. 899, s. 1; 1985, c. 757, s. 179(d); 1989, c. 76, s. 26; c. 727, s. 8; c. 751, s. 7(28); 1991 (Reg. Sess., 1992), c. 959, s. 52; 1993, c. 321, s. 313(b); 1998-217, s. 19; 2000-140, s. 76(j); 2001-193, s. 11; 2004-199, s. 27(d); 2010-180, s. 7(f); 2011-145, s. 14.6(g); 2011-401, s. 1.5; 2012-120, s. 3(g); 2013-360, s. 15.10(e).)

Part 1A. Housing Coordination and Policy Council.

§§ 143B-433.1 through 143B-433.3: Repealed by Session Laws 1993, c. 321, s. 305(c).

Part 2. Economic Development.

§ 143B-434. Economic Development Board - creation, duties, membership.

(a) Creation and Duties. - There is created within the Department of Commerce an Economic Development Board. The Board shall have the following duties:

(1) To provide economic and community development planning for the State.

(2) To recommend economic development policy to the Secretary of Commerce, the General Assembly, and the Governor. The recommendations may cover the following issues as well as any other economic development policy issues:

a. Use of tax abatements and other incentives to motivate economic development.

b. Definition of which specific activities and programs should be considered economic development activities and programs for the purpose of receiving State appropriations.

c. The role of institutions of higher education in economic development.

d. The use of State funds to leverage private nonprofit economic development initiatives.

e. The linkage of workforce preparedness activities and initiatives, and economic development planning.

(3) To recommend annually to the Governor biennial and annual appropriations for economic development programs.

(4) To develop and update annually a comprehensive strategic economic development plan, as provided in G.S. 143B-434.1.

The Board shall meet at least quarterly at the call of its chair or the Secretary. Each quarter the Secretary shall report to the Board on the program and progress of this State's economic development.

(b) Membership. - The Economic Development Board shall consist of 39 members. The Secretary of Commerce shall serve ex officio as a member and as the secretary of the Economic Development Board. The Secretary of Revenue shall serve as an ex officio, nonvoting member. The Secretary of the Department of Cultural Resources shall serve as an ex officio, nonvoting member. Four members of the House of Representatives appointed by the Speaker of the House of Representatives, four members of the Senate appointed by the President Pro Tempore of the Senate, the Superintendent of Public Instruction, or designee, the President of The University of North Carolina, or designee, the President of the North Carolina Community College System, or designee, the Secretary of State, and the President of the Senate (or the designee of the President of the Senate), shall serve as members of the Board. The Governor shall appoint the remaining 23 members of the Board. Effective with the terms beginning July 1, 1997, one of the Governor's appointees shall be a representative of a nonprofit organization involved in economic development and two of the Governor's appointees shall be county economic development representatives. The Governor shall designate a chair and a vice-chair from among the members of the Board. Appointments to the Board made by the Governor for terms beginning July 1, 1997, and appointments to the Board made by the Speaker of the House of Representatives and the President Pro Tempore of the Senate for terms beginning July 9, 1993, should reflect the ethnic and gender diversity of the State as nearly as practical.

The initial appointments to the Board shall be for terms beginning on July 9, 1993. Of the initial appointments made by the Governor, the terms shall expire July 1, 1997. Of the initial appointments made by the Speaker of the House of Representatives and by the President Pro Tempore of the Senate two appointments of each shall be designated to expire on July 1, 1995; the remaining terms shall expire July 1, 1997. Thereafter, all appointments shall be for a term of four years.

The appointing officer shall make a replacement appointment to serve for the unexpired term in the case of a vacancy.

The members of the Economic Development Board shall receive per diem and necessary travel and subsistence expenses payable to members of State Boards and agencies generally pursuant to G.S. 138-5 and G.S. 138-6, as the case may be. The members of the Economic Development Board who are members of the General Assembly shall not receive per diem but shall receive necessary travel and subsistence expenses at rates prescribed by G.S. 120-3.1.

(c) Advice and Staff. - The Secretaries of Administration, State, and Transportation, the Commissioners of Agriculture and Labor, and the State Treasurer, or their designees, shall advise the Board on economic development activities within the responsibility of their respective departments. Clerical and professional staff support to the Economic Development Board shall be provided by an Interagency Economic Development Group composed of representatives of the following State agencies:

(1) The Department of Administration.

(2) The Department of Agriculture and Consumer Services.

(3) The Division of Employment Security.

(4) The Department of Labor.

(5) The Department of Transportation.

The Department of Commerce shall have the responsibility for coordinating the activities and efforts of the Interagency Economic Development Group. (1977, c. 198, s. 1; 1981, c. 47, s. 6; 1981 (Reg. Sess., 1982), c. 1191, s. 18; 1983, c. 717, s. 83; 1989, c. 751, ss. 7(29), 9(c); 1991 (Reg. Sess., 1992), c. 959, s. 85; c. 1038, s. 22; 1993, c. 321, s. 313(a); c. 561, s. 12; 1993 (Reg. Sess., 1994), c. 773, s. 15.1; 1997-261, s. 105; 2001-487, s. 32; 2001-513, s. 13; 2010-184, s. 6; 2011-121, s. 1; 2011-401, s. 5.1.)

§ 143B-434.01. Comprehensive Strategic Economic Development Plan.

(a) Definitions. - The following definitions apply in this section:

(1) Board. - The Economic Development Board.

(2) Department. - The Department of Commerce.

(3) Economic distress. - The presence of at least one trend indicator or at least one status indicator:

a. Trend indicators:

1. Weighted average age of industrial plants exceeding statewide average age.

2. Loss of population over the most recent three- to five-year period.

3. Below average job growth over the most recent three- to five-year period.

4. Outmigration over the most recent three- to five-year period.

5. Decline in real wages over the most recent three- to five-year period.

6. Above average rate of business failures over the most recent three- to five-year period.

b. Status indicators:

1. Per capita income below the State average.

2. Earnings or wages per job below the State average.

3. Unemployment above the State average.

4. Poverty rate above the State average.

5. Below average fiscal capacity.

(4) Plan. - The Comprehensive Strategic Economic Development Plan.

(5) Region. - One of the major geographic regions of the State defined in the Plan as an economic region based on compatible economic development factors.

(b) Board to Prepare Plan. - The Board shall prepare the Plan by April 1, 1994. The Board shall review and update this Plan by April 1 of each year. The original Plan shall cover a period of four years and each annual update shall extend the time frame by one year so that a four-year plan is always in effect. The Board shall provide copies of the Plan and each annual update to the Governor and the Joint Legislative Commission on Governmental Operations. The Plan shall encompass all of the components set out in this section.

(c) Purpose. - The purpose of this section is to require the Board to apply strategic planning principles to its economic development efforts. This requirement is expected to result in:

(1) The selection of a set of priority development objectives that recognizes the increasingly competitive economic environment and addresses the changing needs of the State in a more comprehensive manner.

(2) The effective utilization of available and limited resources.

(3) A commitment to achieve priority objectives and to sustain the process.

(d) (1) Public and Private Input. - At each stage as it develops and updates the Plan, the Board shall solicit input from all parties involved in economic development in North Carolina, including:

a. Each of the programs and organizations that, for State budget purposes, identifies economic development as one of its global goals.

b. Local economic development departments and regional economic development organizations.

c. The Board of Governors of The University of North Carolina.

(2) The Board shall also hold hearings in each of the Regions to solicit public input on economic development before the initial Plan is completed. The purposes of the public hearings are to:

a. Assess the strengths and weaknesses of recent regional economic performance.

b. Examine the status and competitive position of the regional resource base.

c. Identify and seek input on issues that are key to improving the economic well-being of the Region.

The Board shall hold additional hearings from time to time to solicit public input regarding economic development activities.

(3) Each component of the Plan shall be based on this broad input and, to the extent possible, upon a consensus among all affected parties. The Board shall coordinate its planning process with any State capital development planning efforts affecting State infrastructure such as roads and water and sewer facilities.

(e) Environmental Scan. - The first step in developing the Plan shall be to develop an environmental scan based on the input from economic development parties and the public and on information about the economic environment in North Carolina. To prepare the scan, the Board shall gather the following information and ensure that the information is updated periodically. The updated information may be provided in whatever format and through whatever means is most efficient.

(1) Compilation of the latest economic and demographic data on North Carolina by State, Region, and county including population, population projections, employment, and employment projections, income and earnings status and outlook, migration and commuting patterns, unemployment, poverty, and other similar data.

(2) Compilation of the latest data on the strength of the business environment by State, Region, and county with emphasis on the dynamics of job creation: start-ups, expansions, locations, contractions, and failures. Special assessments are to be made of rural, small, and minority business components of overall activity.

(3) Compilation of the latest data on labor compensation, construction costs, utility rates, payroll costs, taxes, and other cost data normally considered by manufacturing firms and new businesses and shall be tabulated by State, Region, and county.

(4) Compilation of data on assets within the State and by Region and county to include the following:

a. Available buildings, bona fide industrial parks, and sites.

b. Characteristics of the available labor force (number, demographic attributes, skill levels, etc.).

c. Special labor situations, such as military base discharges and large plant closings.

d. Available infrastructure capacities by county and Region including water, sewer, electrical, natural gas, telecommunication, highway access, and other pertinent services.

e. The fiscal capacity of counties and localities within counties to support the infrastructure development necessary to participate in the development process.

f. Analyses of assimilative capacity of riverine, estuarine, or ocean outfalls, or other environmental cost considerations.

g. Proximity analyses of counties in close alignment with major urban areas in bordering states.

h. Special educational and research capabilities.

i. Special transportation situations such as major airports, ports, and railyards.

j. Available data on the performance, contribution, and impact each economic sector (including, but not limited to, agriculture, finance, manufacturing, public utilities, trade, services, tourism, and government) is having on individual counties, Regions, and the State.

k. Available tourist and service assets.

l. Analyses of seasonal population and absentee ownership in resort and tourism areas and their impact on the delivery of public services.

m. Cost and availability of natural gas and electricity.

(5) Compilation and analyses of data on economic and industrial changes in competitor states by Region, as applicable. This data shall be entered into a database and kept current. It shall include, specifically, all new plant location information such as origin of the plant, Standard Industrial Classification Code, employment, and investment.

(6) Compilation of cost data, policies, and strategies in competitive Southeastern states as well as other United States regions and foreign countries.

(7) Compilation of incentives and special programs being offered by other states.

(8) Compilation and analyses of other data relating to economic development such as regulatory or legal matters, structural problems, and social considerations, e.g. unemployment, underemployment, poverty, support services, equity concerns, etc.

(9) The cost of doing business in North Carolina and other competing states, as it may affect decisions by firms to locate in this State.

(10) Competitive assets within the State and by Region and county, including infrastructure, tourist assets, natural resources, labor, educational and research resources, and transportation.

(11) Other information relating to economic development such as regulatory or legal matters and social considerations.

(f) Repealed by Session Laws 2012-142, s. 13.4(a), effective July 1, 2012.

(g) Vision and Mission Statements. - The Board shall develop a vision statement for economic development that would describe the preferred future for North Carolina and what North Carolina would be like if all economic development efforts were successful. The Board shall then develop a mission statement that outlines the basic purpose of each of North Carolina's economic development programs. Because special purpose nonprofit organizations are uniquely situated to conduct the entrepreneurial and high-risk activity of investing in and supporting new business creation in the State, they should be assigned a dominant role in this key component of economic development activity.

(h) Goals and Objectives. - The Board using data from the public input and the environmental scan, shall formulate a list of goals and objectives. Goals shall be long-range, four years or more, and shall address both needs of economically distressed Regions and counties as well as opportunities for Regions and counties not distressed. The goals shall be developed with realism but should also be selected so as to encourage every Region and county within the State to develop to its maximum potential. Objectives shall be one year or less in scope and shall, if achieved, lead to the realization of the goals formulated by the Board as provided in this section.

Both goals and objectives should be stated largely in economic terms, that is, they should be related to specific population, employment, demographic targets, or economic sector targets. Both efficiency and equity considerations are to be addressed and balanced with special emphasis placed on the needs of disadvantaged or economically distressed populations and communities. The goals and objectives should not state how the economic targets are to be reached, but rather what the economic conditions will be if they are obtained. So that the progress of North Carolina's economic development efforts can be monitored, the Board shall set objectives for each goal that allow measurement of progress toward the goal. Objectives should be quantifiable and time-specific in order to serve as performance indicators.

(i) Formulation of Economic Development Strategy. - The Plan shall have as its action component a strategy set forth in a blueprint for directing resources of time and dollars toward the satisfaction of the goals and objectives stated in subsection (h) of this section. As a practical consequence of the economic environment, a focus on the competitiveness of indigenous industries and entrepreneurial development is required. The Plan shall include a strategy for the coordination of initiatives and activities for workforce preparedness, funded by federal or State sources, including, but not limited to, vocational education, applied technology education, remedial education, and job training, and the achievement of the economic development goals of the Plan. A balance of opportunity between rural and urban regions and between majority and minority populations should be an overriding consideration. Equity of opportunity for counties and communities across the State will involve the explicit consideration of local fiscal capacity and the fiscal ability to support development activities.

The concept of differentiation should be employed. The Plan should recognize the various strengths and weaknesses of the State and its component regions, subregions, and, in some cases, individual counties. The concept of market segmentation should be employed. Different Regions and subregions of the State should be promoted to different markets.

(j) Implementation Plan. - Based upon all of the foregoing steps, the Board shall establish an implementation plan assigning to the appropriate parties specific responsibilities for meeting measurable objectives. The implementation plan shall contain all necessary elements so that it may be used as a means to monitor performance, guide appropriations, and evaluate the outcomes of the parties involved in economic development in the State.

(k) Annual Evaluation. - The Board shall annually evaluate the State's economic performance based upon the statistics listed in this subsection and upon the Board's stated goals and objectives in its Plan. The statistics upon which the evaluation is made should be available to policymakers. The information may be provided in whatever format and through whatever means is most efficient.

(1) The net job change (expansions minus contractions) by the various economic sectors of the county, Region, and State.

(2) Realized capital investment in plants and equipment by new and expanding industry in each county, Region, and State.

(3) Manufacturing changes by county, Region, and State that affect the value of firms, total payrolls, average wages, value of shipments, contributions to gross State product, and value added.

(4) The net change in the number of firms by county, Region, and State with statistics on the dynamics of change: relocations in versus relocations out; births versus deaths; and expansions versus contractions.

(5) A measure of the status and performance of all sectors of the county, Region, and State economy including, but not limited to, manufacturing, agriculture, trade, finance, communications, transportation, utilities, services, and travel and tourism.

(6) An assessment of the relative status and performance of rural business development as opposed to that in urban areas.

(7) An analysis of the status of minority-owned businesses throughout the State.

(8) An assessment of the development capability of the various Regions of the State in terms of their environmental, fiscal, and administrative capacity. Those areas that are handicapped by barriers to development should be highlighted.

(9) Repealed by Session Laws 2012-142, s. 13.4(a), effective July 1, 2012.

(l) Accountability. - The Board shall make all data, plans, and reports available to the General Assembly, the Joint Legislative Commission on

Governmental Operations, the Joint Legislative Economic Development and Global Engagement Oversight Committee, the Senate Appropriations Committee on Natural and Economic Resources, and the House of Representatives Appropriations Subcommittee on Natural and Economic Resources at appropriate times and upon request. The Board shall prepare and make available on an annual basis public reports on each of the major sections of the Plan and the Annual Report indicating the degree of success in attaining each development objective. (1993, c. 321, s. 313(c); 1997-456, s. 27; 2012-142, s. 13.4(a).)

§ 143B-434.1. The North Carolina Travel and Tourism Board - creation, duties, membership.

(a) There is created within the Department of Commerce the North Carolina Travel and Tourism Board. The Secretary of Commerce and the Director of the Division of Tourism, Film, and Sports Development will work with the Board to fulfill the duties and requirements set forth in this section, and to promote the sound development of the travel and tourism industry in North Carolina.

(b) The function and duties of the Board shall be:

(1) To advise the Secretary of Commerce in the formulation of policy and priorities for the promotion and development of travel and tourism in the State.

(2) To advise the Secretary of Commerce in the development of a budget for the Division of Tourism, Film, and Sports Development.

(3) To recommend programs to the Secretary of Commerce that will promote the State as a travel and tourism destination and that will develop travel and tourism opportunities throughout the State.

(4) To advise the Secretary of Commerce every three months as to the effectiveness of agencies with which the Department has contracted for advertising and regarding the selection of an advertising agency that will assist the Department in the promotion of the State as a travel and tourism destination.

(5) To name a three-member subcommittee, with one member from each of the eastern, central, and western regions of the State, to make recommendations to the Secretary of Commerce regarding any revisions in the matching funds tourism grants program, project applications, and criteria for projects that qualify for participation in the program.

(6) To advise the Secretary of Commerce from time to time as to the effectiveness of the overall operations of the Division of Tourism, Film, and Sports Development.

(7) To promote the exchange of ideas and information on travel and tourism between State and local governmental agencies, and private organizations and individuals.

(8) To advise the Secretary of Commerce upon any matter that the Secretary, Governor, or Director of the Division of Tourism, Film, and Sports Development may refer to it.

(c) The Board shall consist of 29 members as follows:

(1) The Secretary of Commerce, who shall not be a voting member.

(2) The Director of the Division of Tourism, Film, and Sports Development, who shall not be a voting member.

(3) Two members designated by the Board of Directors of the North Carolina Restaurant and Lodging Association, representing the lodging sector.

(4) Two members designated by the Board of Directors of the North Carolina Restaurant and Lodging Association, representing the restaurant sector.

(5) Three Directors of Convention and Visitor Bureaus designated by the Board of Directors of the North Carolina Association of Convention and Visitor Bureaus.

(6) The Chairperson of the Travel and Tourism Coalition or the Chairperson's designee.

(7) The President of the North Carolina Travel Industry Association.

(8) A member designated by the Board of Directors of the North Carolina Travel Industry Association.

(9) The President of the North Carolina Chamber.

(10) One member designated by the North Carolina Petroleum Marketers Association.

(11) One person associated with tourism attractions in North Carolina, appointed by the Speaker of the House of Representatives. One person who is not a member of the General Assembly, appointed by the Speaker of the House of Representatives.

(12) One person associated with the tourism-related transportation industry, appointed by the President Pro Tempore of the Senate. One person who is not a member of the General Assembly, appointed by the President Pro Tempore of the Senate.

(13) Four public members each interested in matters relating to travel and tourism, two appointed by the Governor (one from a rural area and one from an urban area), one appointed by the Speaker of the House, and one appointed by the President Pro Tempore of the Senate.

(14) One member associated with the major cultural resources and activities of the State in North Carolina, appointed by the Governor.

(15) Two members of the House of Representatives, appointed by the Speaker of the House of Representatives.

(16) Two members of the Senate, appointed by the President Pro Tempore of the Senate.

(17) Two members designated by the Board of Directors of North Carolina Watermen United who represent the charter boat/headboat industry.

(d) The members of the Board shall serve the following terms: the Secretary of Commerce, the Director of the Division of Tourism, Film, and Sports Development, the Chairperson of the Travel and Tourism Coalition, the President of the North Carolina Travel Industry Association, and the President of the North Carolina Chamber shall serve on the Board while they hold their respective offices. Each member of the Board appointed by the Governor shall serve during his or her term of office. The members of the Board appointed by the General Assembly shall serve two-year terms beginning on January 1 of odd-numbered years and ending on December 31 of the following year. The first such term shall begin on January 1, 1991, or as soon thereafter as the member is appointed to the Board, and end on December 31, 1992. All other members of the Board shall serve a term which consists of the portion of calendar year 1991 that remains following their appointment or designation and, thereafter, two-year terms which shall begin on January 1 of an even-numbered year and end on December 31 of the following year. The first such two-year term shall begin on January 1, 1992, and end on December 31, 1994.

(e)   No member of the Board, except a member serving by virtue of his or her office, shall serve during more than five consecutive calendar years, except that a member shall continue to serve until his or her successor is appointed.

(f)   Appointments to fill vacancies in the membership of the Board that occur due to resignation, dismissal, death, or disability of a member shall be for the balance of the unexpired term and shall be made by the same appointing authority that made the initial appointment.

(g)   Board members who are employees of the State shall receive travel allowances at the rate set forth in G.S. 138-6. Board members who are legislators shall be reimbursed for travel and subsistence in accordance with G.S. 120-3.1. All other Board members, except those serving pursuant to subdivisions (3) through (10) of subsection (c) of this section, shall receive per diem, subsistence, and travel expenses at the rate set forth in G.S. 138-5. Board members serving pursuant to subdivisions (3) through (10) of subsection (c) of this section shall not receive per diem, subsistence, or travel expenses. The expenses set forth in this section shall be paid by the Division of Tourism, Film, and Sports Development of the Department of Commerce.

(h)   At its first meeting in 1991, the Board shall elect one of its voting members to serve as Chairperson during calendar year 1991. At its last regularly scheduled meeting in 1991, and at its last regularly scheduled meeting in each year thereafter, the Board shall elect one of its voting members to serve as Chairperson for the coming calendar year. No person shall serve as Chairperson during more than three consecutive calendar years. The Chairperson shall continue to serve until his or her successor is elected.

(i)   A majority of the current voting membership shall constitute a quorum.

(j)   The Secretary of Commerce shall provide clerical and other services as required by the Board. (1991, c. 406, s. 1; 1991 (Reg. Sess., 1992), c. 959, s. 54; 1997-495 s. 89(a); 2000-140, s. 79(a); 2007-67, s. 1; 2007-484, ss. 32(a), (b); 2009-550, s. 7; 2009-570, s. 8(f), (g).)

§ 143B-434.2. Travel and Tourism Policy Act.

(a)   This section shall be known as the Travel and Tourism Policy Act.

(b)   The General Assembly of North Carolina finds that:

(1)   The State of North Carolina is endowed with great scenic beauty, historical sites, and cultural resources, and with a population whose ethnic diversity and traditions are attractive to visitors.

(2)   These resources should be preserved and nurtured, not only because they are appreciated by other Americans and by visitors from other lands, but because they are valued by the State's own residents.

(3)   Tourism provides economic well-being by contributing to employment and economic development, generating State revenues and receipts for local businesses, and increasing international trade.

(4)   Tourism is an educational and informational medium for personal growth which informs residents about their State's geography and history, their political institutions, their cultural resources, and their environment, and about each other.

(5)   Tourism instills State pride and a sense of common interest among the people of the State.

(6)   Tourism enhances the quality of life and well-being of the State's residents by affording recreation, new experiences, and opportunities for relief from job stress.

(7)   Tourism promotes international understanding and goodwill, and contributes to intercultural appreciation.

(8)   Tourism engenders appreciation of the State's cultural, architectural, technological, and industrial achievements.

(9)   The development and promotion of tourism to and within the State is in the interest of the people of North Carolina.

(10)   Tourism should develop in an orderly manner in order to provide the maximum benefit to the State and its residents.

(11) A comprehensive tourism policy is essential if tourism is to grow in an orderly way.

(c) The policy of the State of North Carolina is to:

(1) Encourage the orderly growth and development of travel and tourism to and within the State.

(2) Promote the State's travel and tourism resources to the residents of the State, and to potential visitors from other states and other countries.

(3) Instill a sense of history in the State's young people by encouraging family visits to State historic sites, and by promoting the preservation and restoration of historic sites, trails, buildings, and districts.

(4) Promote the mental, emotional, and physical well-being of the people of North Carolina by encouraging outdoor recreational activities within the State.

(5) Strengthen a sense of common interest among the residents of the State by encouraging them to visit each other's communities and discover each other's traditions and ways of life.

(6) Increase national and international awareness of the State's cultural contributions by encouraging attendance at orchestral, operatic, dramatic, and other productions by artistic groups performing in the State.

(7) Cultivate the State's commercial interests by encouraging local and county fairs so that visitors may learn about local products and crafts.

(8) Encourage the talents and strengthen the economic independence of State residents by encouraging the preservation of traditional craft skills; the production of handicrafts and folk art by private artisans and craftspeople; and the holding of craft demonstrations.

(9) Provide visitors to the State with a hospitable reception.

(10) Develop and maintain a statewide tourism data base.

(11) Encourage the protection of wildlife and natural resources and the preservation of geological, archaeological, and cultural treasures in tourist areas.

(12) Encourage, assist, and coordinate, where possible, the tourism activities of local and area promotional organizations.

(13) Ensure that the tourism interest of the State is fully considered by State agencies and the General Assembly in their deliberations; and coordinate, to the maximum extent possible, all State activities in support of tourism with the needs of the general public, the political subdivisions of the State, and the tourism industry.

(d) The Department of Commerce, and the Division of Tourism, Film, and Sports Development within that Department, shall implement the policies set forth in this section. The Division of Tourism, Film, and Sports Development shall make an annual report to the General Assembly regarding the status of the travel and tourism industry in North Carolina; the report shall be submitted to the General Assembly by October 15 of each year beginning October 15, 2011. The duties and responsibilities of the Department of Commerce through the Division of Tourism, Film, and Sports Development shall be to:

(1) Organize and coordinate programs designed to promote tourism within the State and to the State from other states and foreign countries.

(2) Measure and forecast tourist volume, receipts, and impact, both social and economic.

(3) Develop a comprehensive plan to promote tourism to the State.

(4) Encourage the development of the State's tourism infrastructure, facilities, services, and attractions.

(5) Cooperate with neighboring states and the federal government to promote tourism to the State from other countries.

(6) Develop opportunities for professional education and training in the tourism industry.

(7) Provide advice and technical assistance to local public and private tourism organizations in promoting tourism to the State.

(8) Encourage cooperation between State agencies and private individuals and organizations to advance the State's tourist interests and seek the views of

these agencies and the private sector in the development of State tourism programs and policies.

(9)   Give leadership to all concerned with tourism in the State.

(10)   Perform other functions necessary to the orderly growth and development of tourism.

(11)   Develop informational materials for visitors which, among other things, shall:

a.   Describe the State's travel and tourism resources and the State's history, economy, political institutions, cultural resources, outdoor recreational facilities, and principal festivals.

b.   Urge visitors to protect endangered species, natural resources, archaeological artifacts, and cultural treasures.

c.   Instill the ethic of stewardship of the State's natural resources.

(12)   Foster an understanding among State residents and civil servants of the economic importance of hospitality and tourism to the State.

(13)   Work with local businesses, including banks and hotels, with educational institutions, and with the United States Travel and Tourism Administration, to provide special services for international visitors, such as currency exchange facilities.

(14)   Encourage the reduction of architectural and other barriers which impede travel by physically handicapped persons. (1991, c. 144, ss. 1-4; 1991 (Reg. Sess., 1992), c. 959, s. 85; 2000-140, s. 79(b); 2011-145, s. 14.3.)

§ 143B-434.3: Repealed by Session Laws 2003-284, s. 12.6A.(a), effective on and after August 2, 2000.

§ 143B-434.4: Repealed by Session Laws 2005-276, s. 39.1(d), effective July 1, 2005.

§ 143B-435. Publications.

The Department of Commerce may also cause to be prepared for publication, from time to time, reports and statements, with illustrations, maps and other descriptions, which may adequately set forth the natural and material resources of the State and its industrial and commercial developments, with a view to furnishing information to educate the people with reference to the material advantages of the State, to encourage and foster existing industries, and to present inducements for investment in new enterprises. Such information shall be published and distributed as the Department of Commerce may direct. The costs of publishing and distributing such information shall be paid from:

(1) State funds as other public documents; or

(2) Private funds received:

a. As donations, or

b. From the sale of appropriate advertising in such published information. (1925, c. 122, s. 11; 1973, c. 1262, s. 28; 1977, c. 198, ss. 20, 26; 1989, c. 751, s. 7(30); 1989 (Reg. Sess., 1990), c. 1066, s. 55; 1991 (Reg. Sess., 1992), c. 959, s. 55.)

§ 143B-435.1. Clawbacks.

(a) Clawback Defined. - For the purpose of this Article, a clawback is a requirement that all or part of an economic development incentive will be returned or forfeited if the recipient business does not fulfill its responsibilities under the incentive law, contract, or both.

(b) Findings. - The General Assembly finds that in order for a clawback to be effective, there must be monitoring and reporting regarding the business's performance of its responsibilities and a mechanism for obtaining repayment if the clawback requiring the return of previously disbursed funding is triggered. Clawback provisions are essential to protect the State's investment in a private business and ensure that the public benefits from the incentive will be secured.

(c) Catalog. - The Department of Commerce shall catalog all clawbacks in State and federal programs it administers, whether provided by statute, by rule, or under a contract. The catalog must include a description of each clawback, the program to which it applies, and a citation to its source. The Department shall publish the catalog on its Web site and update it every six months.

(d) Report. - By April 1 and October 1 of each year, the Department of Commerce shall report to the Revenue Laws Study Committee, the Joint Legislative Commission on Governmental Operations, the Senate Appropriations Committee on Natural and Economic Resources, the House of Representatives Appropriations Subcommittee on Natural and Economic Resources, and the Fiscal Research Division of the Legislative Services Commission on (i) all clawbacks that have been triggered under the One North Carolina Fund established pursuant to G.S. 143B-437.71, the Job Development Investment Grant Program established pursuant to G.S. 143B-437.52, Job Maintenance and Capital Development Fund established pursuant to G.S. 143B-437.012, the Utility Account established pursuant to G.S. 143B-437.01, and the Site Infrastructure Fund established pursuant to G.S. 143B-437.02 and (ii) its progress on obtaining repayments. The report must include the name of each business, the event that triggered the clawback, and the amount forfeited or to be repaid. (2007-515, s. 6; 2012-142, s. 13.4(b); 2013-360, s. 15.18(d).)

§ 143B-436. Advertising of State resources and advantages.

It is hereby declared to be the duty of the Department of Commerce to map out and to carry into effect a systematic plan for the nationwide advertising of North Carolina, properly presenting, by the use of any available advertising media, the true facts concerning the State of North Carolina and all of its resources. (1937, c. 160; 1953, c. 808, s. 4; 1973, c. 1262, s. 86; 1977, c. 198, ss. 20, 26; 1989, c. 751, s. 7(31); 1991 (Reg. Sess., 1992), c. 959, s. 56.)

§ 143B-437. Investigation of impact of proposed new and expanding industry.

The Department of Commerce shall conduct an evaluation in conjunction with the Department of Environment and Natural Resources of the effects on the State's natural and economic environment of any new or expanding industry or manufacturing plant locating in North Carolina. (1971, c. 824; 1973, c. 1262, ss. 28, 86; 1977, c. 198, ss. 19, 26; c. 771, s. 4; 1989, c. 727, s. 218(153); c. 751, s. 7(32); 1991 (Reg. Sess., 1992), c. 959, s. 57; 1997-443, s. 11A.119(a).)

§ 143B-437.01. Industrial Development Fund Utility Account.

(a) Creation and Purpose of Fund. - There is created in the Department of Commerce a special account to be known as the Industrial Development Fund Utility Account ("Utility Account") to provide funds to assist the local government units of the most economically distressed counties in the State in creating jobs. The Department of Commerce shall adopt rules providing for the administration of the program. Those rules shall include the following provisions, which shall apply to each grant from the account:

(1) The funds shall be used for construction of or improvements to new or existing water, sewer, gas, telecommunications, high-speed broadband, electrical utility distribution lines or equipment, or transportation infrastructure for existing or new or proposed buildings. To be eligible for funding, the water, gas, telecommunications, high-speed broadband, electrical utility lines or facilities, or transportation infrastructure shall be located on the site of the building or, if not located on the site, shall be directly related to the operation of the job creation activity. To be eligible for funding, the sewer infrastructure shall be located on the site of the building or, if not located on the site, shall be directly related to the operation of the job creation activity, even if the sewer infrastructure is located in a county other than the county in which the building is located.

(1a) The funds shall be used for projects located in economically distressed counties except that the Secretary of Commerce may use up to one hundred thousand dollars ($100,000) to provide emergency economic development assistance in any county that is documented to be experiencing a major economic dislocation.

(2) The funds shall be used by the city and county governments for projects that are reasonably anticipated to result in the creation of new jobs. There shall be no maximum funding amount per new job to be created or per project.

(3) There shall be no local match requirement if the project is located in a county that has one of the 25 highest rankings under G.S. 143B-437.08.

(4) The Department may authorize a local government that receives funds under this section to use up to two percent (2%) of the funds, if necessary, to verify that the funds are used only in accordance with law and to otherwise administer the grant or loan.

(5) No project subject to the Environmental Policy Act, Article 1 of Chapter 113A of the General Statutes, shall be funded unless the Secretary of Commerce finds that the proposed project will not have a significant adverse effect on the environment. The Secretary of Commerce shall not make this finding unless the Secretary has first received a certification from the Department of Environment and Natural Resources that concludes, after consideration of avoidance and mitigation measures, that the proposed project will not have a significant adverse effect on the environment.

(6) The funds shall not be used for any nonmanufacturing project that does not meet the wage standard set out in G.S. 105-129.4(b) or for any retail, entertainment, or sports projects.

(7) Priority for the use of funds shall be given to eligible industries.

(a1) Definitions. - The following definitions apply in this section:

(1) Air courier services. - The furnishing of air delivery of individually addressed letters and packages for compensation, in interstate commerce, except by the United States Postal Service.

(2) Repealed by Session Laws 2006-252, s. 2.4, effective January 1, 2007.

(2a) Company headquarters. - A corporate, subsidiary, or regional managing office, as defined by NAICS in United States industry 551114, that is responsible for strategic or organizational planning and decision making for the business on an international, national, or multistate regional basis.

(3) Repealed by Session Laws 2006-252, s. 2.4, effective January 1, 2007.

(4) Economically distressed county. - A county that is defined as a development tier one or two area under G.S. 143B-437.08 after the adjustments of that section are applied.

(5) Eligible industry. - A company headquarters or a person engaged in the business of air courier services, information technology and services, manufacturing, or warehousing and wholesale trade.

(6) Information technology and services. - An industry in one of the following, as defined by NAICS:

a. Data processing industry group 518.

b. Software publishers industry group 5112.

c. Computer systems design and related services industry group 5415.

d. An Internet activity included in industry group 519130.

(7) Major economic dislocation. - The actual or imminent loss of 500 or more manufacturing jobs in the county or of a number of manufacturing jobs equal to at least ten percent (10%) of the existing manufacturing workforce in the county.

(8) Manufacturing. - An industry in manufacturing sectors 31 through 33, as defined by NAICS, but not including quick printing or retail bakeries.

(9) Reserved.

(10) Warehousing. - An industry in warehousing and storage subsector 493 as defined by NAICS.

(11) Wholesale trade. - An industry in wholesale trade sector 42 as defined by NAICS.

(b) Repealed by Session Laws 1996, Second Extra Session, c. 13, s. 3.5.

(b1) Repealed by Session Laws 2013-360, s. 15.18(a), effective July 1, 2013, and applicable to projects for which funds are initially provided on or after July 1, 2013.

(c), (c1) Repealed by Session Laws 2012-142, s. 13.4(c), effective July 1, 2012.

(d) Repealed by Session Laws 1996, Second Extra Session, c. 13, s. 3.5. (1989, c. 751, s. 9(c); c. 754, s. 54; 1991 (Reg. Sess., 1992), c. 959, s. 60; 1993, c. 444, s. 1; 1996, 2nd Ex. Sess., c. 13, s. 3.5; 1997-456, s. 27; 1998-55, s. 6; 1999-360, s. 17; 2000-56, s. 3(b); 2002-172, ss. 2.2(a), (b); 2003-416, s. 2; 2005-276, s. 13.5; 2006-252, s. 2.4; 2007-323, s. 13.18(i); 2009-523, s. 1(a)-(c); 2010-31, s. 14.9; 2012-74, s. 4; 2012-142, s. 13.4(c); 2013-360, s. 15.18(a).)

§ 143B-437.02. Site infrastructure development.

(a) Findings. - The General Assembly finds that:

(1) It is the policy of the State of North Carolina to stimulate economic activity and to create new jobs for the citizens of the State by encouraging and promoting the expansion of existing business and industry within the State and by recruiting and attracting new business and industry to the State.

(2) Both short-term and long-term economic trends at the State, national, and international levels have made the successful implementation of the State's economic development policy and programs both more critical and more challenging; and the decline in the State's traditional industries, and the resulting adverse impact upon the State and its citizens, have been exacerbated in recent years by adverse national and State economic trends that contribute to the reduction in the State's industrial base and that inhibit the State's ability to sustain or attract new and expanding businesses.

(3) The economic condition of the State is not static and recent changes in the State's economic condition have created economic distress that requires the enactment of a new program as provided in this section that is designed to stimulate new economic activity and to create new jobs within the State.

(4) The enactment of this section is necessary to stimulate the economy, facilitate economic recovery, and create new jobs in North Carolina and this section will promote the general welfare and confer, as its primary purpose and effect, benefits on citizens throughout the State through the creation of new jobs, an enlargement of the overall tax base, an expansion and diversification of the State's industrial base, and an increase in revenue to the State and its political subdivisions.

(5) The purpose of this section is to stimulate economic activity and to create new jobs within the State.

(b) Fund. - The Site Infrastructure Development Fund is created as a restricted reserve in the Department of Commerce. Funds in the fund do not revert but remain available to the Department for these purposes. The Department may use the funds in the fund only for the following purposes:

(1) For site development in accordance with this section.

(2) To acquire options and hold options for the purchase of land in accordance with subsection (m) of this section.

(c) Definitions. - The definitions in G.S. 143B-437.51 apply in this section. In addition, the following definitions apply in this section:

(1) Department. - The Department of Commerce.

(2) Site development. - Any of the following:

a. A restricted grant or a forgivable loan made to a business to enable the business to acquire land, improve land, or both.

b. A grant to one or more State agencies or nonprofit corporations to enable the grantees to acquire land, improve land, or both and to lease the property to a business.

c. A grant to one or more local government units to enable the units to acquire land, improve land, or both and to lease the property to a business.

(d) Eligibility. - To be eligible for consideration for site development for a project, a business must meet both of the following conditions:

(1) The business will invest at least one hundred million dollars ($100,000,000) of private funds in the project.

(2) The project will employ at least 100 new employees.

(e) Health Insurance. - A business is eligible for consideration for site development under this section only if the business provides health insurance for all of the full-time employees of the project with respect to which the application is made. For the purposes of this subsection, a business provides health insurance if it pays at least fifty percent (50%) of the premiums for health care coverage that equals or exceeds the minimum provisions of the basic health care plan of coverage recommended by the Small Employer Carrier Committee pursuant to G.S. 58-50-125.

Each year that a contract for site development under this section is in effect, the business must provide the Department of Commerce a certification that the business continues to provide health insurance for all full-time employees of the project governed by the contract. If the business ceases to provide health insurance to all full-time employees of the project, Department shall provide for reimbursement of an appropriate portion of the site development funds provided to the business.

(f) Safety and Health Programs. - In order for a business to be eligible for consideration for site development under this section, the business must have no citations under the Occupational Safety and Health Act that have become a final order within the past three years for willful serious violations or for failing to abate serious violations with respect to the location for which the grant is made. For the purposes of this subsection, "serious violation" has the same meaning as in G.S. 95-127.

(g) Environmental Impact. - A business is eligible for consideration for site development under this part only if the business certifies that, at the time of the application, the business satisfies the environmental impact standard under G.S. 105-129.83.

(h) Selection. - The Department of Commerce shall administer the selection of projects to receive site development. The selection process shall include the following components:

(1) Criteria. - The Department of Commerce must develop criteria to be used to identify and evaluate eligible projects for possible site development.

(2) Initial evaluation. - The Department must evaluate major competitive projects to determine if site development is merited and to determine whether the project is eligible and appropriate for consideration for site development.

(3) Application. - The Department must require a business to submit an application in order for a project to be considered for site development. The Department must prescribe the form of the application, the application process, and the information to be provided, including all information necessary to evaluate the project in accordance with the applicable criteria.

(4) Committee. - The Department must submit to the Economic Investment Committee the applications for projects the Department considers eligible and appropriate for consideration for site development. In evaluating each application, the Committee must consider all of the factors set out in Section 2.1(b) of S.L. 2002-172.

(5) Findings. - In order to recommend a project for site development, the Committee must make all of the following findings:

a. The conditions for eligibility have been met.

b. Site development for the project is necessary to carry out the public purposes provided in subsection (a) of this section.

c. The project is consistent with the economic development goals of the State and of the area where it will be located.

d. The affected local governments have participated in recruitment and offered incentives in a manner appropriate to the project.

e. The price and nature of any real property to be acquired is appropriate to the project and not unreasonable or excessive.

f. Site development under this section is necessary for the completion of the project in this State.

(6) Recommendations. - If the Committee recommends a project for site development, it must recommend the amount of State funds to be committed, the preferred form and details of the State participation, and the performance criteria and safeguards to be required in order to protect the State's investment.

(i) Agreement. - Unless the Secretary of Commerce determines that the project is no longer eligible or appropriate for site development, the Department shall enter into an agreement to provide site development within available funds for a project recommended by the Committee. Each site development agreement is binding and constitutes a continuing contractual obligation of the State and the business. The site development agreement must include all of the performance criteria, remedies, and other safeguards recommended by the Committee or required by the Department to secure the State's investment. Each site development agreement must contain a provision prohibiting a business from receiving a payment or other benefit under the agreement at any time when the business has received a notice of an overdue tax debt and the overdue tax debt has not been satisfied or otherwise resolved. Nothing in this section constitutes or authorizes a guarantee or assumption by the State of any debt of any business or authorizes the taxing power or the full faith and credit of the State to be pledged.

The Department shall cooperate with the Department of Administration and the Attorney General's Office in preparing the documentation for the site development agreement. The Attorney General shall review the terms of all proposed agreements to be entered into under this section. To be effective against the State, an agreement entered into under this section must be signed personally by the Attorney General.

(j)   Safeguards. - To ensure that public funds are used only to carry out the public purposes provided in this section, the Department shall require that each business that receives State-funded site development must agree to meet performance criteria to protect the State's investment and assure that the projected benefits of the project are secured. The performance criteria to be required shall include creation and maintenance of an appropriate level of employment and investment over the term of the agreement and any other criteria the Department considers appropriate. The agreement must require the business to repay or reimburse an appropriate portion of the State funds expended for the site development, based on the extent of any failure by the business to meet the performance criteria. The agreement must provide a method for securing these payments from the business, such as structuring the site development as a conditional grant, a forgivable loan, or a revocable lease.

(k)   Monitoring and Reports. - The Department is responsible for monitoring compliance with the performance criteria under each site development agreement and for administering the repayment in case of default. The Department shall pay for the cost of this monitoring from funds appropriated to it for that purpose or for other economic development purposes.

On September 1 of each year until all funds have been expended, the Department shall report to the Joint Legislative Commission on Governmental Operations regarding the Site Infrastructure Development Program. This report shall include a listing of each agreement negotiated and entered into during the preceding year, including the name of the business, the cost/benefit analysis conducted by the Committee during the application process, a description of the project, and the amount of the site development incentive expected to be paid under the agreement during the current fiscal year. The report shall also include detailed information about any defaults and repayment during the preceding year and the information contained in the report required by G.S. 105-277.15A(g). The Department shall publish this report on its web site and shall make printed copies available upon request.

(l)   Reserved for future codification purposes.

(m) Options. - The Department of Commerce may acquire options and hold options for the purchase of land for an anticipated industrial site if all of the following conditions are met:

(1) The options are necessary to provide a large, regional industrial site that cannot be assembled by local governments.

(2) The acquisition of the options is approved by the Committee. (2003-435, 2nd Ex. Sess., s. 1; 2004-124, s. 6.26(a), (b); 2009-451, s. 14.5(a); 2010-147, s. 1.5; 2013-130, s. 4.)

§ 143B-437.03. Allocation of economic development responsibilities.

The Economic Development Board created in G.S. 143B-434 shall coordinate economic development efforts among the various agencies and entities, including those created by executive order of the Governor, that receive economic development appropriations and the Board shall recommend to the Governor and to the General Assembly the assignment of key responsibilities for different aspects of economic development. The Board shall recommend to the Governor and to the General Assembly resource allocation and planning designed to encourage each agency to focus on its area of primary responsibility and not diffuse its resources by conducting activities assigned to other agencies. (1993, c. 321, s. 313(e); 1997-456, s. 27.)

§ 143B-437.04. Community development block grants.

(a) The Department of Commerce shall adopt guidelines for the awarding of Community Development Block Grants to ensure that:

(1) No local match is required for grants awarded for projects located in counties that have one of the 25 highest rankings under G.S. 143B-437.08 or counties that have a population of less than 50,000 and more than nineteen percent (19%) of its population below the federal poverty level according to the most recent federal decennial census.

(2) To the extent practicable, priority consideration for grants is given to projects located in counties that have met the conditions of subdivision (a)(1) of this section or in urban progress zones that have met the conditions of subsection (b) of this section.

(3) Priority consideration is given to projects located in areas annexed by a municipality under Article 4A of Chapter 160A of the General Statutes in order to provide water or sewer services to low-income residents. For purposes of this section, low-income residents are those with a family income that is eighty percent (80%) or less of median family income.

(b) In order to qualify for the benefits of this section, after an area is designated an urban progress zone under G.S. 143B-437.09, the governing body of the city in which the zone is located must adopt a strategy to improve the zone and establish an urban progress zone committee to oversee the strategy. The strategy and the committee must conform with requirements established by the Secretary of Commerce. (1996, 2nd Ex. Sess., c. 13, s. 3.6; 1997-456, s. 27; 1998-55, s. 3; 2006-252, s. 2.5; 2007-323, s. 13.18(h); 2011-396, s. 11.1.)

§ 143B-437.05. Regional Development.

The Department of Commerce shall review the Economic Development Board's annual report on economic development to evaluate the progress of development in each of the economic regions defined by the Board in its Comprehensive Strategic Economic Development Plan. In its recruitment and development work, the Department shall strive for balance and equality among the economic regions and shall use its best efforts to locate new industries in the less developed areas of the State. (1996, 2nd Ex. Sess., c. 13, s. 3.10; 1997-456, s. 27.)

§ 143B-437.06: Repealed by Session Laws 2004-124, s. 13.6(c) effective July 1, 2004.

§ 143B-437.07. Economic development grant reporting.

(a) Report. - The Department of Commerce must publish on or before October 1 of each year the information required by this subsection, itemized by business entity, for each business or joint private venture to which the State has, in whole or in part, granted one or more economic development incentives during the previous fiscal year. The information in the report must include all of the following:

(1)   A unique project identification number and a unique descriptor or title.

(2)   The date of the award and the date of the award agreement.

(3)   The name, mailing address, telephone number, and Web site of the business recipient, or recipients if a joint venture, and the physical location of the site receiving the incentive. If the physical location of the site is undecided, then the name of the county in which the site will be located.

(4)   The development tier designation of the county in which the site is located on the date the incentive is awarded.

(5)   The NAICS six-digit code and NAICS category of business receiving the incentive. The term "NAICS" has the same meaning as defined in G.S. 105-164.3.

(6)   The sources and dollar value of eligible State incentives by program name.

(7)   The sources and dollar value of local government funds provided by any locality and the nature of the local funding. Examples of the nature of local funding include cash, fee-waivers, in-kind services, and donation of land, buildings, or other assets.

(8)   The intended use of the incentive by any category or categories to which State law restricts or limits uses of incentive funds. If the use of the incentive funds is not restricted, then the intended purpose of the funds.

(9)   The amount of incentive monies disbursed taken during the period.

(10)   The amount of potential future liability under the applicable incentive program.

(11)   The number, type, and wage level of jobs required to be created or retained to receive a disbursement of incentive monies.

(12)   The actual full-time equivalent jobs employed by the recipient during the period.

(13)   The projected cost per job created or retained, including State and local funds.

(14) Any amount recaptured from the business entity during the period for failure to satisfy the terms of the grant agreement.

(b) Online Posting/Written Submission. - The Department of Commerce must post on its Internet Web site a summary of the report compiled in subsection (a) of this section. The summary report must include the information required by subdivisions (2), (9), (11), and (12) of subsection (a) of this section. By October 1 of each year, the Department of Commerce must submit the written report required by subsection (a) of this section to the Joint Legislative Commission on Governmental Operations, the Revenue Laws Study Committee, the Senate Appropriations Committee on Natural and Economic Resources, the House of Representatives Appropriations Subcommittee on Natural and Economic Resources, and the Fiscal Research Division of the General Assembly.

(c) Economic Development Incentive. - An economic development incentive includes any grant from the following programs: Job Development Investment Grant Program; the Job Maintenance and Capital Development Fund; One North Carolina Fund; and the Utility Account. The State also incents economic development through the use of tax expenditures in the form of tax credits and refunds. The Department of Revenue must report annually on these statutory economic development incentives, as required under G.S. 105-256. (2005-429, s. 1.3; 2011-145, s. 14.2(b); 2012-142, s. 13.4(d); 2013-360, s. 15.18(e).)

§ 143B-437.08. Development tier designation.

(a) Tiers Defined. - A development tier one area is a county whose annual ranking is one of the 40 highest in the State. A development tier two area is a county whose annual ranking is one of the next 40 highest in the State. A development tier three area is a county that is not in a lower-numbered development tier.

(b) Development Factor. - Each year, on or before November 30, the Secretary of Commerce shall assign to each county in the State a development factor that is the sum of the following:

(1) The county's rank in a ranking of counties by average rate of unemployment from lowest to highest, for the most recent 12 months for which data are available.

(2) The county's rank in a ranking of counties by median household income from highest to lowest, for the most recent 12 months for which data are available.

(3) The county's rank in a ranking of counties by percentage growth in population from highest to lowest, for the most recent 36 months for which data are available.

(4) The county's rank in a ranking of counties by adjusted assessed property value per capita as published by the Department of Public Instruction, from highest to lowest, for the most recent taxable year.

(c) Annual Ranking. - After computing the development factor as provided in this section and making the adjustments required in this section, the Secretary of Commerce shall rank all the counties within the State according to their development factor from highest to lowest. The Secretary shall then identify all the areas of the State by development tier and publish this information. A development tier designation is effective only for the calendar year following the designation.

(d) Data. - In measuring rates of unemployment and median household income, the Secretary shall use the latest available data published by a State or federal agency generally recognized as having expertise concerning the data. In measuring population and population growth, the Secretary shall use the most recent estimates of population certified by the State Budget Officer. For the purposes of this section, population statistics do not include people incarcerated in federal or State prisons.

(e) Adjustment for Certain Small Counties. - Regardless of the actual development factor, any county that has a population of less than 12,000 shall automatically be ranked one of the 40 highest counties, any county that has a population of less than 50,000 shall automatically be ranked one of the 80 highest counties, and any county that has a population of less than 50,000 and more than nineteen percent (19%) of its population below the federal poverty level according to the most recent federal decennial census shall automatically be ranked one of the 40 highest counties.

(f) Adjustment for Development Tier One Areas. - Regardless of the actual development factor, a county designated as a development tier one area shall automatically be ranked one of the 40 highest counties until it has been a development tier one area for at least two consecutive years.

(g) Exception for Two-County Industrial Park. - An eligible two-county industrial park has the lower development tier designation of the designations of the two counties in which it is located if it meets all of the following conditions:

(1) It is located in two contiguous counties, one of which has a lower development tier designation than the other.

(2) At least one-third of the park is located in the county with the lower tier designation.

(3) It is owned by the two counties or a joint agency of the counties, is under contractual control of designated agencies working on behalf of both counties, or is subject to a development agreement between both counties and third-party owners.

(4) The county with the lower tier designation contributed at least the lesser of one-half of the cost of developing the park or a proportion of the cost of developing the park equal to the proportion of land in the park located in the county with the lower tier designation.

(5) Expired, effective July 1, 2012, pursuant to Session Laws 2009-524, s. 2.

(h) Exception for Certain Multijurisdictional Industrial Parks. - An eligible industrial park created by interlocal agreement under G.S. 158-7.4, and parcels of land located within the industrial park that are subsequently transferred and used for industrial or commercial purposes authorized for cities and counties under G.S. 158-7.1, have the lowest development tier designation of the designations of the counties in which they are located if all of the following conditions are satisfied:

(1) The industrial park is located, at one or more sites, in three or more contiguous counties.

(2) At least one of the counties in which the industrial park is located is a development tier one area.

(3) The industrial park is owned by three or more units of local government or a nonprofit corporation owned or controlled by three or more units of local government.

(4) In each county in which the industrial park is located, the park has at least 250 developable acres. A transfer of acreage that reduces the number of developable acres below 250 developable acres in a county does not affect an industrial park's eligibility under this subsection if the transfer is to an owner who uses or develops the acreage for industrial or commercial purposes authorized for cities and counties under G.S. 158-7.1. For the purposes of this subdivision, "developable acres" includes acreage that is owned directly by the industrial park or its owners or that is the subject of a development agreement between the industrial park or its owners and a third-party owner.

(5) The total population of all of the counties in which the industrial park is located is less than 200,000.

(6) In each county in which the industrial park is located, at least sixteen and eight-tenths percent (16.8%) of the population was Medicaid eligible for the 2003-2004 fiscal year based on 2003 population estimates.

(i) Expired, effective July 1, 2013, pursuant to Session Laws 2009-505, s. 2, as amended by Session Laws 2012-36, s. 1.

(j) Exception for Eco-Industrial Park. - An Eco-Industrial Park has a development tier one designation. An Eco-Industrial Park is an industrial park that the Secretary of Commerce has certified meets the following requirements:

(1) It has at least 100 developable acres.

(2) It is located in a county that is not required under G.S. 143-215.107A to perform motor vehicle emissions inspections.

(3) Each building located in the industrial park is constructed in accordance with energy-efficiency and water-use standards established in G.S. 143-135.37 for construction of a major facility.

(4) Each business located in the park is in a clean-industry sector according to the Toxic Release Inventory by the United States Environmental Protection Agency.

(k) Report. - By November 30 of each year, the Secretary of Commerce shall submit a written report to the Joint Legislative Commission on Governmental Operations, the Senate Appropriations Committee on Natural and Economic Resources, the House of Representatives Appropriations

Subcommittee on Natural and Economic Resources, and the Fiscal Research Division of the General Assembly on the tier rankings required by subsection (c) of this section, including a map of the State whereupon the tier ranking of each county is designated. (2006-252, s. 1.2; 2008-147, s. 1; 2009-505, s. 1; 2009-524, s. 1; 2010-147, s. 5.1; 2012-36, s. 1; 2012-142, s. 13.4(e).)

§ 143B-437.09. Urban progress zone designation.

(a) Urban Progress Zone Defined. - An urban progress zone is an area that meets all of the following conditions:

(1) It is comprised of part or all of one or more contiguous census tracts, census block groups, or both, in the most recent federal decennial census.

(2) All of the area is located in whole within the primary corporate limits of a municipality with a population in excess of 10,000 according to the most recent annual population estimates certified by the State Budget Officer.

(3) Every census tract and census block group that comprises the area meets at least one of the following conditions:

a. It has a population that meets the poverty level threshold. The population of a census tract or census block group meets the poverty level threshold if more than twenty percent (20%) of its population is below the poverty level according to the most recent federal decennial census.

b. It is located adjacent to a census tract or census block group whose population meets the poverty level threshold and at least fifty percent (50%) of the part of it that is included in the area is zoned as nonresidential. No more than thirty-five percent (35%) of the area of a zone may consist of census tracts or census block groups that satisfy this condition only.

c. It has a population that has a poverty level that is greater than the poverty level of the population of the State and a per capita income that is at least ten percent (10%) below the per capita income of the State according to the most recent federal decennial census, and it has experienced a major plant closing and layoff within the past 10 years. A census tract or census block group has experienced a major plant closing and layoff if one of its industries has closed one or more facilities in the census tract or census block group resulting in a layoff of at least 3,000 employees working in the census tract or census block group and if the number of employees laid off is greater than seven percent (7%) of the population of the municipality according to the most recent federal decennial census.

(b) Limitations. - No census tract or block group may be located in more than one urban progress zone. The total area of all zones within a municipality may not exceed fifteen percent (15%) of the total area of the municipality unless the smallest possible area in the municipality satisfying all of the conditions of subsection (a) of this section exceeds fifteen percent (15%) of the total area of the municipality. In the case of a municipality where the smallest possible area in the municipality satisfying all of the conditions of subsection (a) of this section exceeds fifteen percent (15%) of the total area of the municipality, the smallest possible area in the municipality satisfying all of the conditions of subsection (a) of this section may be designated as an urban poverty zone.

(c) Designation. - Upon application of a local government, the Secretary of Commerce shall make a written determination whether an area is an urban progress zone that satisfies the conditions and limitations of subsections (a) and (b) of this section. The application shall include all of the information listed in this subsection. A determination under this section is effective until December 31 of the year following the year in which the determination is made. The Department of Commerce shall publish annually a list of all urban progress zones with a description of their boundaries.

(1) A map showing the census tracts and block groups that would comprise the zone.

(2) A detailed description of the boundaries of the area that would comprise the zone.

(3) A zoning map for the municipality with the proposed zone clearly delineated upon it.

(4) A certification regarding the size of the proposed zone and the areas within the proposed zone zoned as nonresidential.

(5) Detailed census information on the municipality and the proposed zone.

(6) A resolution of the governing body of the municipality requesting the designation of the area as an urban progress zone.

(7)   Any other material required by the Secretary of Commerce.

(d)   Parcel of Property Partially in Urban Progress Zone. - For the purposes of this section, a parcel of property that is located partially within an urban progress zone is considered entirely within the zone if all of the following conditions are satisfied:

(1)   At least fifty percent (50%) of the parcel is located within the zone.

(2)   The parcel was in existence and under common ownership prior to the most recent federal decennial census.

(3)   The parcel is a portion of land made up of one or more tracts or tax parcels of land that is surrounded by a continuous perimeter boundary. (2006-252, s. 1.2; 2007-515, s. 2.)

§ 143B-437.010. Agrarian growth zone designation.

(a)   Agrarian Growth Zone Defined. - An agrarian growth zone is an area that meets all of the following conditions:

(1)   It is comprised of one or more contiguous census tracts, census block groups, or both, in the most recent federal decennial census.

(2)   All of the area is located in whole within a county that has no municipality with a population in excess of 10,000.

(3)   Every census tract and census block group that comprises the area either has more than twenty percent (20%) of its population below the poverty level or is adjacent to another census tract or census block group in the zone that has more than twenty percent (20%) of its population below the poverty level according to the most recent federal decennial census.

(4)   The zone as a whole has more than twenty percent (20%) of its population below the poverty level according to the most recent federal decennial census.

(b)   Limitation and Designation. - The area of a county that is included in one or more agrarian growth zones shall not exceed five percent (5%) of the total area of the county. Upon application of a county, the Secretary of Commerce shall make a written determination whether an area is an agrarian growth zone that satisfies the conditions of subsection (a) of this section. The application shall include all of the information listed in this subsection. A determination under this section is effective until December 31 of the year following the year in which the determination is made. The Department of Commerce shall publish annually a list of all agrarian growth zones with a description of their boundaries.

(1) A map showing the census tracts and block groups that would comprise the zone.

(2) A detailed description of the boundaries of the area that would comprise the zone.

(3) A certification regarding the size of the proposed zone.

(4) Detailed census information on the county and the proposed zone.

(5) A resolution of the board of county commissioners requesting the designation of the area as an agrarian growth zone.

(6) Any other material required by the Secretary of Commerce.

(c) Parcel of Property Partially in Agrarian Growth Zone. - For the purposes of this section, a parcel of property that is located partially within an agrarian growth zone is considered entirely within the zone if all of the following conditions are satisfied:

(1) At least fifty percent (50%) of the parcel is located within the zone.

(2) The parcel was in existence and under common ownership prior to the most recent federal decennial census.

(3) The parcel is a portion of land made up of one or more tracts or tax parcels of land that is surrounded by a continuous perimeter boundary. (2006-252, s. 1.2; 2007-484, s. 33(a); 2007-515, s. 3; 2010-147, s. 1.2.)

§ 143B-437.011: Repealed by Session Laws 2010-31, s. 14.6(b), effective July 1, 2010.

§ 143B-437.012. Job Maintenance and Capital Development Fund.

(a)   Findings. - The General Assembly finds that:

(1)   It is the policy of the State of North Carolina to stimulate economic activity, to maintain high-paying jobs for the citizens of the State, and to encourage capital investment by encouraging and promoting the maintenance of existing business and industry within the State.

(2)   The economic condition of the State is not static, and recent changes in the State's economic condition have created economic distress that requires the enactment of a new program as provided in this section that is designed to encourage the retention of significant numbers of high-paying jobs and the addition of further large-scale capital investment.

(3)   The enactment of this section is necessary to stimulate the economy and maintain high-quality jobs in North Carolina, and this section will promote the general welfare and confer, as its primary purpose and effect, benefits on citizens throughout the State through the maintenance of high-quality jobs, an enlargement of the overall tax base, continued diversity in the State's industrial base, and an increase in revenue to the State's political subdivisions.

(4)   The purpose of this section is to stimulate economic activity and to maintain high-paying jobs within the State while increasing the property tax base for local governments.

(5)   The benefits that flow to the State from job maintenance and capital investment are many and include increased tax revenues related to the capital investment, increased corporate income and franchise taxes due to the placement of additional resources in the State, a better trained, highly skilled workforce, and the continued receipt of personal income tax withholdings from workers who remain employed in high-paying jobs.

(b)   Fund. - The Job Maintenance and Capital Development Fund is created as a restricted reserve in the Department of Commerce. Monies in the Fund do not revert but remain available to the Department for these purposes. The Department may use monies in the Fund only to encourage businesses to maintain high-paying jobs and make further capital investments in the State as provided in this section, and funds are hereby appropriated for these purposes in accordance with G.S. 143C-1-2.

(c) Definitions. - The definitions in G.S. 143B-437.51 apply in this section. In addition, as used in this section, the term "Department" means the Department of Commerce.

(d) Eligibility. - A business is eligible for consideration for a grant under this section if it satisfies the conditions of either subdivision (1) or (2) of this subsection and satisfies the conditions of both subdivisions (3) and (4) of this subsection:

(1) The business is a major employer. A business is a major employer if the business meets the following requirements:

a. The Department certifies that the business has invested or intends to invest at least two hundred million dollars ($200,000,000) of private funds in improvements to real property and additions to tangible personal property in the project within a six-year period beginning with the time the investment commences.

b. The business employs at least 2,000 full-time employees or equivalent full-time contract employees at the project that is the subject of the grant at the time the application is made, and the business agrees to maintain at least 2,000 full-time employees or equivalent full-time contract employees at the project for the full term of the grant agreement.

(2) The business is a large manufacturing employer. A business is a large manufacturing employer if the business meets the following requirements:

a. The business is in manufacturing, as defined in G.S. 143B-437.01, and is converting its manufacturing process to change the product it manufactures.

b. The Department certifies that the business has invested or intends to invest at least sixty-five million dollars ($65,000,000) of private funds in improvements to real property and additions to tangible personal property in the project within a three-year period beginning with the time the investment commences.

c. The business employs at least 320 full-time employees at the project that is the subject of the grant at the time the application is made, and the business agrees to maintain at least 320 full-time employees at the project for the full term of the grant.

(3) The project is located in a development tier one area at the time the business applies for a grant.

(4) All newly hired employees of the business must be citizens of the United States, or have proper identification and documentation of their authorization to reside and work in the United States.

(e) Wage Standard. - A business is eligible for consideration for a grant under this section only if the business satisfies a wage standard at the project that is the subject of the agreement. A business satisfies the wage standard if it pays an average weekly wage that is at least equal to one hundred forty percent (140%) of the average wage for all insured private employers in the county. The Department of Commerce shall annually publish the wage standard for each county. In making the wage calculation, the business shall include any jobs that were filled for at least 1,600 hours during the calendar year, regardless of whether the jobs are full-time positions or equivalent full-time contract positions. Each year that a grant agreement is in effect, the business shall provide the Department a certification that the business continues to satisfy the wage standard. If a business fails to satisfy the wage standard for a year, the business is not eligible for a grant payment for that year.

(f) Health Insurance. - A business is eligible for consideration for a grant under this section only if the business makes available health insurance for all of the full-time employees and equivalent full-time contract employees of the project with respect to which the application is made. For the purposes of this subsection, a business makes available health insurance if it pays at least fifty percent (50%) of the premiums for health care coverage that equals or exceeds the minimum provisions of the basic health care plan of coverage under G.S. 58-50-125.

Each year that a grant agreement under this section is in effect, the business shall provide the Department a certification that the business continues to make available health insurance for all full-time employees of the project governed by the agreement. If a business fails to satisfy the requirements of this subsection, the business is not eligible for a grant payment for that year.

(g) Safety and Health Programs. - A business is eligible for consideration for a grant under this section only if the business has no citations under the Occupational Safety and Health Act that have become a final order within the last three years for willful serious violations or for failing to abate serious violations with respect to the location for which the grant is made. For the purposes of this subsection, "serious violation" has the same meaning as in G.S. 95-127.

(h) Environmental Impact. - A business is eligible for consideration for a grant under this section only if the business certifies that, at the time of the application, the business satisfies the environmental impact standard under G.S. 105-129.83.

(i) Selection. - The Department shall administer the selection of projects to receive grants under this section. The selection process shall include the following components:

(1) Criteria. - The Department shall develop criteria to be used to identify and evaluate eligible projects for possible grants under this section.

(2) Initial evaluation. - The Department shall evaluate projects to determine if a grant under this section is merited and to determine whether the project is eligible and appropriate for consideration for a grant under this section.

(3) Application. - The Department shall require a business to submit an application in order for a project to be considered for a grant under this section. The Department shall prescribe the form of the application, the application process, and the information to be provided, including all information necessary to evaluate the project in accordance with the applicable criteria.

(4) Committee. - The Department shall submit to the Economic Investment Committee the applications for projects the Department considers eligible and appropriate for a grant under this section. The Committee shall evaluate applications to choose projects to receive a grant under this section. In evaluating each application, the Committee shall consider all criteria adopted by the Department under this section and, to the extent applicable, the factors set out in Section 2.1(b) of S.L. 2002-172.

(5) Findings. - The Committee shall make all of the following findings before recommending a project receive a grant under this section:

a. The conditions for eligibility have been met.

b. A grant under this section for the project is necessary to carry out the public purposes provided in subsection (a) of this section.

c. The project is consistent with the economic development goals of the State and of the area where it is located.

d. The affected local governments have participated in retention efforts and offered incentives in a manner appropriate to the project.

e. A grant under this section is necessary for the sustainability and maintenance of the project in this State.

(6) Recommendations. - If the Committee recommends a project for a grant under this section, it shall recommend the amount of State funds to be committed, the preferred form and details of the State participation, and the performance criteria and safeguards to be required in order to protect the State's investment.

(j) Agreement. - Unless the Secretary of Commerce determines that the project is no longer eligible or appropriate for a grant under this section, the Department shall enter into an agreement to provide a grant or grants for a project recommended by the Committee. Each grant agreement is binding and constitutes a continuing contractual obligation of the State and the business. The grant agreement shall include the performance criteria, remedies, and other safeguards recommended by the Committee or required by the Department.

Each grant agreement shall contain a provision prohibiting a business from receiving a payment or other benefit under the agreement at any time when the business has received a notice of an overdue tax debt and the overdue tax debt has not been satisfied or otherwise resolved. Each grant agreement for a business that is a major employer under subdivision (1) of subsection (d) of this section shall contain a provision requiring the business to maintain the employment level at the project that is the subject of the agreement that is the lesser of the level it had at the time it applied for a grant under this section or that it had at the time that the investment required under subsection (d) of this section began. For the purposes of this subsection, the employment level includes full-time employees and equivalent full-time contract employees. The agreement shall further specify that the amount of a grant shall be reduced in proportion to the extent the business fails to maintain employment at this level and that the business shall not be eligible for a grant in any year in which its employment level is less than eighty percent (80%) of that required.

Each grant agreement for a business that is a large manufacturing employer under subdivision (2) of subsection (d) of this section shall contain a provision requiring the business to maintain the employment level required under that subdivision at the project that is the subject of the grant. The agreement shall further specify that the business is not eligible for a grant in any year in which the business fails to maintain the employment level.

A grant agreement may obligate the State to make a series of grant payments over a period of up to 10 years. Nothing in this section constitutes or authorizes a guarantee or assumption by the State of any debt of any business or authorizes the taxing power or the full faith and credit of the State to be pledged.

The Department shall cooperate with the Attorney General's office in preparing the documentation for the grant agreement. The Attorney General shall review the terms of all proposed agreements to be entered into under this section. To be effective against the State, an agreement entered into under this section shall be signed personally by the Attorney General.

(k)   Safeguards. - To ensure that public funds are used only to carry out the public purposes provided in this section, the Department shall require that each business that receives a grant under this section shall agree to meet performance criteria to protect the State's investment and ensure that the projected benefits of the project are secured. The performance criteria to be required shall include maintenance of an appropriate level of employment at specified levels of compensation, maintenance of health insurance for all full-time employees, investment of a specified amount over the term of the agreement, and any other criteria the Department considers appropriate. The agreement shall require the business to repay or reimburse an appropriate portion of the grant based on the extent of any failure by the business to meet the performance criteria. The agreement shall require the business to repay all amounts received under the agreement and to forfeit any future grant payments if the business fails to satisfy the investment eligibility requirement of subdivision (d)(1) or (d)(2) of this section. The use of contract employees shall not be used to reduce compensation at the project that is the subject of the agreement.

(l)   Calculation of Grant Amounts. - The Committee shall consider the following factors in determining the amount of a grant that would be appropriate, but is not necessarily limited to these factors:

(1)   Ninety-five percent (95%) of the privilege and sales and use taxes paid by the business on machinery and equipment installed at the project that is the subject of the agreement.

(2) Ninety-five percent (95%) of the sales and use taxes paid by the business on building materials used to construct, renovate, or repair facilities at the project that is the subject of the agreement.

(3) Ninety-five percent (95%) of the additional income and franchise taxes that are not offset by tax credits. For the purposes of this subdivision, "additional income and franchise taxes" are the additional taxes that would be due because of the investment in machinery and equipment and real property at the project that is the subject of the agreement during the investment period specified in subsection (d) of this section.

(4) Ninety-five percent (95%) of the sales and use taxes paid on electricity and the excise tax paid on piped natural gas.

(5) One hundred percent (100%) of worker training expenses, including wages paid for on-the-job training, associated with the project that is the subject of the agreement.

(6) One hundred percent (100%) of any State permitting fees associated with the capital expansion at the project that is the subject of the agreement.

(m) Monitoring and Reports. - The Department is responsible for monitoring compliance with the performance criteria under each grant agreement and for administering the repayment in case of default. The Department shall pay for the cost of this monitoring from funds appropriated to it for that purpose or for other economic development purposes.

On September 1 of each year until all funds have been expended, the Department shall report to the Joint Legislative Commission on Governmental Operations regarding the Job Maintenance and Capital Development Fund. This report shall include a listing of each grant awarded and each agreement entered into under this section during the preceding year, including the name of the business, the cost/benefit analysis conducted by the Committee during the application process, a description of the project, and the amount of the grant expected to be paid under the agreement during the current fiscal year. The report shall also include detailed information about any defaults and repayment during the preceding year. The Department shall publish this report on its Web site and shall make printed copies available upon request.

(n) Limitations. - The Department may enter into no more than five agreements under this section. The total aggregate cost of all agreements entered into under this section may not exceed sixty-nine million dollars ($69,000,000). The total annual cost of an agreement entered into under this section may not exceed six million dollars ($6,000,000). (2007-552, 1st Ex. Sess., s. 1; 2008-187, s. 26(a); 2009-451, s. 14.5(b); 2009-520, s. 1; 2010-95, ss. 37(a), 38(a); 2010-147, s. 1.6; 2013-360, s. 15.18(c).)

§ 143B-437.013. Port enhancement zone designation.

(a) Port Enhancement Zone Defined. - A port enhancement zone is an area that meets all of the following conditions:

(1) It is comprised of part or all of one or more contiguous census tracts, census block groups, or both, in the most recent federal decennial census.

(2) All of the area is located within 25 miles of a State port and is capable of being used to enhance port operations.

(3) Every census tract and census block group that comprises the area has at least eleven percent (11%) of households with incomes of fifteen thousand dollars ($15,000) or less.

(b) Limitations and Designation. - The area of a county that is included in one or more port enhancement zones shall not exceed five percent (5%) of the total area of the county. Upon application of a county, the Secretary of Commerce shall make a written determination whether an area is a port enhancement zone that satisfies the conditions of subsection (a) of this section. The application shall include all of the information listed in this subsection. A determination under this section is effective until December 31 of the year following the year in which the determination is made. The Department of Commerce shall publish annually a list of all port enhancement zones with a description of their boundaries.

(1) A map showing the census tracts and block groups that would comprise the zone.

(2) A detailed description of the boundaries of the area that would comprise the zone.

(3) A certification regarding the size of the proposed zone.

(4)   Detailed census information on the county and the proposed zone.

(5)   A resolution of the board of county commissioners requesting the designation of the area as a port enhancement zone.

(6)   Any other material required by the Secretary of Commerce. (2011-302, s. 5; 2012-74, s. 6(a); 2012-187, s. 15.2(a).)

§ 143B-437.020. Utilization of economic development incentive programs to support new and expanded natural gas service and to support propane gas service for agricultural projects.

(a)   Definitions. -

(1)   Agriculture. - Activities defined in G.S. 106-581.1, whether performed on or off the farm.

(2)   Economic development incentive programs. - All economic development incentives set forth in G.S. 143B-437.07(c).

(3)   Eligible project. - A discrete and specific economic development project that would expand agricultural production or processing capabilities that requires new or expanded natural gas or propane gas service.

(4)   Excess infrastructure costs. - Any project carrying costs incurred by a natural gas local distribution company to provide new or expanded natural gas service to an eligible project that exceed the income the infrastructure generates for the local natural gas distribution company, including any standard rates, special contract rates, minimum margin agreements, and contributions in aid of construction collected by the natural gas local distribution company.

(5)   Project carrying costs. - All costs, including depreciation, taxes, operation and maintenance expenses, and, for a natural gas local distribution company, a return on investment equal to the rate of return approved by the Utilities Commission in the natural gas local distribution company's most recent general rate case under G.S. 62-133.

(b)   Facilitation of New and Expanded Natural Gas Service to Agricultural Projects. - Economic development incentive programs may utilize funds for agricultural projects for the following purposes:

(1) To allow the owner of an eligible project to pay for excess infrastructure costs associated with the eligible project.

(2) To allow the owner of an eligible project to pay for cost-effective alternatives that would reduce excess infrastructure costs, including:

a. Relocating equipment that uses natural gas to a different location on the property nearer existing natural gas lines to reduce or eliminate the project carrying costs.

b. Adding supplemental uses of natural gas to increase annual volume throughput and enhance the feasibility of new natural gas service, including fuel for tractors and equipment, greenhouses, plant or animal production, feed grain drying, and natural gas powered irrigation pumps.

(c) Facilitation of New and Expanded Propane Gas Service to Agricultural Production. - Economic development incentive programs may utilize funds for agricultural projects to allow the owner of an eligible project to pay for cost-effective alternatives that would reduce infrastructure costs or that would increase energy efficiency by adding supplemental uses of propane gas to increase annual volume throughput, reduce energy consumption, reduce energy costs, or to enhance the feasibility of the project or the provision of propane gas service, including the conversion or repowering of tractors, trucks, vehicles, and mowers to use propane gas, or to provide propane gas powered tractors, equipment, appliances, irrigation pumps, and dryers to service agricultural production facilities or operations, or to provide a dispensing station for the project owner's use.

(d) Use of Incentive Funds. - Incentive funds utilized in accordance with subsections (b) and (c) of this section shall be paid directly to the owner of the eligible project.

(e) Termination. - Incentive funds utilized in accordance with subsection (b) of this section shall terminate when there are no longer excess infrastructure costs.

(f) Reimbursement. - The owner of an eligible project who receives incentive funds in accordance with subsections (b) or (c) of this section shall be responsible for reimbursing the incentive funds if, for any reason, the eligible project does not maintain business operations for a period of at least five years from the date of the initial utilization of incentive funds.

(g) Limits on Eligible Project Incentive Funds. - Total incentive funds for all eligible projects under subsections (b) and (c) of this section shall not cumulatively exceed five million dollars ($5,000,000) per biennium. The managers of economic development incentive programs shall promptly report payments made in accordance with subsections (b) and (c) of this section to the Department of Commerce, and the Department of Commerce shall promptly notify the managers of economic development incentive programs when the limitation provided by this subsection has been reached for the biennium.

(h) Mechanism not Exclusive. - The utilization of incentive funds in accordance with subsections (b) or (c) of this section is intended to supplement other available mechanisms for the extension of service to new or expanding customers and may be used in conjunction with special contract arrangements, minimum margin agreements, and contributions in aid of construction. (2013-367, s. 1.)

Part 2A. Community Development Council.

§ 143B-437.1. Community Development Council - creation; powers and duties.

There is hereby created the Community Development Council to be located in the Department of Commerce. The Community Development Council shall have the following functions and duties:

(1) To advise the Secretary of Commerce with respect to promoting and assisting in the orderly development of North Carolina counties and communities.

(2) To advise the Secretary of Commerce with respect to the type and effectiveness of planning and management services provided to local government.

(3), (4) Repealed by Session Laws 1977, c. 198, s. 13.

(5) The Council shall consider and advise the Secretary of Commerce upon any matter the Secretary may refer to it. (1973, c. 1262, s. 48; 1977, c. 198, ss. 13, 14; c. 771, ss. 4, 8; 1989, c. 727, ss. 199, 200; c. 751, ss. 7(33), 8(19); 1991 (Reg. Sess., 1992), c. 959, s. 58.)

§ 143B-437.2. Community Development Council - members; chairman; selection; removal; compensation; quorum; services.

(a) The Community Development Council shall consist of 11 members appointed by the Governor. The composition of the Council shall be as follows: one member who shall be a local government official, one member who shall be the Executive Secretary of the League of Municipalities, one member who shall be the Executive Secretary of the County Commissioners Association, one member who shall represent industry, one member who shall represent labor, and six members at large.

(b)   The Governor shall designate one member of the Council to serve as Chairman at the pleasure of the Governor.

(c)   The initial members of the Council other than those members serving in an ex officio capacity shall be appointed to serve for terms of four years and until their successors are appointed and qualify. Any appointment to fill a vacancy on the Council created by the resignation, dismissal, death or disability of a member shall be for the balance of the unexpired term.

(d)   The Governor shall have the power to remove any member of the Council from office in accordance with the provisions of G.S. 143B-16 of the Executive Organization Act of 1973.

(e)   Members of the Council shall receive per diem and necessary travel and subsistence expenses in accordance with the provisions of G.S. 138-5.

(f)   A majority of the Council shall constitute a quorum for the transaction of business.

(g)   All clerical and other services required by the Council shall be supplied by the Secretary of Commerce. (1973, c. 1262, s. 49; 1977, c. 198, s. 14; c. 771, ss. 4, 9; 1989, c. 727, ss. 199, 201; c. 751, s. 8(20); 1991 (Reg. Sess., 1992), c. 959, s. 59.)

§ 143B-437.3. Community Development Council - meetings.

The Community Development Council shall meet at least semiannually and may hold special meetings at any time and place within the State at the call of the chairman or upon the written request of at least a majority of the members. (1973, c. 1262, s. 50; 1977, c. 198, s. 14; 1989, c. 727, s. 199.)

Part 2B. NC Green Business Fund.

§ 143B-437.4. NC Green Business Fund and grant program.

(a) Fund. - The NC Green Business Fund is established as a special revenue fund in the Department of Commerce, and the Department shall be responsible for administering the Fund.

(b) Purposes. - Moneys in the NC Green Business Fund shall be allocated pursuant to this subsection. The Department of Commerce shall make grants from the Fund to private businesses with less than 100 employees, nonprofit organizations, local governments, and State agencies to encourage the expansion of small to medium size businesses with less than 100 employees to help grow a green economy in the State. Moneys in the NC Green Business Fund shall be used for projects that will focus on the following three priority areas listed in this subsection. In selecting between projects that are within a priority area, a project that is located in an Eco-Industrial Park certified under G.S. 143B-437.08 has priority over a comparable project that is not located in a certified Eco-Industrial Park. The priority areas are:

(1) To encourage the development of the biofuels industry in the State. The Department of Commerce may make grants available to maximize development, production, distribution, retail infrastructure, and consumer purchase of biofuels in North Carolina, including grants to enhance biofuels workforce development.

(2) To encourage the development of the green building industry in the State. The Department of Commerce may make grants available to assist in the development and growth of a market for environmentally conscious and energy efficient green building processes. Grants may support the installation, certification, or distribution of green building materials; energy audits; and marketing and sales of green building technology in North Carolina, including grants to enhance workforce development for green building processes.

(3) To attract and leverage private-sector investments and entrepreneurial growth in environmentally conscious clean technology and renewable energy

products and businesses, including grants to enhance workforce development in such businesses.

(c) Cap and Matching Funds. - The Department of Commerce may set a cap on a grant from the NC Green Business Fund and may require a private business to provide matching funds for a grant from the Fund. A grant to a project located in an Eco-Industrial Park certified under G.S. 143B-437.08 is not subject to a cap or a requirement to provide matching funds. (2007-323, s. 13.2(a); 2010-147, s. 5.2.)

§ 143B-437.5. Green Business Fund Advisory Committee.

The Department of Commerce may establish an advisory committee to assist in the development of the specific selection criteria and the grant-making process of the NC Green Business Fund. (2007-323, s. 13.2(a).)

§ 143B-437.6. Agreements required.

Funds may be disbursed from the NC Green Business Fund only in accordance with agreements entered into between the Department of Commerce and an eligible grantee. Each agreement must contain the following provisions:

(1) A description of the acceptable uses of grant proceeds. The agreement may limit the use of funds to specific purposes or may allow the funds to be used for any lawful purposes.

(2) A provision allowing the Department of Commerce to inspect all records of the business that may be used to confirm compliance with the agreement or with the requirements of this Part.

(3) A provision establishing the method for determining compliance with the agreement.

(4) A provision establishing a schedule for disbursement of funds under the agreement.

(5) A provision requiring recapture of grant funds if a grantee subsequently fails to comply with the terms of the agreement.

(6) Any other provision the State finds necessary to ensure the proper use of State funds. (2007-323, s. 13.2(a).)

§ 143B-437.7. Program guidelines.

The Department of Commerce shall develop guidelines related to the administration of the NC Green Business Fund and to the selection of projects to receive allocations from the Fund, including project evaluation measures. At least 20 days before the effective date of any guidelines or nontechnical amendments to guidelines, the Department of Commerce must publish the proposed guidelines on the Department's Web site and provide notice to persons who have requested notice of proposed guidelines. In addition, the Department must accept oral and written comments on the proposed guidelines during the 15 business days beginning on the first day that the Department has completed these notifications. For the purpose of this section, a technical amendment is either of the following:

(1) An amendment that corrects a spelling or grammatical error.

(2) An amendment that makes a clarification based on public comment and could have been anticipated by the public notice that immediately preceded the public comment. (2007-323, s. 13.2(a).)

§ 143B-437.8. Reports.

Grants made to non-State entities through the NC Green Business Fund shall be subject to the oversight and reporting requirements of G.S. 143C-6-23. The Department of Commerce shall publish a report on the commitment, disbursement, and use of funds allocated from the NC Green Business Fund at the end of each fiscal year. The report is due no later than September 1 and must be submitted to the following:

(1) The Joint Legislative Commission on Governmental Operations.

(2)   The chairs of the House of Representatives and Senate Finance Committees.

(3)   The chairs of the House of Representatives and Senate Appropriations Committees.

(4)   The Fiscal Research Division of the General Assembly. (2007-323, s. 13.2(a).)

§ 143B-437.9. Reserved for future codification purposes.

§ 143B-437.10: Recodified as G.S. 143B-437.010 by Session Laws 2007-484, s.33(a), effective July 1, 2007.

§ 143B-437.11: Recodified as G.S. 143B-437.012 by Session Laws 2008-187, s. 26(a), effective August 7, 2008.

§ 143B-437.13. Reserved for future codification purposes.

Part 2C. Energy Loan Fund.

§§ 143B-437.14 through 143B-437.16: Recodified as Part 32 of Article 7 of Chapter 143B, G.S. 143B-344.42 through G.S. 143B-344.44, by Session Laws 2013-360, s. 15.22(b), effective July 1, 2013.

§ 143B-437.17. Reserved for future codification purposes.

§ 143B-437.18. Reserved for future codification purposes.

§ 143B-437.19. Reserved for future codification purposes.

Part 2D. North Carolina Rural Redevelopment Authority.

§ 143B-437.20: Repealed by Session Laws 2008-134, s. 73(a).

§ 143B-437.21: Repealed by Session Laws 2008-134, s. 73(a).

§ 143B-437.22: Repealed by Session Laws 2008-134, s. 73(a).

§ 143B-437.23: Repealed by Session Laws 2008-134, s. 73(a).

§ 143B-437.24. Reserved for future codification purposes.

§ 143B-437.25. Reserved for future codification purposes.

§ 143B-437.26: Repealed by Session Laws 2008-134, s. 73(a).

§ 143B-437.27: Repealed by Session Laws 2008-134, s. 73(a).

§ 143B-437.28: Repealed by Session Laws 2008-134, s. 73(a).

§ 143B-437.29: Repealed by Session Laws 2008-134, s. 73(a).

§ 143B-437.30: Repealed by Session Laws 2008-134, s. 73(a).

§ 143B-437.31: Repealed by Session Laws 2008-134, s. 73(a).

§ 143B-437.32: Repealed by Session Laws 2008-134, s. 73(a).

§ 143B-437.33: Repealed by Session Laws 2008-134, s. 73(a).

§§ 143B-437.34 through 143B-437.39. Reserved for future codification purposes.

Part 2E. North Carolina Rural Internet Access Authority

(Repealed effective December 31, 2003).

§§ 143B-437.40 through 143B-437.43: Repealed by Session Laws 2000-149, s. 5, as amended by Session Laws 2003-425, s. 3, effective December 31, 2003.

Part 2F.

E-NC Initiative.

§§ 143B-437.44 through 143B-437.47: Repealed by Session Laws 2003-425, s. 4, as amended by Session Laws 2006-66, s. 12.3(a), effective December 31, 2011.

§ 143B-437.48: Reserved for future codification purposes.

§ 143B-437.49: Reserved for future codification purposes.

Part 2G. Job Development Investment Grant Program.

§ 143B-437.50. Legislative findings and purpose.

The General Assembly finds that:

(1) It is the policy of the State of North Carolina to stimulate economic activity and to create new jobs for the citizens of the State by encouraging and promoting the expansion of existing business and industry within the State and by recruiting and attracting new business and industry to the State.

(2) Both short-term and long-term economic trends at the State, national, and international levels have made the successful implementation of the State's economic development policy and programs both more critical and more challenging; and the decline in the State's traditional industries, and the resulting adverse impact upon the State and its citizens, have been exacerbated in recent years by adverse national and State economic trends that contribute to the reduction in the State's industrial base and that inhibit the State's ability to sustain or attract new and expanding businesses.

(3) The economic condition of the State is not static and recent changes in the State's economic condition have created economic distress that requires a reevaluation of certain existing State programs and the enactment of a new program as provided in this Part that are designed to stimulate new economic activity and to create new jobs within the State.

(4) The enactment of this Part is necessary to stimulate the economy, facilitate economic recovery, and create new jobs in North Carolina; and this Part will promote the general welfare and confer, as its primary purpose and effect, benefits on citizens throughout the State through the creation of new jobs, an enlargement of the overall tax base, an expansion and diversification of the State's industrial base, and an increase in revenue to the State and its political subdivisions.

(5) The purpose of this Part is to stimulate economic activity and to create new jobs within the State.

(6) It is not the intent of the General Assembly that grants provided through this Part be used as venture capital funds, business incubator funds, or business start-up funds or to otherwise fund the initial capitalization needs of new businesses.

(7) Nothing in this Part shall be construed to constitute a guarantee or assumption by the State of any debt of any business or to authorize the taxing power or the full faith and credit of the State to be pledged. (2002-172, s. 2.1(a); 2003-416, s. 2.)

§ 143B-437.51. Definitions.

The following definitions apply in this Part:

(1) Agreement. - A community economic development agreement under G.S. 143B-437.57.

(2) Base period. - The period of time set by the Committee during which new employees are to be hired for the positions on which the grant is based.

(3) Business. - A corporation, sole proprietorship, cooperative association, partnership, S corporation, limited liability company, nonprofit corporation, or other form of business organization, located either within or outside this State.

(4) Committee. - The Economic Investment Committee established pursuant to G.S. 143B-437.54.

(4a) Development tier. - The classification assigned to an area pursuant to G.S. 143B-437.08.

(5) Eligible position. - A position created by a business and filled by a new full-time employee in this State during the base period.

(6) Full-time employee. - A person who is employed for consideration for at least 35 hours a week, whose wages are subject to withholding under Article 4A of Chapter 105 of the General Statutes, and who is determined by the Committee to be employed in a permanent position according to criteria it develops in consultation with the Attorney General. The term does not include any person who works as an independent contractor or on a consulting basis for the business.

(7) New employee. - A full-time employee who represents a net increase in the number of the business's employees statewide.

(8) Overdue tax debt. - Defined in G.S. 105-243.1.

(9) Related member. - Defined in G.S. 105-130.7A.

(10) Withholdings. - The amount withheld by a business from the wages of employees in eligible positions under Article 4A of Chapter 105 of the General Statutes. (2002-172, s. 2.1(a); 2003-416, s. 2; 2003-435, 2nd Ex. Sess., s. 2.1; 2006-168, s. 1.1; 2006-252, s. 2.6; 2006-264, s. 69(a).)

§ 143B-437.52. Job Development Investment Grant Program.

(a) Program. - There is established the Job Development Investment Grant Program to be administered by the Economic Investment Committee. In order to foster job creation and investment in the economy of this State, the Committee may enter into agreements with businesses to provide grants in accordance with the provisions of this Part. The Committee, in consultation with the Attorney General, shall develop criteria to be used in determining whether the conditions of this section are satisfied and whether the project described in the application is otherwise consistent with the purposes of this Part. Before entering into an agreement, the Committee must find that all the following conditions are met:

(1) The project proposed by the business will create, during the term of the agreement, a net increase in employment in this State by the business.

(2) The project will benefit the people of this State by increasing opportunities for employment and by strengthening this State's economy by, for example, providing worker training opportunities, constructing and enhancing critical infrastructure, increasing development in strategically important industries, or increasing the State and local tax base.

(3) The project is consistent with economic development goals for the State and for the area where it will be located.

(4) A grant under this Part is necessary for the completion of the project in this State.

(5) The total benefits of the project to the State outweigh its costs and render the grant appropriate for the project.

(b) Priority. - In selecting between applicants, a project that is located in an Eco-Industrial Park certified under G.S. 143B-437.08 has priority over a comparable project that is not located in a certified Eco-Industrial Park.

(c) Awards. - The maximum amount of total annual liability for grants awarded in any single calendar year under this Part, including amounts transferred to the Utility Account pursuant to G.S. 143B-437.61, is fifteen million dollars ($15,000,000). No agreement may be entered into that, when considered together with other existing agreements governing grants awarded during a single calendar year, could cause the State's potential total annual liability for grants awarded in a single calendar year to exceed this amount. The Department shall make every effort to ensure that the average percentage of withholdings of eligible positions for grants awarded under this Part does not exceed the average of the range provided in G.S. 143B-437.56(a).

(d) Measuring Employment. - For the purposes of subdivision (a)(1) of this section and G.S. 143B-437.51(5), 143B-437.51(7), and 143B-437.57(a)(11), the Committee may designate that the increase or maintenance of employment is measured at the level of a division or another operating unit of a business, rather than at the business level, if both of the following conditions are met:

(1) The Committee makes an explicit finding that the designation is necessary to secure the project in this State.

(2) The agreement contains terms to ensure that the business does not create eligible positions by transferring or shifting to the project existing

positions from another project of the business or a related member of the business. (2002-172, s. 2.1(a); 2003-416, s. 2; 2003-435, 2nd Ex. Sess., s. 2.2; 2004-124, ss. 32G.1(b), 32G.1(c), 32G.1(e); 2006-168, s. 1.2; 2006-264, s. 69(b); 2009-394, s. 1; 2010-147, s. 5.3; 2012-142, s. 13.6(g); 2013-360, s. 15.19(a).)

§ 143B-437.53. Eligible projects.

(a) Minimum Number of Eligible Positions. - A business may apply to the Committee for a grant for any project that creates the minimum number of eligible positions as set out in the table below. If the project will be located in more than one development tier area, the location with the highest development tier area designation determines the minimum number of eligible positions that must be created.

Development Tier Area	Number of Eligible Positions
Tier One	10
Tier Two	20
Tier Three	20

(b) Ineligible Businesses. - A project that consists solely of retail facilities is not eligible for a grant under this Part. If a project consists of both retail facilities and nonretail facilities, only the portion of the project consisting of nonretail facilities is eligible for a grant, and only the withholdings from employees in eligible positions that are employed exclusively in the portion of the project that represents nonretail facilities may be used to determine the amount of the grant. If a warehouse facility is part of a retail facility and supplies only that retail facility, the warehouse facility is not eligible for a grant. For the purposes of this Part, catalog distribution centers are not retail facilities.

A project that consists of a professional or semiprofessional sports team or club, other than a professional motorsports racing team, is not eligible for a grant under this Part.

(c) Health Insurance. - A business is eligible for a grant under this Part only if the business provides health insurance for all of the applicable full-time employees of the project with respect to which the grant is made. For the purposes of this subsection, an applicable full-time employee is one who earns from the business less than one hundred fifty thousand dollars ($150,000) in taxable compensation on an annualized basis or three and one-half times the annualized average State wage for all insured private employers in the State employing between 250 and 1,000 employees, whichever is greater. For the purposes of this subsection, a business provides health insurance if it pays at least fifty percent (50%) of the premiums for health care coverage that equals or exceeds the minimum provisions of the basic health care plan of coverage recommended by the Small Employer Carrier Committee pursuant to G.S. 58-50-125.

Each year that a business receives a grant under this Part, the business must provide with the submission required under G.S. 143B-437.58 a certification that the business continues to provide health insurance, as required by this subsection, for all applicable full-time employees of the project with respect to which the grant is made. If the business ceases to provide the required health insurance, the Committee shall amend or terminate the agreement as provided in G.S. 143B-437.59.

(d) Repealed by Session Laws 2003-435, 2nd Ex. Sess., s. 2.3, effective December 16, 2003.

(e) Safety and Health Programs. - In order for a business to be eligible for a grant under this Part, the business must have no citations under the Occupational Safety and Health Act that have become a final order within the past three years for willful serious violations or for failing to abate serious violations with respect to the location for which the grant is made. For the purposes of this subsection, "serious violation" has the same meaning as in G.S. 95-127. (2002-172, s. 2.1(a); 2003-416, s. 2; 2003-435, Ex. Sess., s. 2.3; 2005-241, s. 5; 2006-168, s. 1.3; 2006-252, s. 2.7.)

§ 143B-437.54. Economic Investment Committee established.

(a) Membership. - The Economic Investment Committee is established. The Committee consists of the following members:

(1) The Secretary of Commerce.

(2) The Secretary of Revenue.

(3) The Director of the Office of State Budget and Management.

(4) One member appointed by the General Assembly upon the recommendation of the Speaker of the House of Representatives.

(5) One member appointed by the General Assembly upon the recommendation of the President Pro Tempore of the Senate.

The members of the Committee appointed by the General Assembly may not be members of the General Assembly. The members of the Committee appointed by the General Assembly serve two-year terms that begin upon appointment.

(b) Decision Required. - The Committee may act only upon a decision of three of its five members.

(c) Conflict of Interest. - It is unlawful for a current or former member of the Committee to, while serving on the Committee or within two years after the end of service on the Committee, provide services for compensation, as an employee, consultant, or otherwise, to any business or a related member of the business that is awarded a grant under this Part or under G.S. 143B-437.02 while the member is serving on the Committee. Violation of this subsection is a Class 1 misdemeanor. In addition to the penalties imposed under G.S. 15A-1340.23, the court shall also make a finding as to what compensation was received by the defendant for services in violation of this section and shall order the defendant to forfeit that compensation.

If a person is convicted under this section, the person shall not provide services for compensation, as an employee, consultant, or otherwise, to any business or a related member of the business that was awarded a grant under this Part or under G.S. 143B-437.02 while the member was serving on the Committee until two years after the person's conviction under this section.

(d) Public Notice. - At least 20 days before the effective date of any criteria or nontechnical amendments to criteria, the Committee must publish the proposed criteria on the Department of Commerce's web site and provide notice to persons who have requested notice of proposed criteria. In addition, the Committee must accept oral and written comments on the proposed criteria during the 15 business days beginning on the first day that the Committee has completed these notifications. For the purpose of this subsection, a technical amendment is either of the following:

(1)   An amendment that corrects a spelling or grammatical error.

(2)   An amendment that makes a clarification based on public comment and could have been anticipated by the public notice that immediately preceded the public comment.

(e)   Sunshine. - Meetings of the Committee are subject to the open meetings requirements of Article 33C of Chapter 143 of the General Statutes. All documents of the Committee, including applications for grants, are public records governed by Chapter 132 of the General Statutes and any applicable provisions of the General Statutes protecting confidential information. (2002-172, s. 2.1(a); 2003-416, ss. 2, 25; 2003-435, 2nd Ex. Sess., ss. 1.4, 2.4.)

§ 143B-437.55.   Applications; fees; reports; study.

(a)   Application. - A business shall apply, under oath, to the Committee for a grant on a form prescribed by the Committee that includes at least all of the following:

(1)   The name of the business, the proposed location of the project, and the type of activity in which the business will engage at the project site or sites.

(2)   The names and addresses of the principals or management of the business, the nature of the business, and the form of business organization under which it is operated.

(3)   The financial statements of the business prepared by a certified public accountant and any other financial information the Committee considers necessary.

(4)   The number of eligible positions proposed to be created for the project and the salaries for these positions.

(5)   An estimate of the total withholdings.

(6) Certification that the business will provide health insurance to full-time employees of the project as required by G.S. 143B-437.53(c).

(7) Information concerning other locations, including locations in other states and countries, being considered for the project and the nature of any benefits that would accrue to the business if the project were to be located in one of those locations.

(8) Information concerning any other State or local government incentives for which the business is applying or that it has an expectation of receiving.

(9) Any other information necessary for the Committee to evaluate the application.

A business may apply, in one consolidated application in a form and manner determined by the Committee, for a grant that may include performance by related members of the business who may qualify under this Part.

The Committee will consider an application by a business for a grant that includes performance of its related members only if the related members for whom the application is submitted assign to the business any claim of right the related members may have under this Part to apply for grants individually during the term of the agreement and agree to cooperate with the business in providing to the Committee all the information required for the initial application and the agreement, and any other information the Committee may require for the purposes of this Part. The applicant business is responsible for providing to the Committee all the information required under this Part.

If a business applies for a grant that includes performance by its related members, the related members included in the application may be permitted to meet the qualifications for a grant collectively by participating in a project that meets the requirements of this Part. The amount of a grant may be calculated under the terms of this Part as if the related members were all collectively one business entity. Any conditions for a grant, other than the number of eligible positions created, apply to each related member who is listed in the application as participating in the project. The grant awarded shall be paid to the approved grantee business only. A grant received under this Part by a business may be apportioned to the related members in a manner determined by the business. In order for an agreement to be executed, each related member included in the application must sign the agreement and agree to abide by its terms.

(b) Application Fee. - When filing an application under this section, the business must pay the Committee a fee of ten thousand dollars ($10,000). The fee is due at the time the application is filed. The Secretary of Commerce, the Secretary of Revenue, and the Director of the Office of State Budget and Management shall determine the allocation of the fee imposed by this section among their agencies. The proceeds of the fee are receipts of the agency to which they are credited. Within 30 days of receipt of an application under this section but prior to any award being made, the Department of Commerce shall notify each governing body of an area where a submitted application proposes locating a project of the information listed in this subsection, provided that the governing body agrees, in writing, to any confidentiality requirements imposed by the Department under G.S. 132-6(d). The information required by this subsection includes all of the following:

(1) The estimated amount of the grant anticipated to be awarded to the applicant for the project.

(2) Any economic impact data submitted with the application or prepared by the Department.

(3) Any economic impact estimated by the Department to result from the project.

(c) Annual Reports. - The Committee shall publish a report on the Job Development Investment Grant Program on or before April 30 of each year. The Committee shall submit the report electronically to the House of Representatives Finance Committee, the Senate Finance Committee, the House of Representatives Appropriations Subcommittee on Natural and Economic Resources, the Senate Appropriations Committee on Natural and Economic Resources, and the Fiscal Research Division. The report shall include the following:

(1) A listing of each grant awarded during the preceding calendar year, including the name of the business, the cost/benefit analysis conducted by the Committee during the application process, a description of the project, the term of the grant, the percentage of withholdings used to determine the amount of the grant, the annual maximum State liability under the grant, and the maximum total lifetime State liability under the grant.

(2) An update on the status of projects under grants awarded before the preceding calendar year.

(3)   The number and development tier area of eligible positions to be created by projects with respect to which grants have been awarded.

(3a)   A listing of the employment level for all businesses receiving a grant and any changes in those levels from the level of the next preceding year.

(4)   The wage levels of all eligible positions to be created by projects with respect to which grants have been awarded, aggregated and listed in increments of ten thousand dollars ($10,000) or other appropriate increments.

(5)   The amount of new income tax revenue received from withholdings related to the projects for which grants have been awarded.

(6)   For the first annual report after adoption of the criteria developed by the Committee, in consultation with the Attorney General, to implement this Part, a copy of such criteria, and, for subsequent reports, identification of any changes in those criteria from the previous calendar year.

(7)   The number of awards made to new businesses and the number of awards made to existing, expanding businesses in the preceding calendar year.

(8)   The environmental impact of businesses that have received grants under the program.

(9)   The geographic distribution of grants, by number and amount, awarded under the program.

(10)   Repealed by Session Laws 2009-394, s. 2, effective July 31, 2009.

(11)   A listing of all businesses making an application under this Part and an explanation of whether each business ultimately located the project in this State regardless of whether the business was awarded a grant for the project under this Part.

(12)   Repealed by Session Laws 2006-168, s. 1.4, effective July 27, 2006.

(13)   The total amount transferred to the Utility Account under this Part during the preceding year.

(d)   Repealed by Session Laws 2012-142, s. 13.4(f), effective July 1, 2012.

(e) Study. - The Committee shall conduct a study to determine the minimum funding level required to implement the Job Development Investment Grant Program successfully. The Committee shall report the results of this study to the House of Representatives Finance Committee, the Senate Finance Committee, the House of Representatives Appropriations Subcommittee on Natural and Economic Resources, the Senate Appropriations Committee on Natural and Economic Resources, and the Fiscal Research Division no later than April 1 of each year. (2002-172, s. 2.1(a); 2003-416, s. 2; 2005-429, s. 2.1; 2006-168, s. 1.4; 2006-252, s. 2.8; 2006-264, s. 69(c); 2009-394, s. 2; 2010-31, s. 14.8; 2012-142, s. 13.4(f); 2013-360, ss. 15.18(f), 15.19(b), 15.20(a).)

§ 143B-437.56. Calculation of minimum and maximum grants; factors considered.

(a) Subject to the limitations of subsection (d) of this section, the amount of the grant awarded in each case shall be a percentage of the withholdings of eligible positions. The percentage shall be no less than ten percent (10%) and no more than seventy-five percent (75%) of the withholdings of the eligible positions for a period of years. The percentage used to determine the amount of the grant shall be based on criteria developed by the Committee, in consultation with the Attorney General, after considering at least the following:

(1) The number of eligible positions to be created.

(2) The expected duration of those positions.

(3) The type of contribution the business can make to the long-term growth of the State's economy.

(4) The amount of other financial assistance the project will receive from the State or local governments.

(5) The total dollar investment the business is making in the project.

(6) Whether the project utilizes existing infrastructure and resources in the community.

(7) Whether the project is located in a development zone.

(8) The number of eligible positions that would be filled by residents of a development zone.

(9) The extent to which the project will mitigate unemployment in the State and locality.

(b) The term of the grant shall not exceed 12 years starting with the first year a grant payment is made. The first grant payment must be made within six years after the date on which the grant was awarded. The number of years in the base period for which grant payments may be made shall not exceed five years.

(c) The grant may be based only on eligible positions created during the base period.

(d) For any eligible position that is located in a development tier three area, seventy-five percent (75%) of the annual grant approved for disbursement shall be payable to the business, and twenty-five percent (25%) shall be payable to the Utility Account pursuant to G.S. 143B-437.61. For any eligible position that is located in a development tier two area, eighty-five percent (85%) of the annual grant approved for disbursement shall be payable to the business, and fifteen percent (15%) shall be payable to the Utility Account pursuant to G.S. 143B-437.61. A position is located in the development tier area that has been assigned to the county in which the project is located at the time the application is filed with the Committee.

(e) A business that is receiving any other grant by operation of State law may not receive an amount as a grant pursuant to this Part that, when combined with any other grants, exceeds seventy-five percent (75%) of the withholdings of the business, unless the Committee makes an explicit finding that the additional grant is necessary to secure the project.

(f) The amount of a grant associated with any specific eligible position, including any amount transferred to the Utility Account pursuant to G.S. 143B-437.61, may not exceed six thousand five hundred dollars ($6,500) in any year. (2002-172, s. 2.1(a); 2003-416, s. 2; 2003-435, 2nd Ex. Sess., s. 2.5; 2006-168, s. 1.5; 2006-252, s. 2.9(a), (b); 2006-264, s. 69(d).)

§ 143B-437.57. Community economic development agreement.

(a) Terms. - Each community economic development agreement shall include at least the following:

(1) A detailed description of the proposed project that will result in job creation and the number of new employees to be hired during the base period.

(2) The term of the grant and the criteria used to determine the first year for which the grant may be claimed.

(3) The number of eligible positions that are subjects of the grant and a description of those positions and the location of those positions.

(4) The amount of the grant based on a percentage of withholdings.

(5) A method for determining the number of new employees hired during a grant year.

(6) A method for the business to report annually to the Committee the number of eligible positions for which the grant is to be made.

(7) A requirement that the business report to the Committee annually the aggregate amount of withholdings during the grant year.

(8) A provision permitting an audit of the payroll records of the business by the Committee from time to time as the Committee considers necessary.

(9) A provision that requires the Committee to reduce the amount or term of a grant pursuant to G.S. 143B-437.59.

(10) A provision that requires the business to maintain operations at the project location or another location approved by the Committee for at least one hundred fifty percent (150%) of the term of the grant and a provision to permit the Committee to recapture all or part of the grant at its discretion if the business does not remain at the site for the required term.

(11) A provision that requires the business to maintain employment levels in this State at the level of the year immediately preceding the base period.

(12) A provision establishing the conditions under which the grant agreement may be terminated, in addition to those under G.S. 143B-437.59, and under which grant funds may be recaptured by the Committee.

(13)   A provision stating that unless the agreement is terminated pursuant to G.S. 143B-437.59, the agreement, including any amendments pursuant to G.S. 143B-437.59, is binding and constitutes a continuing contractual obligation of the State and the business.

(14)   A provision setting out any allowed variation in the terms of the agreement that will not subject the business to grant reduction, amendment, or termination of the agreement under G.S. 143B-437.59.

(15)   A provision that prohibits the business from manipulating or attempting to manipulate employee withholdings with the purpose of increasing the amount of the grant and that requires the Committee to terminate the agreement and take action to recapture grant funds if the Committee finds that the business has manipulated or attempted to manipulate withholdings with the purpose of increasing the amount of the grant.

(16)   A provision requiring that the business engage in fair employment practices as required by State and federal law and a provision encouraging the business to use small contractors, minority contractors, physically handicapped contractors, and women contractors whenever practicable in the conduct of its business.

(17)   A provision encouraging the business to hire North Carolina residents.

(18)   A provision encouraging the business to use the North Carolina State Ports.

(19)   A provision stating that the State is not obligated to make any annual grant payment unless and until the State has received withholdings from the business in an amount that exceeds the amount of the grant payment.

(20)   A provision describing the manner in which the amount of a grant will be measured and administered to ensure compliance with the provisions of G.S. 143B-437.52(c).

(21)   A provision stating that any recapture of a grant and any reduction in the amount of the grant or the term of the agreement must, at a minimum, be proportional to the failure to comply measured relative to the condition or criterion with respect to which the failure occurred.

(22)   A provision stating that any disputes over interpretation of the agreement shall be submitted to binding arbitration.

(23)   A provision stating that the amount of a grant associated with any specific eligible position, including any amount transferred to the Utility Account pursuant to G.S. 143B-437.61, may not exceed six thousand five hundred dollars ($6,500) in any year.

(24)   A provision stating that the business agrees to submit to an audit at any time that the Committee requires one.

(25)   A provision encouraging the business to contract with small businesses headquartered in the State for goods and services.

(b)   Approval of Attorney General. - The Attorney General shall review the terms of all proposed agreements entered into by the Committee. To be effective against the State, an agreement entered into under this Part must be signed personally by the Attorney General.

(c)   Agreement Binding. - A community economic development agreement is a binding obligation of the State and is not subject to State funds being appropriated by the General Assembly. (2002-172, s. 2.1(a); 2003-416, s. 2; 2004-124, ss. 32G.1(f), 32G.1(g); 2006-168, s. 1.6; 2006-264, s. 69(e); 2009-394, s. 3.)

§ 143B-437.58. Grant recipient to submit records.

(a)   No later than March 1 of each year, for the preceding grant year, every business that is awarded a grant under this Part shall submit to the Committee an annual payroll report showing withholdings as a condition of its continuation in the grant program and identifying eligible positions that have been created during the base period that remain filled at the end of each year of the grant. Annual reports submitted to the Committee shall include social security numbers of individual employees identified in the reports. Upon request of the Committee, the business shall also submit a copy of its State and federal tax returns. Payroll and tax information, including social security numbers of individual employees and State and federal tax returns, submitted under this subsection is tax information subject to G.S. 105-259. Aggregated payroll or withholding tax information submitted or derived under this subsection is not tax information subject to G.S. 105-259. When making a submission under this section, the business must pay the Committee a fee of the greater of two thousand five hundred dollars ($2,500) or three one-hundredths of one percent (.03%) of an amount equal to the grant less the maximum amount to be transferred pursuant to G.S. 143B-437.61. The fee is due at the time the submission is made. The Secretary of Commerce, the Secretary of Revenue, and the Director of the Office of State Budget and Management shall determine the allocation of the fee imposed by this section among their agencies. The proceeds of the fee are receipts of the agency to which they are credited.

(b)   The Committee may require any information that it considers necessary to effectuate the provisions of this Part.

(c)   The Committee may require any business receiving a grant to submit to an audit at any time.

(d)   The reporting procedures of this section are in lieu of any other general reporting requirements relating to private entities that receive State funds. (2002-172, s. 2.1(a); 2003-416, s. 2; 2004-124, s. 32G.1(d); 2006-168, s. 1.7; 2006-264, s. 69(f); 2009-394, s. 4; 2013-360, s. 15.21(a).)

§ 143B-437.59. Failure to comply with agreement.

(a)   If the business receiving a grant fails to meet or comply with any condition or requirement set forth in an agreement or with criteria developed by the Committee in consultation with the Attorney General, the Committee shall reduce the amount of the grant or the term of the agreement, may terminate the agreement, or both. The reduction in the amount or the term must, at a minimum, be proportional to the failure to comply measured relative to the condition or criterion with respect to which the failure occurred. The Committee may reduce the amount or term of a grant by formally approving a motion to reduce such grant in accordance with program policies adopted by the Committee for the treatment of failures by businesses to meet or comply with a condition or requirement set forth in the grant agreement, and it shall not be necessary to execute an amendment to the applicable grant agreement. The Committee shall notify any such affected business of the reduction to its grant payment, reflected in any such motion.

(b) If a business fails to maintain employment at the levels stipulated in the agreement or otherwise fails to comply with any condition of the agreement for any two consecutive years:

(1) If the business is still within the base period established by the Committee, the Committee shall withhold the grant payment for any consecutive year after the second consecutive year remaining in the base period in which the business fails to comply with any condition of the agreement, and the Committee may extend the base period for up to 24 additional months. Under no circumstances may the Committee extend the base period by more than a total of 24 months. In no event shall the term of the grant be extended beyond the date set by the Committee at the time the Committee awarded the grant.

(2) If the business is no longer within the base period established by the Committee, the Committee shall terminate the agreement.

(c) Notwithstanding the provisions of subsections (a) and (b) of this section, if the Committee finds that the business has manipulated or attempted to manipulate employee withholdings with the purpose of increasing the amount of a grant, the Committee shall immediately terminate the agreement and take action to recapture any grant funds disbursed in any year in which the Committee finds the business manipulated or attempted to manipulate employee withholdings with the purpose of increasing the amount of the grant. (2002-172, s. 2.1(a); 2003-416, s. 2; 2006-168, s. 1.8; 2009-394, s. 5; 2010-91, s. 8.)

§ 143B-437.60. Disbursement of grant.

A business may not receive an annual disbursement of a grant if, at the time of disbursement, the business has received a notice of an overdue tax debt and that overdue tax debt has not been satisfied or otherwise resolved. A business may receive an annual disbursement of a grant only after the Committee has certified that there are no outstanding overdue tax debts and that the business has met the terms and conditions of the agreement. No amount shall be disbursed to a business as a grant under this Part in any year until the Secretary of Revenue has certified to the Committee (i) that there are no outstanding overdue tax debts of the business and (ii) the amount of withholdings received in that year by the Department of Revenue from the business. A business that has met the terms of the agreement shall make an annual certification of this to the Committee. The Committee shall require the business to provide any necessary evidence of compliance to verify that the terms of the agreement have been met. The Committee shall certify the grant amount for which the business is eligible under the agreement and the grant amount for which the business would be eligible under the agreement without regard to G.S. 143B-437.56(d). The Department of Commerce shall remit a check to the business in the amount of the certified grant amount within 90 days of receiving the certification of the Committee. (2002-172, s. 2.1(a); 2003-416, s. 2; 2006-168, s. 1.9.)

§ 143B-437.61. Transfer to Industrial Development Fund Utility Account.

At the time the Department of Commerce remits a check to a business under G.S. 143B-437.60, the Department of Commerce shall transfer to the Utility Account an amount equal to the amount certified by the Committee as the difference between the amount of the grant and the amount of the grant for which the business would be eligible without regard to G.S. 143B-437.56(d). (2002-172, s. 2.1(a); 2003-416, s. 2; 2006-168, s. 1.10; 2013-360, s. 15.18(g).)

§ 143B-437.62. Expiration.

The authority of the Committee to award new grants expires January 1, 2016. (2002-172, s. 2.1(a); 2003-416, s. 2; 2004-124, s. 32G.1(a); 2005-241, s. 3; 2006-168, s. 1.11; 2009-394, s. 6.)

§ 143B-437.63. JDIG Program cash flow requirements.

Notwithstanding any other provision of law, grants made through the Job Development Investment Grant Program, including amounts transferred pursuant to G.S. 143B-437.61, shall be budgeted and funded on a cash flow basis. The Office of State Budget and Management shall periodically transfer funds from the JDIG Reserve established pursuant to G.S. 143C-9-6 to the Department of Commerce in an amount sufficient to satisfy grant obligations and amounts to be transferred pursuant to G.S. 143B-437.61 to be paid during the fiscal year. (2004-124, s. 6.12(b); 2009-445, s. 40; 2009-570, s. 22.)

§ 143B-437.64: Reserved for future codification purposes.

§ 143B-437.65: Reserved for future codification purposes.

§ 143B-437.66: Reserved for future codification purposes.

§ 143B-437.67: Reserved for future codification purposes.

§ 143B-437.68: Reserved for future codification purposes.

§ 143B-437.69: Reserved for future codification purposes.

Part 2H. One North Carolina Fund.

§ 143B-437.70. Legislative findings and purpose.

The General Assembly finds that:

(1)   It is the policy of the State of North Carolina to stimulate economic activity and to create new jobs for the citizens of the State by encouraging and promoting the retention and expansion of existing business and industry within the State and by recruiting and attracting new business and industry to the State.

(2)   Both short-term and long-term economic trends at the State, national, and international levels have made the successful implementation of the State's economic development policy and programs both more critical and more challenging; and the decline in the State's traditional industries, and the resulting adverse impact upon the State and its citizens, have been exacerbated in recent years by adverse national and State economic trends that contribute to the reduction in the State's industrial base and that inhibit the State's ability to sustain or attract new and expanding businesses.

(3)   The purpose of this Part is to stimulate economic activity and to create new jobs within the State.

(4)   The enactment of this Part will maintain consistency and accountability in a key economic development program and will ensure that the program benefits the State and its citizens.

(5) Nothing in this Part shall be construed to constitute a guarantee or assumption by the State of any debt of any business or to authorize the taxing power or the full faith and credit of the State to be pledged. (2004-88, s. 1(d).)

§ 143B-437.71. One North Carolina Fund established as a special revenue fund.

(a) Establishment. - The One North Carolina Fund is established as a special revenue fund in the Department of Commerce.

(b) Purposes. - Moneys in the One North Carolina Fund may only be allocated pursuant to this subsection. Moneys may be allocated to local governments for use in connection with securing commitments for the recruitment, expansion, or retention of new and existing businesses and to the One North Carolina Small Business Account created pursuant to subsection (c) of this section in an amount not to exceed three million dollars ($3,000,000). Moneys in the One North Carolina Fund allocated to local governments shall be used for the following purposes only:

(1) Installation or purchase of equipment.

(2) Structural repairs, improvements, or renovations to existing buildings to be used for expansion.

(3) Construction of or improvements to new or existing water, sewer, gas, or electric utility distribution lines or equipment for existing buildings.

(4) Construction of or improvements to new or existing water, sewer, gas, or electric utility distribution lines or equipment for new or proposed buildings to be used for manufacturing and industrial operations.

(5) Any other purposes specifically provided by an act of the General Assembly.

(b1) Awards. - The amounts committed in Governor's Letters issued in a single fiscal biennium may not exceed twenty-eight million dollars ($28,000,000).

(c)   There is created in the One North Carolina Fund a special account, the One North Carolina Small Business Account, to be used for the North Carolina SBIR/STTR Incentive Program and the North Carolina SBIR/STTR Matching Funds Program, as specified in Part 2I of Article 10 of Chapter 143B of the General Statutes. (2004-88, s. 1(d); 2005-276, s. 13.14(a); 2006-162, s. 19; 2012-142, s. 13.6(b); 2013-360, s. 15.16A.)

§ 143B-437.72. Agreements required; disbursement of funds.

(a)   Agreements Required. - Funds may be disbursed from the One North Carolina Fund only in accordance with agreements entered into between the State and one or more local governments and between the local government and a grantee business.

(b)   Company Performance Agreements. - An agreement between a local government and a grantee business must contain the following provisions:

(1)   A commitment to create or retain a specified number of jobs within a specified salary range at a specific location and commitments regarding the time period in which the jobs will be created or retained and the minimum time period for which the jobs must be maintained.

(2)   A commitment to provide proof satisfactory to the local government and the State of new jobs created or existing jobs retained and the salary level of those jobs.

(3)   A provision that funds received under the agreement may be used only for a purpose specified in G.S. 143B-437.71(b).

(4)   A provision allowing the State or the local government to inspect all records of the business that may be used to confirm compliance with the agreement or with the requirements of this Part.

(5)   A provision establishing the method for determining compliance with the agreement.

(6)   A provision establishing a schedule for disbursement of funds under the agreement that allows disbursement of funds only in proportion to the amount of performance completed under the agreement.

(6a) A provision establishing that a business that has completed performance and become entitled to a final disbursement of funds under the agreement must timely request, in writing to the Secretary of Commerce, a disbursement of funds within not more than one year from the date of completed performance or forfeit the disbursement.

(6b) A provision establishing that a business that anticipates becoming entitled to a disbursement of funds under the agreement shall notify the Secretary of Commerce of the potential payment no later than March 1 of the fiscal year preceding the fiscal year in which the performance is anticipated to be completed.

(7) A provision requiring recapture of grant funds if a business subsequently fails to comply with the terms of the agreement.

(8) Any other provision the State or the local government finds necessary to ensure the proper use of State or local funds.

(c) Local Government Grant Agreement. - An agreement between the State and one or more local governments shall contain the following provisions:

(1) A commitment on the part of the local government to match the funds allocated by the State. A local match may include cash, fee waivers, in-kind services, the donation of assets, the provision of infrastructure, or a combination of these.

(2) A provision requiring the local government to recapture any funds to which the local government is entitled under the company performance agreement.

(3) A provision requiring the local government to reimburse the State for any funds improperly disbursed or funds recaptured by the local government.

(4) A provision allowing the State access to all records possessed by the local government necessary to ensure compliance with the company performance agreement and with the requirements of this Part.

(5) A provision establishing a schedule for the disbursement of funds from the One North Carolina Fund to the local government that reflects the disbursement schedule established in the company performance agreement.

(6) Any other provision the State finds necessary to ensure the proper use of State funds.

(d) Disbursement of Funds. - Funds may be disbursed from the One North Carolina Fund to the local government only after the local government has demonstrated that the business has complied with the terms of the company performance agreement. The State shall disburse funds allocated under the One North Carolina Fund to a local government in accordance with the disbursement schedule established in the local government grant agreement. (2004-88, s. 1(d); 2012-142, s. 13.6(c).)

§ 143B-437.73. Program guidelines.

The Department of Commerce, in conjunction with the Governor's Office, shall develop guidelines related to the administration of the One North Carolina Fund and to the selection of projects to receive allocations from the Fund. At least 20 days before the effective date of any guidelines or nontechnical amendments to guidelines, the Department of Commerce must publish the proposed guidelines on the Department's Web site and provide notice to persons who have requested notice of proposed guidelines. In addition, the Department must accept oral and written comments on the proposed guidelines during the 15 business days beginning on the first day that the Department has completed these notifications. For the purpose of this section, a technical amendment is either of the following:

(1) An amendment that corrects a spelling or grammatical error.

(2) An amendment that makes a clarification based on public comment and could have been anticipated by the public notice that immediately preceded the public comment. (2004-88, s. 1(d).)

§ 143B-437.74. Reports; study.

(a) Reports. - The Department of Commerce shall publish a report on the use of funds in the One North Carolina Fund at the end of each fiscal quarter. The report shall contain information on the commitment, disbursement, and use of funds allocated under the One North Carolina Fund. The report is due no later than one month after the end of the fiscal quarter and must be submitted to the following:

(1)   The Joint Legislative Commission on Governmental Operations.

(2)   The chairs of the House of Representatives and Senate Finance Committees.

(3)   The chairs of the House of Representatives and Senate Appropriations Committees.

(4)   The Fiscal Research Division of the General Assembly.

(b)   Study. - The Department of Commerce shall conduct a study to determine the minimum funding level required to implement the One North Carolina Fund successfully. The Department shall report the results of this study to the House of Representatives Finance Committee, the Senate Finance Committee, the House of Representatives Appropriations Subcommittee on Natural and Economic Resources, the Senate Appropriations Committee on Natural and Economic Resources, and the Fiscal Research Division no later than April 1 of each year. (2004-88, s. 1(d); 2012-142, s. 13.6(d).)

§ 143B-437.75. Cash flow requirements.

Notwithstanding any other provision of law, moneys allocated from the One North Carolina Fund shall be budgeted and funded on a cash flow basis. The Office of State Budget and Management shall periodically transfer funds from the One North Carolina Fund established pursuant to G.S. 143B-437.71 to the Department of Commerce in an amount sufficient to satisfy Fund allocations to be transferred pursuant to G.S. 143B-437.72 to be paid during the fiscal year. (2012-142, s. 13.6(e).)

§ 143B-437.76. Reserved for future codification purposes.

§ 143B-437.77. Reserved for future codification purposes.

§ 143B-437.78. Reserved for future codification purposes.

§ 143B-437.79. Reserved for future codification purposes.

Part 2I. One North Carolina Small Business Program.

§ 143B-437.80. North Carolina SBIR/STTR Incentive Program.

(a)   Program. - There is established the North Carolina SBIR/STTR Incentive Program to be administered by the North Carolina Board of Science and Technology. In order to foster job creation and economic development in the State, the Board may provide grants to eligible businesses to offset costs associated with applying to the United States Small Business Administration for Small Business Innovative Research (SBIR) grants or Small Business Technology Transfer Research (STTR) grants. The grants shall be paid from the One North Carolina Small Business Account established in G.S. 143B-437.71.

(b)   Eligibility. - In order to be eligible for a grant under this section, a business must satisfy all of the following conditions:

(1)   The business must be a for-profit, North Carolina-based business. For the purposes of this section, a North Carolina-based business is one that has its principal place of business in this State.

(2)   The business must have submitted a qualified SBIR/STTR Phase I proposal to a participating federal agency in response to a specific federal solicitation.

(3)   The business must satisfy all federal SBIR/STTR requirements.

(4)   The business shall not receive concurrent funding support from other sources that duplicates the purpose of this section.

(5)   The business must certify that at least fifty-one percent (51%) of the research described in the federal SBIR/STTR Phase I proposal will be conducted in this State and that the business will remain a North Carolina-based business for the duration of the SBIR/STTR Phase I project.

(6)   The business must demonstrate its ability to conduct research in its SBIR/STTR Phase I proposal.

(c) Grant. - The North Carolina Board of Science and Technology may award grants to reimburse an eligible business for up to fifty percent (50%) of the costs of preparing and submitting a SBIR/STTR Phase I proposal, up to a maximum of three thousand dollars ($3,000). A business may receive only one grant under this section per year. A business may receive only one grant under this section with respect to each federal proposal submission. Costs that may be reimbursed include costs incurred directly related to preparation and submission of the grant such as word processing services, proposal consulting fees, project-related supplies, literature searches, rental of space or equipment related to the proposal preparation, and salaries of individuals involved with the preparation of the proposals. Costs that shall not be reimbursed include travel expenses, large equipment purchases, facility or leasehold improvements, and legal fees.

(d) Application. - A business shall apply, under oath, to the North Carolina Board of Science and Technology for a grant under this section on a form prescribed by the Board that includes at least all of the following:

(1) The name of the business, the form of business organization under which it is operated, and the names and addresses of the principals or management of the business.

(2) An acknowledgement of receipt of the Phase I proposal by the relevant federal agency.

(3) An itemized statement of the costs that may be reimbursed.

(4) Any other information necessary for the Board to evaluate the application. (2005-276, s. 13.14(b).)

§ 143B-437.81. North Carolina SBIR/STTR Matching Funds Program.

(a) Program. - There is established the North Carolina SBIR/STTR Matching Funds Program to be administered by the North Carolina Board of Science and Technology. In order to foster job creation and economic development in the State, the Board may provide grants to eligible businesses to match funds received by a business as a SBIR or STTR Phase I award and to encourage businesses to apply for Phase II awards.

(b) Eligibility. - In order to be eligible for a grant under this section, a business must satisfy all of the following conditions:

(1) The business must be a for-profit, North Carolina-based business. For the purposes of this section, a North Carolina-based business is one that has its principal place of business in this State.

(2) The business must have received a SBIR/STTR Phase I award from a participating federal agency in response to a specific federal solicitation. To receive the full match, the business must also have submitted a final Phase I report, demonstrated that the sponsoring agency has interest in the Phase II proposal, and submitted a Phase II proposal to the agency.

(3) The business must satisfy all federal SBIR/STTR requirements.

(4) The business shall not receive concurrent funding support from other sources that duplicates the purpose of this section.

(5) The business must certify that at least fifty-one percent (51%) of the research described in the federal SBIR/STTR Phase II proposal will be conducted in this State and that the business will remain a North Carolina-based business for the duration of the SBIR/STTR Phase II project.

(6) The business must demonstrate its ability to conduct research in its SBIR/STTR Phase II proposal.

(c) Grant. - The North Carolina Board of Science and Technology may award grants to match the funds received by a business through a SBIR/STTR Phase I proposal up to a maximum of one hundred thousand dollars ($100,000). Seventy-five percent (75%) of the total grant shall be remitted to the business upon receipt of the SBIR/STTR Phase I award and application for funds under this section. Twenty-five percent (25%) of the total grant shall be remitted to the business upon submission by the business of the Phase II application to the funding agency and acceptance of the Phase I report by the funding agency. A business may receive only one grant under this section per year. A business may receive only one grant under this section with respect to each federal proposal submission. Over its lifetime, a business may receive a maximum of five awards under this section.

(d) Application. - A business shall apply, under oath, to the North Carolina Board of Science and Technology for a grant under this section on a form prescribed by the Board that includes at least all of the following:

(1) The name of the business, the form of business organization under which it is operated, and the names and addresses of the principals or management of the business.

(2) An acknowledgement of receipt of the Phase I report and Phase II proposal by the relevant federal agency.

(3) Any other information necessary for the Board to evaluate the application. (2005-276, s. 13.14(b).)

§ 143B-437.82. Program guidelines.

The Department of Commerce shall develop guidelines related to the administration of the One North Carolina Small Business Program. At least 20 days before the effective date of any guidelines or nontechnical amendments to guidelines, the Department of Commerce must publish the proposed guidelines on the Department's Web site and provide notice to persons who have requested notice of proposed guidelines. In addition, the Department must accept oral and written comments on the proposed guidelines during the 15 business days beginning on the first day that the Department has completed these notifications. For the purpose of this section, a technical amendment is either of the following:

(1) An amendment that corrects a spelling or grammatical error.

(2) An amendment that makes a clarification based on public comment and could have been anticipated by the public notice that immediately preceded the public comment. (2005-276, s. 13.14(b).)

§ 143B-437.83. Reports.

The Department of Commerce shall publish a report on the use of funds in the One North Carolina Small Business Account on September 1 of each year until all funds have been expended. The report shall contain information on the disbursement and use of funds allocated under the One North Carolina Small Business Program. The report must be submitted to the following:

(1)   The Joint Legislative Commission on Governmental Operations.

(2)   The chairs of the House of Representatives and Senate Finance Committees.

(3)   The chairs of the House of Representatives and Senate Appropriations Committees.

(4)   The Fiscal Research Division of the General Assembly. (2005-276, s. 13.14(b); 2009-451, s. 14.5(c).)

§ 143B-437.84. Reserved for future codification purposes.

§ 143B-437.85. Reserved for future codification purposes.

§ 143B-437.86. Reserved for future codification purposes.

§ 143B-437.87. Reserved for future codification purposes.

§ 143B-437.88. Reserved for future codification purposes.

§ 143B-437.89. Reserved for future codification purposes.

Part 2J. Wine and Grape Growers Council.

§ 143B-437.90: Recodified as Article 62A of Chapter 106, G.S. 106-755.1 and G.S. 106-755.2, by Session Laws 2012-142, s. 13.9A(b), effective July 1, 2012.

§ 143B-437.91: Recodified as Article 62A of Chapter 106, G.S. 106-755.1 and G.S. 106-755.2, by Session Laws 2012-142, s. 13.9A(b), effective July 1, 2012.

§ 143B-437.92. Reserved for future codification purposes.

§ 143B-437.93. Reserved for future codification purposes.

§ 143B-437.94. Reserved for future codification purposes.

§ 143B-437.95. Reserved for future codification purposes.

§ 143B-437.96. Reserved for future codification purposes.

§ 143B-437.97. Reserved for future codification purposes.

§ 143B-437.98. Reserved for future codification purposes.

§ 143B-437.99. Reserved for future codification purposes.

Part 2K. North Carolina Certified Retirement Community Program.

§ 143B-437.100. North Carolina Certified Retirement Community Program - creation; powers and duties.

(a) Program. - There is established the North Carolina Certified Retirement Community Program as part of the North Carolina Department of Commerce. The Department shall coordinate the development and planning of the North Carolina Certified Retirement Community Program with other State and local groups interested in participating in and promoting the North Carolina Certified Retirement Community Program. The Department shall adopt administrative rules to implement the provisions of this Part. For purposes of this Part, "Department" means the North Carolina Department of Commerce, and "Program" means the North Carolina Certified Retirement Community Program.

(b) Purpose. - The purpose of the Program is to encourage retirees and those planning to retire to make their homes in North Carolina. In order to further this purpose, the Department shall engage in the following activities:

(1) Promote the State as a retirement destination to retirees and those persons and families who are planning retirement both in and outside of North Carolina.

(2) Assist North Carolina communities in their efforts to market themselves as retirement locations and to develop communities that retirees would find attractive for a retirement lifestyle.

(3) Assist in the development of retirement communities and continuing care facilities under Article 64 of Chapter 58 of the General Statutes in order to promote economic development and a potential workforce to enrich North Carolina communities.

(4) Encourage mature market travel and tourism to North Carolina to evaluate future retirement desirability and to visit those who have chosen to retire in North Carolina.

(c) Factors. - The Department shall identify factors that are of interest to retirees or potential retirees in order to inform them of the benefits of living in North Carolina. These factors shall be used to develop a scoring system to determine whether an applicant will qualify as a North Carolina certified retirement community and may include the following:

(1) North Carolina's State and local tax structure.

(2) Housing opportunities and cost.

(3) Climate.

(4) Personal safety.

(5) Working opportunities.

(6) Health care and continuing care services.

(7) Transportation.

(8) Continuing education.

(9) Leisure living.

(10) Recreation.

(11) The performing arts.

(12) Festivals and events.

(13) Sports.

(14) Other services and facilities necessary to enable persons to age in the community with a minimum of restrictions.

(d) Certification. - The Department shall establish criteria for qualifying as a North Carolina certified retirement community. To be eligible to obtain certification as a North Carolina certified retirement community, the community shall meet each of the following requirements:

(1) Be located within 30 miles of a hospital and of emergency medical services.

(2) Take steps to gain the support of churches, clubs, businesses, media, and other entities whose participation will increase the Program's success in attracting retirees or potential retirees.

(3) Establish a retiree attraction committee. The retiree attraction committee shall fulfill or create subcommittees to fulfill each of the following:

a. Conduct a retiree desirability assessment analyzing the community with respect to each of the factors identified by the Department and submit a report of the analysis to the Department.

b. Send a representative of the retirement attraction committee to attend State training meetings conducted by the Department during the certification process.

c. Raise funds necessary to run the Program, organize special events, and promote and coordinate the Program with local entities.

d. Establish a community image, evaluate target markets, and develop a marketing and public relations plan designed to accomplish the purpose of the Program.

e. Develop a system that identifies and makes contact with existing and prospective retirees, that provides tour guides when prospects visit the community, and that responds to inquiries, logs contacts made, invites prospects to special community events, and maintains continual contact with prospects until the prospect makes a retirement location decision.

(4) Remit an application fee to the Department equal to the greater of ten thousand dollars ($10,000) or the product of fifty cents (50¢) multiplied by the population of the community, as determined by the most recent census.

(5) Submit the completed marketing and public relations plan designed to accomplish the purpose of the Program to the Department.

(6) Submit a long-term plan outlining the steps the community will undertake to maintain or improve its desirability as a destination for retirees, including corrections to any services or facilities identified in the retiree desirability assessment. (2008-188, s. 1; 2011-145, s. 14.3C.)

§ 143B-437.101. North Carolina Certified Retirement Community Program - administration.

(a) Administration and Support. - Upon being certified as a North Carolina certified retirement community, the Department shall provide the following assistance to the community:

(1) Assistance in the training of local Program staff and volunteers.

(2) Ongoing oversight and guidance in marketing and updating on national retirement trends.

(3) Inclusion in the State's national advertising and public relations campaigns and travel show promotions, including a prominent feature on the Department's Web site.

(4) Eligibility for State financial assistance for brochures, support material, and advertising.

(5) An annual evaluation and progress assessment on maintaining and improving the community's desirability as a home for retirees.

(b) Expiration. - A community's certification under this section expires on the fifth anniversary of the date the initial certification is issued. To be considered for recertification by the Department, an applicant community shall submit the following:

(1) A completed new application in accordance with the requirements of this Part.

(2) Data demonstrating the success or failure of the community's efforts to market and promote itself as a desirable location for retirees and potential retirees.

(3) The fee required by G.S. 143B-437.100(d)(4). (2008-188, s. 1; 2011-145, s. 14.3C.)

Part 3. Labor Force Development.

§ 143B-438: Repealed by Session Laws 1981, c. 380, s. 1.

Part 3A. Employment and Training Act of 1985.

§§ 143B-438.1 through 143B-438.6. Repealed by Session Laws 1999-237. s. 16.15(a).

§ 143B-438.7. Reserved for future codification purposes.

§ 143B-438.8. Reserved for future codification purposes.

§ 143B-438.9. Reserved for future codification purposes.

Part 3B. Workforce Development.

§ 143B-438.10. Commission on Workforce Development.

(a) Creation and Duties. - There is created within the Department of Commerce the North Carolina Commission on Workforce Development. The Commission shall have the following powers and duties:

(1) To develop strategies to produce a skilled, competitive workforce that meets the needs of the State's changing economy.

(2) To advise the Governor, the General Assembly, State and local agencies, and the business sector regarding policies and programs to enhance the State's workforce by submitting annually a comprehensive report on workforce development initiatives in the State.

(3) To coordinate and develop strategies for cooperation between the academic, governmental, and business sectors.

(4) To establish, develop, and provide ongoing oversight of the "One-Stop Delivery System" for employment and training services in the State.

(5) To develop a unified State plan for workforce training and development.

(6) To review and evaluate the plans and programs of agencies, boards, and organizations operating federally funded or State-funded workforce development programs for effectiveness, duplication, fiscal accountability, and coordination.

(7) To develop and continuously improve performance measures to assess the effectiveness of workforce training and employment in the State. The Commission shall assess and report on the performance of workforce development programs administered by the Department of Commerce, the Department of Health and Human Services, the Community Colleges System Office, the Department of Administration, and the Department of Public Instruction in a manner that addresses at least all of the following:

a. Actual performance and costs of State and local workforce development programs.

b. Expected performance levels for State and local workforce development programs based on attainment of program goals and objectives.

c. Program outcomes, levels of employer participation, and satisfaction with employment and training services.

d. Information already tracked through the common follow-up information management system created pursuant to G.S. 96-32, such as demographics, program enrollment, and program completion.

(7a) To issue annual reports that, at a minimum, include the information listed in sub-subdivisions a. through d. of subdivision (7) of this section on the performance of workforce development programs administered by the entities listed in that subdivision. The first annual report shall be delivered to the General Assembly by January 15, 2014.

(8) To submit to the Governor and to the General Assembly by April 1, 2000, and biennially thereafter, a comprehensive Workforce Development Plan that shall include at least the following:

a. Goals and objectives for the biennium.

b. An assessment of current workforce programs and policies.

c. An assessment of the delivery of employment and training services to special populations, such as youth and dislocated workers.

d. Recommendations for policy, program, or funding changes.

(9) To serve as the State's Workforce Investment Board for purposes of the federal Workforce Investment Act of 1998.

(10) To take the lead role in developing the memorandum of understanding for workforce development programs with the Department of Commerce, the Department of Health and Human Services, the Community Colleges System Office, and the Department of Administration. The memorandum of understanding must be reviewed at least every five years.

(11) To coordinate the activities of workforce development work groups formed under this Part.

(12) To collaborate with the Department of Commerce on the common follow-up information management system.

(b) Membership; Terms. - Effective January 1, 2013, the Commission on Workforce Development shall consist of 25 members appointed as follows:

(1) By virtue of their offices, the following department and agency heads or their respective designees shall serve on the Commission: the Secretary of the Department of Administration, the Secretary of the Department of Health and Human Services, the Superintendent of Public Instruction, the President of the Community Colleges System Office, the Commissioner of the Department of Labor, and the Secretary of the Department of Commerce.

(2) The Governor shall appoint 19 members as follows:

a. Two members representing public, postsecondary, and vocational education.

b. One member representing community-based organizations.

c. Three members representing labor.

d. Thirteen members representing business and industry.

(3) The terms of the members appointed by the Governor shall be for four years.

(c) Appointment of Chair; Meetings. - The Governor shall appoint the Chair of the Commission from among the business and industry members, and that person shall serve at the pleasure of the Governor. The Commission shall meet at least quarterly upon the call of the Chair.

(d) Staff; Funding. - The clerical and professional staff to the Commission shall be provided by the Department of Commerce. Funding for the Commission shall derive from State and federal resources as allowable and from the partner agencies to the Commission. Members of the Commission shall receive necessary travel and subsistence in accordance with State law.

(e) Agency Cooperation; Reporting. - Each State agency, department, institution, local political subdivision of the State, and any other State-supported entity identified by or subject to review by the Commission in carrying out its duties under subdivision (6) of subsection (a) of this section must participate fully in the development of performance measures for workforce development programs and shall provide to the Commission all data and information available to or within the agency or entity's possession that is requested by the Commission for its review. Further, each agency or entity required to report information and data to the Commission under this section shall maintain true and accurate records of the information and data requested by the Commission. The records shall be open to the Commission's inspection and copying at reasonable times and as often as necessary.

(f) Confidentiality. - At the request of the Commission, each agency or entity subject to this section shall provide it with sworn or unsworn reports with respect to persons employed or trained by the agency or entity, as deemed necessary by the Commission to carry out its duties pursuant to this section. The information obtained from an agency or entity pursuant to this subsection (i) is not a public record subject to the provisions of Chapter 132 of the General Statutes and (ii) shall be held by the Commission as confidential, unless it is released in a manner that protects the identity and privacy of individual persons and employers referenced in the information.

(g) Advisory Work Group. - The Commission shall appoint an Advisory Work Group composed of representatives from the State and local entities engaged in workforce development activities to assist the Commission with the development of performance measures. (1999-237, s. 16.15(b); 2011-401, s. 1.7; 2012-131, s. 1(a).)

§ 143B-438.11. Local Workforce Development Boards.

(a) Duties. - Local Workforce Development Boards shall have the following powers and duties:

(1) To develop policy and act as the governing body for local workforce development.

(2) To provide planning, oversight, and evaluation of local workforce development programs, including the local One-Stop Delivery System.

(3) To provide advice regarding workforce policy and programs to local elected officials, employers, education and employment training agencies, and citizens.

(4) To develop a local plan in coordination with the appropriate community partners to address the workforce development needs of the service area.

(5) To develop linkages with economic development efforts and activities in the service area and promote cooperation and coordination among public organizations, education agencies, and private businesses.

(6) To review local agency plans and grant applications for workforce development programs for coordination and achievement of local goals and needs.

(7) To serve as the Workforce Investment Board for the designated substate area for the purpose of the federal Workforce Investment Act of 1998.

(7a) To designate through a competitive selection process, by no later than July 1, 2014, the providers of adult and dislocated worker services authorized in the Workforce Investment Act of 1998.

(8) To provide the appropriate guidance and information to Workforce Investment Act consumers to ensure that they are prepared and positioned to make informed choices in selecting a training provider. Each local Workforce Development Board shall ensure that consumer choice is properly maintained in the one-stop centers and that consumers are provided the full array of public and private training provider information.

(9) To provide coordinated regional workforce development planning and labor market data sharing.

(b) Members. - Members of local Workforce Development Boards shall be appointed by local elected officials in accordance with criteria established by the Governor and with provisions of the federal Workforce Investment Act. The local Workforce Development Boards shall have a majority of business members and shall also include representation of workforce and education providers, labor organizations, community-based organizations, and economic development boards as determined by local elected officials. The Chairs of the local Workforce Development Boards shall be selected from among the business members.

(c) Assistance. - The North Carolina Commission on Workforce Development and the Department of Commerce shall provide programmatic, technical, and other assistance to any local Workforce Development Board that realigns its service area with the boundaries of a local regional council of governments established pursuant to G.S. 160A-470. (1999-237, s. 16.15(b); 2010-31, s. 14.4; 2012-131, s. 3(a); 2013-330, s. 1.)

§ 143B-438.12. Federal Program Administration.

(a) Federal Workforce Investment Act. - In accordance with the federal Workforce Investment Act, the Commission on Workforce Development shall develop a Five-Year Strategic Plan to be submitted to the U.S. Secretary of Labor. The Strategic Plan shall describe the workforce development activities to be undertaken in the State to implement the federal Workforce Investment Act and how special populations shall be served.

(b) Other Workforce Grant Applications. - The Commission on Workforce Development may submit grant applications for workforce development initiatives and may manage the initiatives and demonstration projects. (1999-237, s. 16.15(b).)

§ 143B-438.13. Employment and Training Grant Program.

(a) Employment and Training Grant Program. - There is established in the Department of Commerce, Division of Employment and Training, an Employment and Training Grant Program. Grant funds shall be allocated to local Workforce Development Boards for the purposes of enabling recipient agencies to implement local employment and training programs in accordance with existing resources, local needs, local goals, and selected training occupations. The State program of workforce performance standards shall be used to measure grant program outcomes.

(b) Use of Grant Funds. - Local agencies may use funds received under this section for the purpose of providing services, such as training, education, placement, and supportive services. Local agencies may use grant funds to provide services only to individuals who are (i) 18 years of age or older and meet the federal Workforce Investment Act, title I adult eligibility definitions, or meet the federal Workforce Investment Act, title I dislocated worker eligibility definitions, or (ii) incumbent workers with annual family incomes at or below two hundred percent (200%) of poverty guidelines established by the federal Department of Health and Human Services.

(c) Allocation of Grants. - The Department of Commerce may reserve and allocate up to ten percent (10%) of the funds available to the Employment and Training Grant Program for State and local administrative costs to implement the Program. The Division of Employment and Training shall allocate employment and training grant funds to local Workforce Development Boards serving federal Workforce Investment Act local workforce investment areas based on the following formula:

(1) One-half of the funds shall be allocated on the basis of the relative share of the local workforce investment area's share of federal Workforce Investment Act, title I adult funds as compared to the total of all local areas adult shares under the federal Workforce Investment Act, title I.

(2) One-half of the funds shall be allocated on the basis of the relative share of the local workforce investment area's share of federal Workforce Investment

Act, title I dislocated worker funds as compared to the total of all local areas dislocated worker shares under the federal Workforce Investment Act, title I.

(3) Local workforce investment area adult and dislocated shares shall be calculated using the current year's allocations to local areas under the federal Workforce Investment Act, title I.

(d) Repealed by Session Laws 2009-451, s. 14.5(d), effective July 1, 2009.

(e) Nonreverting Funds. - Funds appropriated to the Department of Commerce for the Employment and Training Grant Program that are not expended at the end of the fiscal year shall not revert to the General Fund, but shall remain available to the Department for the purposes established in this section. (1999-237, s. 16.15(b); 2009-451, s. 14.5(d).)

§ 143B-438.14. "No Adult Left Behind" Initiative.

(a) The Commission on Workforce Development, acting as the lead agency, with the cooperation of other participating agencies, including the Department of Labor, the Department of Commerce, the Employment Security Commission, the North Carolina Community College System, The University of North Carolina, and the North Carolina Independent Colleges and Universities shall initiate the "No Adult Left Behind" Initiative (Initiative) geared toward achievement of major statewide workforce development goals. The Initiative may also include community-based nonprofit organizations that provide services or assistance in the areas of worker training, workforce development, and transitioning North Carolinians between industries in the current global labor market.

(b) The first goal of the Initiative is to increase dramatically to forty percent (40%) the percentage of North Carolinians who earn associate degrees, other two-year educational credentials, and baccalaureate degrees. Specific fields of study may be selected for the most intense efforts. The Commission on Workforce Development shall, as the lead agency along with the North Carolina Community College System and The University of North Carolina as key cooperating institutions, do all of the following:

(1) Collaborate to provide model evening-weekend certificate and degree programs designed specifically for working adults and other nontraditional students.

(2) Work together to promote systemic changes designed to increase access and foster success among adult workers and other nontraditional students.

(3) Make it a priority to provide model evening-weekend certificate and degree programs in high-demand disciplines, occupations, and fields closely linked to economic development or that are the focus of public initiatives.

(c) The Commission on Workforce Development and the other lead participating institutions may enter into contracts with other qualified organizations, especially community-based nonprofits, to carry out components of the Initiative set forth in subsection (b) of this section.

(d) The Commission on Workforce Development shall submit to the Governor and to the General Assembly by May 1, 2012, and annually thereafter, details of its implementation of this section that shall include at least the following:

(1) Goals, objectives, and accomplishments for the year toward implementation of this section.

(2) An assessment of current adult educational programs to expand economic opportunities for adult workers as outlined by this section.

(3) Recommendations for policy, program, or funding changes to effectuate the workforce development, adult education, and economic development goals set forth in this section. (2011-327, ss. 2, 3(a)-(c).)

Part 3C. Trade Jobs for Success.

§ 143B-438.15. Legislative findings and purpose.

(a) The General Assembly finds that State, national, and global economic conditions and the passage of international trade agreements have impacted the State workforce adversely and resulted in significant losses in the availability of jobs in manufacturing and the State's other traditional industries. Further, the General Assembly finds that business and plant closings, the weakened State economy, and lengthening periods of unemployment have taken a toll on communities across the State. It is prudent to address the loss of jobs by establishing a statewide initiative to create more jobs for our citizens.

(b) It is the policy of this State to stimulate job growth and hiring by investing in the effective retraining of trade-affected displaced workers while partnering with private business to help those citizens learn new skills for new jobs through on-the-job training and educational assistance.

(c) The purpose of this Part is to establish the Trade Jobs for Success initiative to stimulate job growth and hiring in the State and to assist displaced workers affected by trade-impact business closings. The aim of the Trade Jobs for Success initiative shall be to partner with private business to move displaced workers into new jobs while allowing for a dignified transition from unemployment back to employment. (2004-124, s. 13.7A(d).)

§ 143B-438.16. Trade Jobs for Success initiative established; funds; program components and guidelines.

(a) There is established within the Department of Commerce the Trade Jobs for Success (TJS) initiative. The Department of Commerce shall lead the TJS initiative in cooperation with the Community Colleges System Office.

(b) There is created in the Department of Commerce a special, nonreverting fund called the Trade Jobs for Success Fund (Fund). The Fund shall be used to implement the TJS initiative. The Department of Commerce shall develop guidelines for administration of the TJS initiative and the Fund. An advisory council shall assist the Secretary of Commerce in the administration of the Fund. The members of the advisory council shall include:

(1) The Assistant Secretary of Commerce in charge of the Division of Employment Security or that officer's designee.

(2) The President of the Community Colleges System or that officer's designee.

(3) The State Auditor or that officer's designee.

(4) A representative of a statewide association to further the interests of business and industry in North Carolina designated by the Secretary of Commerce.

(c) At a minimum, the Trade Jobs for Success initiative shall include the following programmatic components:

(1) Displaced workers participating in the TJS initiative shall receive (i) on-the-job training to learn new job skills and (ii) educational assistance or remedial education specifically designed to help displaced workers qualify for new jobs.

(2) Displaced workers participating in the TJS initiative shall not lose their eligibility for unemployment insurance benefits while they are in the program and may receive wage supplements, as appropriate.

(3) In-State relocation assistance, in appropriate instances, where participating individuals must relocate to work for participating employers.

(4) Mentoring, both on and off the job, shall be provided to participants in a dignified manner through telephone assistance and other appropriate means.

(5) Financial assistance and other incentives may be provided to participating employers who provide jobs to participating displaced workers to help defray the costs of providing the on-the-job training opportunities.

(6) Work provided by participating employers as part of the TJS initiative must be full-time employment. Wages paid shall not be less than the hourly entry-level wage normally paid by the employer.

(7) Staff of the Division of the Employment Security, in conjunction with other appropriate staff of the Department of Commerce, shall match participating displaced workers to the most suitable employer.

(8) Local Employment Security offices operated by the Division of Employment Security and community colleges shall enter into partnership agreements with local chambers of commerce, and other appropriate organizations, that would encourage employer participation in the TJS initiative.

(9) Tracking of participating individuals and businesses by the Department of Commerce to assure program integrity and effectiveness and the compilation

of data to generate the reports necessary to evaluate the success of the TJS initiative.

(10)   Coordination and integration of existing programs in the Department of Commerce, the Division of Employment Security, and the North Carolina Community College System in a manner that maximizes the flexibility of these agencies to effectively assist participating individuals and businesses. (2004-124, s. 13.7A(d); 2011-401, s. 1.8.)

§ 143B-438.17. Reporting.

(a),   (b) Repealed by Session Laws 2009-451, s. 14.5(e), effective July 1, 2009.

(c)   Beginning January 1, 2006, the Department of Commerce, in conjunction with the Division of Employment Security and the Community Colleges System Office, shall publish a comprehensive annual written report on the Trade Jobs for Success initiative. The annual report shall include a detailed explanation of outcomes and future planning for the TJS initiative and legislative proposals and recommendations regarding statutory changes needed to maximize the effectiveness and flexibility of the TJS initiative. Copies of the annual report shall be provided to the Governor, to the Joint Legislative Commission on Governmental Operations, to the chairs of the Senate and House of Representatives Appropriations Committees, and to the Fiscal Research Division of the General Assembly. (2004-124, s. 13.7A(d); 2005-276, s. 13.4A(b); 2009-451, s. 14.5(e); 2011-401, s. 1.9.)

Part 4. Credit Union Commission.

§ 143B-439. Credit Union Commission.

(a) There shall be created in the Department of Commerce a Credit Union Commission which shall consist of seven members. The members of the Credit Union Commission shall elect one of its members to serve as chairman of the Commission to serve for a term to be specified by the Commission. On the initial Commission three members shall be appointed by the Governor for terms of two years and three members shall be appointed by the Governor for terms of four years. Thereafter all members of the Commission shall be appointed by the Governor for terms of four years. The Governor shall appoint the seventh member for the same term and in the same manner as the other six members are appointed. In the event of a vacancy on the Commission the Governor shall appoint a successor to serve for the remainder of the term. Three members of the Commission shall be persons who have had three years' or more experience as a credit union director or in management of state-chartered credit unions. At least four members shall be appointed as representatives of the borrowing public and may be members of a credit union but shall not be employees of, or directors of any financial institution or have any interest in any financial institution other than as a result of being a depositor or borrower. No two persons on the Commission shall be residents of the same senatorial district. No person on the Commission shall be on a board of directors or employed by another type of financial institution. The Commission shall meet at least every six months, or more often upon the call of the chairman of the Credit Union Commission or any three members of the Commission. A majority of the members of the Commission shall constitute a quorum. The members of the Commission shall be reimbursed for expenses incurred in the performance of their duties under this Chapter as prescribed in G.S. 138-5. In the event that the composition of the Commission on April 30, 1979, does not conform to that prescribed in the preceding sentences, such composition shall be corrected thereafter by appropriate appointments as terms expire and as vacancies occur in the Commission; provided that no person shall serve on the Commission for more than two complete consecutive terms.

(b) The relationship between the Secretary of Commerce and the Credit Union Commission shall be as defined for a Type II transfer under this Chapter.

(c) The Credit Union Commission is hereby vested with full power and authority to review, approve, or modify any action taken by the Administrator of Credit Unions in the exercise of all powers, duties, and functions vested by law in or exercised by the Administrator of Credit Unions under the credit union laws of this State.

An appeal may be taken to the Commission from any finding, ruling, order, decision or the final action of the Administrator by any credit union which feels aggrieved thereby. Notice of such appeal shall be filed with the chairman of the Commission within 30 days after such finding, ruling, order, decision or other action, and a copy served upon the Administrator. Such notice shall contain a brief statement of the pertinent facts upon which such appeal is grounded. The Commission shall fix a date, time and place for hearing said appeal, and shall notify the credit union or its attorney of record thereof at least 30 days prior to the date of said hearing. (1971, c. 864, s. 17; 1973, cc. 97, 1254; 1975, c. 709, ss. 4-6; 1977, c. 198, s. 26; 1979, c. 478, s. 3; 1989, c. 751, ss. 7(36), 8(22); 1991 (Reg. Sess., 1992), c. 959, s. 63.)

Part 5. North Carolina Board of Science and Technology.

§§ 143B-440 through 143B-441: Recodified as §§ 143B-426.30, 143B-426.31 by Session Laws 1985, c. 757, s. 179(c).

Part 6. North Carolina Science and Technology Research Center.

§ 143B-442. Creation of Center.

There is hereby created the "North Carolina Science and Technology Research Center" at the Research Triangle. (1963, c. 846, s. 1; 1967, c. 69; 1977, c. 198, s. 26.)

§ 143B-443. Administration by Department of Commerce.

The activities of the North Carolina Science and Technology Research Center will be administered by the Department of Commerce. (1963, c. 846, s. 2; 1967, c. 69; 1977, c. 198, ss. 3, 4, 26; 1979, c. 668, s. 3; 1989, c. 751, s. 7(37); 1991 (Reg. Sess., 1992), c. 959, s. 64.)

§ 143B-444. Acceptance of funds.

The North Carolina Science and Technology Research Center is authorized and empowered to accept funds from private sources and from governmental and institutional agencies to be used for construction, operation and maintenance of the Center. (1963, c. 846, s. 4; 1967, c. 69; 1977, c. 198, s. 26.)

§ 143B-445. Applicability of Executive Budget Act.

The North Carolina Science and Technology Research Center is subject to the provisions of Article 1, Chapter 143, of the General Statutes of North Carolina. (1963, c. 846, s. 5; 1967, c. 69; 1977, c. 198, s. 26.)

Part 7. North Carolina National Park, Parkway and Forests Development Council.

§§ 143B-446 through 143B-447.1: Recodified as §§ 143B-324.1 through 143B-324.3 by Session Laws 1997-443, s. 15.36(b).

Part 8. Energy Division.

§§ 143B-448 through 143B-450.1: Repealed by Session Laws 2000-140, s. 76.

Part 9. Navigation and Pilotage Commissions.

§ 143B-451. Navigation and pilotage commissions.

The Board of Commissioners of Navigation and Pilotage for the Cape Fear River as provided for by G.S. 76-1, and the Board of Commissioners of Navigation and Pilotage for Old Topsail Inlet and Beaufort Bar as provided for by G.S. 76-59 are hereby transferred to the Department of Commerce. All powers, duties and authority of the Board of Commissioners of Navigation and Pilotage for the Cape Fear River and Bar and the Board of Commissioners of Navigation and Pilotage for Old Topsail Inlet and Beaufort Bar, as provided for in Chapter 76 of the General Statutes, shall continue to vest in the boards, as now provided by statute, independently of the direction, supervision, and control of the Secretary of Commerce. The commissions shall report their activity to the Governor through the Secretary of Commerce. The appointment to the boards shall continue to be made in the manner as provided by Chapter 76 of the General Statutes. (1975, c. 716, s. 1; 1977, c. 65, s. 4; c. 198, s. 26; 1989, c. 751, s. 8(24); 1991 (Reg. Sess., 1992), c. 959, s. 69.)

Part 10. North Carolina State Ports Authority.

§§ 143B-452 through 143B-467: Recodified as Article 20 of Chapter 136, G.S. 136-260 through G.S. 136-275, by Session Laws 2011-145, s. 14.6(b), effective July 1, 2011.

§ 143B-468: Reserved for future codification purposes.

Part 11. North Carolina Ports Railway Commission.

§§ 143B-469 through 143B-469.3: Repealed.

§ 143B-469.1. Repealed by Session Laws 2002-126, s. 6.6(a)-(f).

§ 143B-469.2. Repealed by Session Laws 2002-126, s. 6.6(a)-(f).

§ 143B-469.3. Repealed by Session Laws 2002-126 s. 6.6(a)-(f).

Part 11A. North Carolina Hazardous Waste Treatment Commission.

§§ 143B-470 through 143B-470.6: Repealed by Session Laws 1989, c. 168, s. 2(a).

Part 12. North Carolina Technological Development Authority.

§§ 143B-471 through 143B-471.5: Repealed by Session Laws 1991, c. 689, s. 154.1(f).

Part 13. Mutual Burial Associations.

§§ 143B-472 through 143B-472.1: Repealed by Session Laws 1997-313, s. 2.

§§ 143B-472.2 through 143B-472.29: Recodified as present G.S. 90-210.80 through 90-210.107 in Article 13E of Chapter 90, by Session Laws 2003-420, s. 17(b), effective October 1, 2003.

Part 14. Business Energy Improvement Program.

§§ 143B-472.30 through 143B-472.34: Repealed by Session Laws 2000-140, s. 76.

Part 15. Main Street Solutions.

§ 143B-472.35. Establishment of fund; use of funds; application for grants; disbursal; repayment; inspections; rules; reports.

(a) A fund to be known as the Main Street Solutions Fund is established in the Department of Commerce. This Fund shall be administered by the Department of Commerce. The Department of Commerce shall be responsible for receipt and disbursement of all funds as provided in this section. Interest earnings shall be credited to the Main Street Solutions Fund.

(a1) The Main Street Solutions Fund is a reimbursable, matching grant program. The Department of Commerce and the North Carolina Main Street Center are authorized to award grants from the Main Street Solutions Fund totaling not more than two hundred thousand dollars ($200,000) to each eligible local government. Funds from eligible local governments, main street organizations, downtown organizations, downtown economic development organizations, and sources other than the State or federal government must be committed to match the amount of any grant from the Main Street Solutions Fund on the basis of a minimum of two non-State dollars ($2.00) for every one dollar ($1.00) provided by the State from the Main Street Solutions Fund.

(a2) Definitions. - For purposes of this section, the following definitions shall apply:

(1) Active North Carolina main street community. - A community in a Tier 1, 2, or 3 county that has been selected by the Department of Commerce to participate in the Main Street Program or the Small Town Main Street Program and that meets the reporting and eligibility requirements of the respective Program.

(2) Designated downtown area. - A designated area within a community that is considered the primary, traditional downtown business district of the community.

(3) Designated micropolitan. - A geographic entity containing an urban core and having a population of between 10,000 and 50,000 people, according to the most recent federal decennial census.

(4) Downtown economic development organization. - An agency that is part of a public-private partnership intended to develop and recruit business opportunities or to undertake economic development projects that will create jobs.

(5) Downtown organization. - An agency that is part of a public-private partnership on the local level and whose core mission is to revitalize a traditional downtown business district.

(6) Eligible local government. - A municipal government that is located in a designated micropolitan or an active North Carolina main street community.

(7) Historic properties. - Properties that have been designated as historically significant by the National Register of Historic Places or a local historic properties commission.

(8) Interlocal small business economic development project. - A project or group of projects in a cluster of communities or counties or in a region that share a common economic development strategy for small business growth and job creation.

(9) Main Street Center. - The agency within the North Carolina Department of Commerce, Office of Urban Development, which receives applications and makes decisions with respect to Main Street Solutions Fund grant applications from eligible local governments.

(10) Main Street Organization. - An agency working in a public-private partnership on the local level, guided by a professional downtown manager, board of directors, or revitalization committee, and charged with administering the local Main Street Program initiative and facilitating revitalization initiatives in the traditional downtown business district through appropriate design, promotion, and economic restructuring activities.

(11) Main Street Program. - The program developed by the National Trust for Historic Preservation to promote downtown revitalization through economic development within the context of historic preservation.

(12) Mixed-use centers. - Areas zoned and developed for a mix of uses, including retail, service, professional, governmental, institutional, and residential.

(13) Private investment. - A project or group of projects in a designated downtown area that will spur private investment and improve property. A project must be owned and maintained by a private entity and must provide a direct benefit to small businesses.

(14) Public improvements and public infrastructure. - The improvement of property or infrastructure that is owned and maintained by a city or county.

(15) Revolving loan programs for private investment. - A property redevelopment or small business assistance fund that is administered on the local level and that may be used to stabilize or appropriately redevelop properties located in the downtown area in connection with private investment or that may be used to provide necessary operating capital for small business creation or expansion in connection with private investment in a designated downtown area.

(16) Small business. - An independently owned and operated business with less than 100 employees and with annual revenues of less than six million dollars ($6,000,000).

(17) Small Town Main Street Program. - A program based upon the Main Street Program developed by the National Trust for Historic Preservation to promote downtown revitalization through economic development within the context of historic preservation. The purpose of the Small Town Main Street Program is to provide guidance to local communities that have a population of less than 7,500 and do not have a downtown manager.

(18) Tier 1, 2, or 3 counties. - North Carolina counties annually ranked by the Department of Commerce based upon the counties' economic well-being and assigned a Tier designation. The 40 most distressed counties are designated as Tier 1, the next 40 as Tier 2, and the 20 least distressed as Tier 3.

(a3) The purpose of the Main Street Program is to provide economic development planning assistance and coordinated grant support to designated micropolitans located in Tier 2 and 3 counties and to active North Carolina main street communities. To achieve the purposes of the Main Street Program, the Main Street Center shall develop criteria for community participation and shall provide technical assistance and strategic planning support to eligible local governments. Local governments, in collaboration with a main street organization, downtown organization, or downtown economic development organization, and the small businesses that will directly benefit from these funds may apply for grants from the Main Street Solutions Fund as provided in this section.

(a4) The Secretary of Commerce, through the Main Street Center, shall award grants from the Main Street Solutions Fund to eligible designated micropolitans and active North Carolina main street communities. Grant funds awarded from the Main Street Solutions Fund shall be used as provided by the provisions of this section and any rules or regulations adopted by the Secretary of Commerce.

(b) Funds in the Main Street Solutions Fund shall be available only to designated micropolitans in Tier 2 and 3 counties and to active North Carolina main street communities in the State. Funds in the Main Street Solutions Fund shall be used for any of the following eligible activities:

(1) Repealed by Session Laws 2010-31, s. 14.6A, effective July 1, 2010.

(1a) Downtown economic development initiatives that do any of the following:

a. Encourage the development or redevelopment of traditional downtown areas by increasing the capacity for mixed-use centers of activity within downtown core areas. Funds may be used to support the rehabilitation of properties, utility infrastructure improvements, new construction, and the development or redevelopment of parking lots or facilities. Projects under this sub-subdivision must foster private investment and provide direct benefit to small business retention, expansion, or recruitment.

b. Attract and leverage private-sector investments and entrepreneurial growth in downtown areas through strategic planning efforts, market studies, and downtown master plans in association with direct benefit to small business retention, expansion, or recruitment.

c. Attract and stimulate the growth of business professionals and entrepreneurs within downtown core areas.

d. Establish revolving loan programs for private investment and small business assistance in downtown historic properties.

e. Encourage public improvement projects that are necessary to create or stimulate private investment in the designated downtown area and provide a direct benefit to small businesses.

(2) Repealed by Session Laws 2010-31, s. 14.6A, effective July 1, 2010.

(2a) Historic preservation initiatives outside of downtown core areas that enhance: (i) community economic development and small business retention, expansion, or recruitment; and (ii) regional or community job creation.

(3) Repealed by Session Laws 2010-31, s. 14.6A, effective July 1, 2010.

(3a) Public improvements and public infrastructure outside of downtown core areas that are consistent with sound municipal planning and that support community economic development, small business retention, expansion, or recruitment, and regional or community job creation.

(4) Repealed by Session Laws 2010-31, s. 14.6A, effective July 1, 2010.

(4a) Interlocal small business economic development projects designed to enhance regional economic growth and job creation.

(5)-(7) Repealed by Session Laws 2010-31, s. 14.6A, effective July 1, 2010.

(c) Repealed by Session Laws 2010-31, s. 14.6A, effective July 1, 2010.

(c1) The application shall include each of the following:

(1) Repealed by Session Laws 2010-31, s. 14.6A, effective July 1, 2010.

(1a) The proposed activities for which the funds are to be used and the projected cost of the project.

(2) The amount of grant funds requested for these activities.

(3)   Projections of the dollar amount of public and private investment that are expected to occur in the designated micropolitan or designated downtown area as a direct result of the proposed activities.

(4)   Repealed by Session Laws 2010-31, s. 14.6A, effective July 1, 2010.

(5)   An explanation of the nature of the private investment in the designated micropolitan or designated downtown area that will result from the proposed activities.

(6)   Projections of the time needed to complete the proposed activities.

(7)   Projections of the time needed to realize the private investment that is expected to result from the proposed activities.

(8)   Repealed by Session Laws 2010-31, s. 14.6A, effective July 1, 2010.

(9)   Any additional or supplemental information requested by the Division.

(d)   A local government whose application is denied may file a new or amended application.

(e)   Repealed by Session Laws 2010-31, s. 14.6A, effective July 1, 2010.

(f)   Repealed by Session Laws 2009-451, s. 14.10, effective July 1, 2009.

(g)   (1)   A local government that has been selected to receive a grant shall use the full amount of the grant for the activities that were approved pursuant to the provisions of this section. Funds are deemed used if the local government is legally committed to spend the funds on the approved activities.

(2)   Repealed by Session Laws 2010-31, s. 14.6A, effective July 1, 2010.

(3)   A local government that fails to satisfy the condition set forth in subdivision (1) of this subsection shall lose any funds that have not been used within three years of being selected. These unused funds shall be credited to the Main Street Solutions Fund. A local government that fails to satisfy the conditions set forth in subdivision (1) of this subsection may file a new application.

(4)   Any funds repaid or credited to the Main Street Solutions Fund pursuant to subdivision (3) of this subsection shall be available to other applicants as long as the Main Street Solutions Fund is in effect.

(h)   Repealed by Session Laws 2009-451, s. 14.10, effective July 1, 2009.

(i)   After a project financed pursuant to this section has been completed, the local government shall report the actual cost of the project to the Department of Commerce.

(j)   Inspection of a project for which a grant has been awarded may be performed by personnel of the Department of Commerce. No person may be approved to perform inspections who is an officer or employee of the unit of local government to which the grant was made or who is an owner, officer, employee, or agent of a contractor or subcontractor engaged in the construction of any project for which the grant was made.

(k)   The Department of Commerce may adopt, modify, and repeal rules establishing the procedures to be followed in the administration of this section and regulations interpreting and applying the provisions of this section, as provided in the Administrative Procedure Act.

(l)   The Department of Commerce and local governments that have been selected to receive a grant from the Main Street Solutions Fund shall prepare and file on or before September 1 of each year with the Joint Legislative Commission on Governmental Operations and the Fiscal Research Division a consolidated report for the preceding fiscal year concerning the allocation of grants authorized by this section.

The portion of the annual report prepared by the Department of Commerce shall set forth for the preceding fiscal year itemized and total allocations from the Main Street Solutions Fund for grants. The Department of Commerce shall also prepare a summary report of all allocations made from the fund for each fiscal year; the total funds received and allocations made and the total unallocated funds in the Fund.

The portion of the report prepared by the local government shall include each of the following:

(1) The total amount of public and private funds that was committed and the amount that was invested in the designated micropolitan or designated downtown area during the preceding fiscal year.

(2) Repealed by Session Laws 2010-31, s. 14.6A, effective July 1, 2010.

(3) The total amount of grants received from the Main Street Solutions Fund during the preceding fiscal year.

(4) Repealed by Session Laws 2009-451, s. 14.10, effective July 1, 2009.

(5) A description of how the grant funds and funds from public and private investors were used during the preceding fiscal year.

(6) Details regarding the types of private investment created or stimulated, the dates of this activity, the amount of public money involved, and any other pertinent information, including any jobs created, businesses started, and number of jobs retained due to the approved activities.

(m) The Department of Commerce may annually use up to seventy-five thousand dollars ($75,000) of the funds in the Main Street Solutions Fund for expenses related to the administration of the Fund. (1989, c. 751, s. 9(c); c. 754, ss. 40(b)-(m); 1991, c. 689, s. 140(a); 1991 (Reg. Sess., 1992), c. 959, s. 72; 1993, c. 553, ss. 50, 51; 1997-456, s. 27; 2009-451, s. 14.10; 2010-31, s. 14.6A.)

§§ 143B-472.36 through 143B-472.39. Reserved for future codification purposes.

Part 16. Information Technology Related State Government Functions.

§§ 143B-472.40 through 143B-472.67: Repealed by Session Laws 2000-174, s. 1.

§ 143B-472.68. Reserved for future codification purposes.

§ 143B-472.69. Reserved for future codification purposes.

Part 17. Electronic Procurement in Government.

§ 143B-472.70: Recodified as § 143-48.3 by Session Laws 2000-140, s. 5.95(a).

§§ 143B-472.71 through 143B-472.79: Reserved for future codification purposes.

Part 18. North Carolina Board of Science and Technology.

§ 143B-472.80. North Carolina Board of Science and Technology; creation; powers and duties.

The North Carolina Board of Science and Technology of the Department of Commerce is created. The Board has the following powers and duties:

(1) To identify, and to support and foster the identification of, important research needs of both public and private agencies, institutions and organizations in North Carolina that relate to the State's economic growth and development;

(2) To make recommendations concerning policies, procedures, organizational structures and financial requirements that will promote effective use of scientific and technological resources in fulfilling the research needs identified and that will promote the economic growth and development of North Carolina;

(3) To allocate funds available to the Board to support research projects, to purchase research equipment and supplies, to construct or modify research facilities, to employ consultants, and for other purposes necessary or appropriate in discharging the duties of the Board;

(4) To advise and make recommendations to the Governor, the General Assembly, the Secretary of Commerce, and the Economic Development Board on the role of science and technology in the economic growth and development of North Carolina.

(5) Repealed by Session Laws 2009-451, s. 14.5(g), effective July 1, 2009. (1973, c. 1262, s. 77; 1977, c. 198, ss. 2, 26; 1979, c. 668, s. 1; 1985, c. 757, s. 179(a), (c); 2001-424, s. 7.6; 2001-486, s. 2.21; 2003-210, s. 1; 2005-276, s. 13.15; 2005-345, s. 25; 2009-451, s. 14.5(g).)

§ 143B-472.81. North Carolina Board of Science and Technology; membership; organization; compensation; staff services.

(a) The North Carolina Board of Science and Technology consists of the Governor, the Secretary of Commerce, and 17 members appointed as follows: the Governor shall appoint one member from the University of North Carolina at Chapel Hill, one member from North Carolina State University at Raleigh, and two members from other components of the University of North Carolina, all nominated by the President of the University of North Carolina; one member from Duke University, nominated by the President of Duke University; one member from a private college or university, other than Duke University, in North Carolina, nominated by the President of the Association of Private Colleges and Universities; one member from the Research Triangle Institute, nominated by the executive committee of the board of that institute; one member from the Microelectronics Center of North Carolina, nominated by the executive committee of the board of that center; one member from the North Carolina Biotechnology Center, nominated by the executive committee of the board of that center; four members from private industry in North Carolina, at least one of whom shall be a professional engineer registered pursuant to Chapter 89C of the General Statutes or a person who holds at least a bachelors degree in engineering from an accredited college or university; and two members from public agencies in North Carolina. Two members shall be appointed by the General Assembly, one shall be appointed upon the recommendation of the President Pro Tempore of the Senate, and one shall be appointed upon the recommendation of the Speaker of the House of Representatives in accordance with G.S. 120-121. The nominating authority for any vacancy on the Board among members appointed by the Governor shall submit to the Governor two nominations for each position to be filled, and the persons so nominated shall represent different disciplines.

(b) Members appointed to the Board by the General Assembly shall serve for two-year terms beginning 1 July of odd-numbered years. Vacancies in appointments made by the General Assembly shall be filled in accordance with G.S. 120-122. The two members from public agencies shall serve for terms expiring at the end of the term of the Governor appointing them. The other 13 members appointed to the Board by the Governor shall serve for four-year terms, and until their successors are appointed and qualified. Of those 13 members, six shall serve for terms that expire on 30 June of years that follow by one year those years that are evenly divisible by four, and seven shall serve for terms that expire on 30 June of years that follow by three years those years that are evenly divisible by four. Any appointment to fill a vacancy on the Board created by the resignation, dismissal, death, or disability of a member shall be for the balance of the unexpired term.

(c) The Governor or the Governor's designee shall serve as chair of the Board. The vice-chair and the secretary of the Board shall be designated by the Governor or the Governor's designee from among the members of the Board.

(d) The Governor may remove any member of the Board from office in accordance with the provisions of G.S. 143B-16.

(e) Members of the Board who are employees of State agencies or institutions shall receive subsistence and travel allowances authorized by G.S. 138-6. Legislative members of the Board shall receive subsistence and travel allowances authorized by G.S. 120-3.1.

(f) A majority of the Board constitutes a quorum for the transaction of business.

(g) The Secretary of Commerce shall provide all clerical and other services required by the Board. (1979, c. 668, s. 1; 1981 (Reg. Sess., 1982), c. 1191, ss. 44-46; 1985, c. 757, s. 179(b), (c); 1989, c. 751, s. 8(17); 1991, c. 573, s. 1; 1995, c. 490, s. 46; 2001-424, s. 7.6; 2001-486, s. 2.21.)

§ 143B-472.82. Reserved for future codification purposes.

§ 143B-472.83. Reserved for future codification purposes.

§ 143B-472.84. Reserved for future codification purposes.

Part 19. Small Business Contractor Act. (Expired).

§§ 143B-472.85 through 143B-472.97: Expired.

§ 143B-472.98. Reserved for future codification purposes.

§ 143B-472.99. Reserved for future codification purposes.

Part 20. Small Business Contractor Act.

§ 143B-472.100. Purpose and intent.

The purpose and intent of this Part is to foster economic development and the creation of jobs by providing financial assistance to financially responsible small businesses that are unable to obtain adequate financing and bonding assistance in connection with contracts. (2007-441, s. 1.)

§ 143B-472.101. Definitions.

The following definitions apply in this Part:

(1) Authority. - The North Carolina Small Business Contractor Authority created in this Part.

(2) Internal Revenue Code. - The Code as defined in G.S. 105-228.90.

(3) Contract term. - The term of a contract, including the maintenance or warranty period required by the contract and the period during which the surety may be liable for latent defects.

(4) Government agency. - The federal government, the State, an agency, or a political subdivision of the federal government or the State, or a utility regulated by the North Carolina Utilities Commission.

(5) Related party. - A party related to the applicant in a manner that would require an attribution of stock to or from the party under section 318 of the Internal Revenue Code.

(6) Secretary. - The Secretary of Commerce. (2007-441, s. 1.)

§ 143B-472.102. Authority creation; powers.

(a) Creation. - The North Carolina Small Business Contractor Authority is created within the Department of Commerce.

(b) Membership. - The Authority consists of 11 members appointed as follows:

(1) Four members appointed by the General Assembly upon the recommendation of the President Pro Tempore of the Senate, one of whom has experience in underwriting surety bonds.

(2) Four members appointed by the General Assembly upon the recommendation of the Speaker of the House of Representatives, one of whom is a present or former governmental employee with experience in administering public contracts.

(3) Three members appointed by the Governor, one of whom is a licensed general contractor and one of whom is experienced in working for private, nonprofit, small, or underutilized businesses.

(c) Terms. - Members serve four-year terms, except initial appointments. There is no prohibition against reappointment for subsequent terms. Initial appointments shall begin on January 1, 2008. Each appointing authority shall designate two of its initial appointments to serve four-year terms and the remainder of its initial appointments to serve three-year terms.

(d) Chair. - The chair shall be elected annually by the members of the Authority from the membership of the Authority and shall be a voting member.

(e) Compensation. - The Authority members shall receive no salary as a result of serving on the Authority but are entitled to per diem and allowances in accordance with G.S. 138-5.

(f) Meetings. - The Secretary shall convene the first meeting of the Authority within 60 days after January 1, 2008. Meetings shall be held as necessary as determined by the Authority.

(g) Quorum. - A majority of the members of the Authority constitutes a quorum for the transaction of business. A vacancy in the membership of the Authority does not impair the right of the quorum to exercise all rights and to perform all duties of the Authority.

(h) Vacancies. - A vacancy on the Authority resulting from the resignation of a member or otherwise is filled in the same manner in which the original appointment was made, for the balance of the unexpired term. Vacancies in appointments made by the General Assembly shall be filled in accordance with G.S. 120-122.

(i) Removal. - Members may be removed in accordance with G.S. 143B-13. A member who misses three consecutive meetings of the Authority may be removed for nonfeasance.

(j) Powers and Duties. - The Authority has the following powers and duties:

(1) To accept grants, loans, contributions, and services.

(2) To employ staff, procure supplies, services, and property, and enter into contracts, leases, or other legal agreements, including the procurement of reinsurance, to carry out the purposes of the Authority.

(3) To acquire, manage, operate, dispose of, or otherwise deal with property, take assignments of rentals and leases, and enter into contracts, leases, agreements, and arrangements that are necessary or incidental to the performance of the duties of the Authority, upon terms and conditions that it considers appropriate.

(4) To specify the form and content of applications, guaranty agreements, or agreements necessary to fulfill the purposes of this Part.

(5) To acquire or take assignments of documents executed, obtained, or delivered in connection with assistance provided by the Authority under this Part.

(6) To fix, determine, charge, and collect any premiums, fees, charges, costs, and expenses in connection with any assistance provided by the Authority under this Part.

(7) To adopt rules, in accordance with Chapter 150B of the General Statutes, to implement this Part.

(8) To take any other action necessary to carry out its purposes.

(9) To report quarterly to the Joint Legislative Commission on Governmental Operations on the activities of the Authority, including the amount of rates, sureties, and bonds. The Authority shall comply with the provisions of this subdivision only in the fiscal years in which funds are appropriated by the State to the Authority to perform the powers and duties authorized in this Part.

(k) Limitations. - Notwithstanding any other provision of this Part, the Authority may not provide financial assistance that constitutes raising money on the credit of the State or pledging the faith and credit or the taxing power of the State directly or indirectly for the payment of any debt. Before providing financial assistance to an applicant under this Part, the Authority must obtain the written certification of the Attorney General that the proposed financial assistance does not constitute raising money on the credit of the State or pledging the faith of the State directly or indirectly for the payment of any debt as provided in Section 3(2) of Article V of the North Carolina Constitution. (2007-441, s. 1; 2012-142, s. 13.3.)

§ 143B-472.103. Eligibility.

To qualify for assistance under this Part, an applicant must meet all of the following requirements:

(1) The applicant must be a small business concern that meets the applicable size standards established by the United States Small Business Administration for business loans based on the industry in which the concern, including its affiliates, is primarily engaged and based on the industry in which the concern, not including its affiliates, is primarily engaged. In addition, in the case of an application for bonding assistance, the applicant, including its affiliates, may not have receipts for construction and service contracts in excess of the maximum amount established by the United States Small Business Administration for surety bond guarantee assistance.

(2) The applicant must be an individual, or be controlled by one or more individuals, with a reputation for financial responsibility, as determined from creditors, employers, and other individuals with personal knowledge. If the applicant is other than a sole proprietorship, at least seventy percent (70%) of the business must be owned by individuals with a reputation for financial responsibility.

(3) The applicant must be a resident of this State or be incorporated in this State and must have its principal place of business in this State.

(4) The applicant must demonstrate to the satisfaction of the Authority that it has been unable to obtain adequate financing or bonding on reasonable terms through an authorized company. If the applicant is applying for a guarantee of a loan, the applicant must have applied for and been denied a loan by a financial institution. (2007-441, s. 1.)

§ 143B-472.104. Small Business Contract Financing Fund.

(a) Creation and Use. - The Small Business Contract Financing Fund is created as a special revenue fund. Revenue in the Fund does not revert at the end of a fiscal year, and interest and other investment income earned by the Fund accrues to the Fund. The Authority shall use the Fund to make direct loans and guaranty payments required by defaults and to pay the portion of the administrative expenses of the Authority related to making these loans and payments.

(b) Content. - The Small Business Contract Financing Fund consists of all of the following revenue:

(1) Funds appropriated to the Fund by the State.

(2) Repayments of principal of and interest on direct loans.

(3) Premiums, fees, and any other amounts received by the Authority with respect to financial assistance provided by the Authority.

(4) Proceeds designated by the Authority from the sale, lease, or other disposition of property or contracts held or acquired by the Authority.

(5) Investment income of the Fund.

(6) Any other moneys made available to the Fund. (2007-441, s. 1.)

§ 143B-472.105. Contract performance assistance authorized.

(a) Type. - The Authority is authorized to provide the following contract performance assistance:

(1) A guarantee of a loan made to the applicant.

(2) If the applicant demonstrates to the satisfaction of the Authority that it is unable to obtain money from any other source, a loan to the applicant.

(b) Qualification. - The Authority shall not lend money to an applicant or guarantee a loan unless all of the following requirements are met:

(1) The applicant meets the requirements of G.S. 143B-472.78.

(2) The loan is to be used to perform an identified contract, of which the majority of funding is provided by a government agency or a combination of government agencies.

(3) The loan is to be used for working capital or equipment needed to perform the contract, the cost of which can be repaid from contract proceeds, if the Authority has entered into an agreement with the applicant necessary to secure the loan or guaranty.

(c) Terms and Conditions. - The Authority shall set the terms and conditions for loans and for the guarantee of loans. When the Authority lends money from the Small Business Contract Financing Fund, it shall prepare loan documents that include all of the following:

(1) The rate of interest on the loan, which shall not exceed any applicable statutory limit for a loan of the same type.

(2) A payment schedule that provides money to the applicant in the amounts and at the times that the applicant needs the money to perform the contract for which the loan is made.

(3) A requirement that, before each advance of money is released to the applicant, the applicant and the Authority must cosign the request for the money.

(4) Provisions for repayment of the loan.

(5) Any other provision the Authority considers necessary to secure the loan, including an assignment of, or a lien on, payment under the contract, if allowable.

(d) Maturity. - A loan made by the Authority shall mature not later than the date the applicant is to receive full payment under the identified contract, unless the Authority determines that a later maturity date is required to fulfill the purposes of this Part.

(e) Diversity. - In selecting applicants for assistance, the Authority must consider the need to serve all geographic and political areas and subdivisions of the State.

(f) Limitation. - The total amount of loan guarantees and loans issued to each recipient during a fiscal year shall not exceed fifteen percent (15%) of the amount of money in the Fund as of the beginning of that fiscal year. (2007-441, s. 1.)

§ 143B-472.106. Small Business Surety Bond Fund.

(a) Creation and Use. - The Small Business Surety Bond Fund is created as a special revenue fund. Revenue in the Fund does not revert at the end of a fiscal year, and interest and other investment income earned by the Fund accrues to the Fund. The Authority shall use the Fund for the purposes of and to pay the expenses of the Authority related to providing bonding assistance.

(b) Content. - The Small Business Surety Bond Fund consists of all of the following revenue:

(1) Funds appropriated to the Fund by the State.

(2) Premiums, fees, and any other amounts received by the Authority with respect to bonding assistance provided by the Authority.

(3) Proceeds designated by the Authority from the sale, lease, or other disposition of property or contracts held or acquired by the Authority.

(4) Investment income of the Fund.

(5) Any other moneys made available to the Fund. (2007-441, s. 1.)

§ 143B-472.107. Bonding assistance authorized.

(a) Guaranty. - Subject to the restrictions of this Part, the Authority, on application, may guarantee a surety for losses incurred under a bid bond, payment bond, or performance bond on an applicant's contract, of which the majority of the funding is provided by a government agency or a combination of government agencies, up to ninety percent (90%) of the surety's losses, or nine hundred thousand dollars ($900,000), whichever is less. The term of a guaranty under this section shall not exceed the contract term. The Authority may vary the terms and conditions of the guaranty from surety to surety, based on the Authority's history of experience with the surety and other factors that the Authority considers relevant.

(b) Notice. - When the Authority provides a guaranty under this section with respect to a contract, it must give the government agencies that are parties to the contract written notice of the guaranty.

(c) Bonds. - The Authority may execute and perform bid bonds, performance bonds, and payment bonds as a surety for the benefit of an applicant in connection with a contract, of which the majority of the funding is provided by a government agency or a combination of government agencies.

(d) Obligation of State. - The total amount of guarantees issued and bonds executed shall not exceed ninety percent (90%) of the amount of money in the Small Business Surety Bond Fund. The Authority shall not pledge any money other than money in the Fund for payment of a loss or bond. No action by the Authority constitutes the creation of a debt secured by a pledge of the taxing power or the faith and credit of the State or any of its political subdivisions. The face of each guarantee issued or bond executed shall contain a statement that the Authority is obligated to pay the guarantee or bond only from the revenue in the Small Business Surety Bond Fund and that neither the taxing power nor the faith and credit of the State or any of its political subdivisions is pledged in payment of the guarantee or bond. Nothing in this subsection limits the ability of the Authority to obtain reinsurance.

(e) Limitation. - The total amount of bonding assistance provided to each recipient during a fiscal year shall not exceed fifteen percent (15%) of the amount of money in the Fund as of the beginning of that fiscal year.

(f) Payment. - If the Authority considers it prudent, it may require that payment be made either to the contractor and lending institution or to the bonding authority. (2007-441, s. 1.)

§ 143B-472.108. Bonding assistance conditions.

(a) Requirements. - To obtain bonding assistance under this Part, an applicant must meet the eligibility requirements of G.S. 143B-472.78 and must demonstrate to the satisfaction of the Authority that all of the following apply:

(1) A bond is required in order to bid on a contract or to serve as a prime contractor or subcontractor.

(2) A bond is not obtainable on reasonable terms and conditions without assistance under this Part.

(3) The applicant will not subcontract more than seventy-five percent (75%) of the face value of the contract.

(b) Default. - If an applicant or a person that is a related party with respect to the applicant has ever defaulted on a bond or guaranty provided by the Authority, the Authority may approve a guaranty or bond under this Part only if one of the following applies:

(1) Five years have elapsed since the time of the default.

(2) Every default by the applicant or related party in any program administered by the Authority has been cured.

(c) Economic Effect. - Before issuing a guaranty or bond, the Authority must determine that the contract for which a bond is sought to be guaranteed or issued has a substantial economic effect. To determine the economic effect of a contract, the Authority must consider all of the following:

(1) The amount of the guaranty obligation.

(2) The terms of the bond to be guaranteed.

(3) The number of new jobs that will be created by the contract to be bonded.

(4) Any other factor that the Authority considers relevant. (2007-441, s. 1.)

§ 143B-472.109. Surety bonding line.

The Authority may, on application, establish a surety bonding line in order to issue or guarantee multiple bonds to an applicant within preapproved terms, conditions, and limitations. (2007-441, s. 1.)

§ 143B-472.110. Application.

To apply for assistance from the Authority under this Part, an applicant and, where applicable, a surety must submit to the Authority an application on a form prescribed by the Authority. The application must include any information and documentation the Authority considers necessary to enable the Authority to evaluate the application in accordance with this Part. The Authority may require an applicant to provide an audited balance sheet unless the Authority determines that such a requirement is not necessary or appropriate to fulfill the purposes of this Part. (2007-441, s. 1.)

§ 143B-472.111. Premiums and fees.

(a) Amount. - The Authority shall by rule set the premiums and fees to be paid for providing assistance under this Part. The premiums and fees set by the Authority shall be payable in the amounts, at the time, and in the manner that the Authority requires. The premiums and fees may vary in amount among transactions and at different stages during the terms of transactions.

(b) Rate Standards. - The rate standards in G.S. 58-40-20 apply to premiums set by the Authority under this section. The Authority may also use the forms and rates of rating or advisory organizations licensed under G.S. 58-40-50 or G.S. 58-40-55. The Authority may vary from these rates in order to broaden participation by small businesses that are unable to obtain adequate financing and bonding assistance in connection with contracts. The premiums set and forms developed by the Authority under this section must be approved by the Commissioner of Insurance before they may be used.

(c) Forms. - The Authority shall develop forms to be used for financing and bonding assistance. (2007-441, s. 1.)

§ 143B-472.112. False statements; penalty.

(a) Documents. - It is unlawful to knowingly make or cause any false statement or report to be made in any application or in any document submitted to the Authority.

(b) Statements. - It is unlawful to make or cause any false statement or report to be made to the Authority for the purpose of influencing the action of the Authority on an application for assistance or affecting assistance, whether or not assistance has been previously extended.

(c) Penalty. - A violation of this section is a Class 2 misdemeanor. (2007-441, s. 1.)

§ 143B-472.113. Reserved for future codification purposes.

§ 143B-472.114. Reserved for future codification purposes.

§ 143B-472.115. Reserved for future codification purposes.

§ 143B-472.116. Reserved for future codification purposes.

§ 143B-472.117. Reserved for future codification purposes.

§ 143B-472.118. Reserved for future codification purposes.

§ 143B-472.119. Reserved for future codification purposes.

§ 143B-472.120. Reserved for future codification purposes.

Part 21. North Carolina Energy Assistance Act for Low-Income Persons.

§§ 143B-472.121 through 143B-472.123: Recodified as Part 34 of Article 7 of Chapter 143B, G.S. 143B-344.48 through G.S. 143B-344.50, by Session Laws 2013-360, s. 15.22(j), effective July 1, 2013.

§ 143B-472.124: Reserved for future codification purposes.

§ 143B-472.125: Reserved for future codification purposes.

Part 22. Rural Economic Development Division.

§ 143B-472.126. Rural Economic Development Division created.

There is hereby created in the Department of Commerce a division to be known as the Rural Economic Development Division. The Secretary shall appoint an Assistant Secretary to administer this Division, who shall be subject to the direction and supervision of the Secretary. The Assistant Secretary, subject to the approval of the Secretary, shall select a professional staff of qualified and competent employees to assist in the administration of the duties and responsibilities prescribed in this Part. (2013-360, s. 15.10(a).)

§ 143B-472.127. Programs administered.

(a) The Rural Economic Development Division shall be responsible for administering the program whereby economic development grants or loans are awarded by the Rural Infrastructure Authority as provided in G.S. 143B-472.128 to local government units. The Rural Infrastructure Authority shall, in awarding economic development grants or loans under the provisions of this subsection, give priority to local government units of the counties that have one of the 80 highest rankings under G.S. 143B-437.08 after the adjustment of that section. The funds available for grants or loans under this program may be used as follows:

(1) To construct critical water and wastewater facilities or to provide other infrastructure needs, including, but not limited to, natural gas, broadband, and rail to sites where these facilities will generate private job-creating investment. The grants under this subdivision shall not be subject to the provisions of G.S. 143-355.4.

(2) To provide matching grants or loans to local government units in an economically distressed county that will productively reuse vacant buildings and properties or construct or expand rural health care facilities with priority given to towns or communities with populations of less than 5,000. For purposes of this section, the term "economically distressed county" has the same meaning as in G.S. 143B-437.01.

(3) Recipients of grant funds under this Part shall contribute a cash match for the grant that is equivalent to at least five percent (5%) of the grant amount. The cash match shall come from local resources and may not be derived from other State or federal grant funds.

(4) In awarding grants under this Part, preference shall be given to a project involving a resident company. For purposes of this Part, the term "resident company" means a company that has paid unemployment taxes or income taxes in this State and whose principal place of business is located in this State. An application for a project that serves an economically distressed area shall have priority over a project that does not. A grant to assist with water infrastructure needs is not subject to the provisions of G.S. 143-355.4.

(5) Under no circumstances shall a grant for a project be awarded in excess of twelve thousand five hundred dollars ($12,500) per projected job created or saved.

(b) In addition to the duties under subsection (a) of this section, the Rural Economic Development Division shall also be responsible for (i) administering the program whereby local government units are awarded funds by the Rural Infrastructure Authority from the Utility Account under G.S. 143B-437.01 and (ii) administering the program whereby local government units are awarded funds by the Rural Infrastructure Authority for economic development projects from community development block grant funds.

(c) The Rural Economic Development Division may make recommendations to the Rural Infrastructure Authority as to any matters related to the administration of the programs under subsections (a) and (b) of this section. (2013-360, s. 15.10(a); 2013-363, s. 5.13(a).)

§ 143B-472.128. Rural Infrastructure Authority created; powers.

(a) Creation. - The Rural Infrastructure Authority is created within the Department of Commerce.

(b) Membership. - The Authority shall consist of 16 members who shall be appointed as follows:

(1) The Secretary of Commerce, who shall serve as a nonvoting ex officio member, except in the case of a tie.

(2) Five members appointed by the General Assembly upon the recommendation of the President Pro Tempore of the Senate, and they shall each represent a Tier 1 or Tier 2 county.

(3) Five members appointed by the General Assembly upon the recommendation of the Speaker of the House of Representatives, and they shall each represent a Tier 1 or Tier 2 county.

(4) Five members appointed by the Governor, and they shall each represent a Tier 1 or Tier 2 county.

(c) Terms. - Members shall serve for a term of three years, except for initial terms as provided in this section. No member of the Authority shall serve for more than two consecutive terms, but a person who has been a member for two consecutive terms may be reappointed after being off the Authority for a period of at least three years. An initial term that is two years or less shall not be counted in determining the limitation on consecutive terms. Initial terms shall commence on July 1, 2013.

In order to provide for staggered terms, two persons appointed to the positions designated in subdivision (b)(2) of this section, one person appointed to the positions designated in subdivision (b)(3) of this section, and two persons appointed to the positions designated in subdivision (b)(4) of this section shall be appointed for initial terms ending on June 30, 2014. One person appointed to the positions designated in subdivision (b)(2) of this section, two persons appointed to the positions designated in subdivision (b)(3) of this section, and two persons appointed to the positions designated in subdivision (b)(4) of this section shall be appointed for initial terms ending on June 30, 2015. Two persons appointed to the positions designated in subdivision (b)(2) of this section, two persons appointed to the positions designated in subdivision (b)(3) of this section, and one person appointed to the positions designated in subdivision (b)(4) of this section shall be appointed for initial terms ending on June 30, 2016.

(d) Officers. - The Authority members shall select from among the membership of the Authority a person to serve as chair and vice-chair. The chair and vice-chair shall each serve for a term of one year, but may be re-elected to serve successive terms.

(e) Compensation. - Authority members shall receive no salary as a result of serving on the Authority, but are entitled to per diem and allowances in accordance with G.S. 138-5 and G.S. 138-6, as appropriate.

(f) Meetings. - The Secretary shall convene the first meeting of the Authority within 30 days after the appointment of Authority members under subsection (b) of this section. Meetings shall be held as necessary as determined by the Authority.

(g) Quorum. - A majority of the members of the Authority constitutes a quorum for the transaction of business. A vacancy in the membership of the Authority does not impair the right of the quorum to exercise all rights and to perform all duties of the Authority.

(h) Vacancies. - A vacancy on the Authority shall be filled in the same manner in which the original appointment was made, and the term of the member filling the vacancy shall be for the balance of the unexpired term. Vacancies in appointments made by the General Assembly shall be filled in accordance with G.S. 120-122.

(i) Removal. - Members may be removed in accordance with G.S. 143B-13. A member who misses three consecutive meetings of the Authority may be removed for nonfeasance.

(j) Powers and Duties. - The Authority has the following powers and duties:

(1) To receive and review applications from local government units for grants or loans authorized under G.S. 143B-472.127.

(2) To award grants or loans as provided in G.S. 143B-472.127. In awarding grants or loans under G.S. 143B-472.127(a), priority shall be given to local government units of the counties that have one of the 80 highest rankings under G.S. 143B-437.08 after the adjustment of that section.

(3) To formulate policies and priorities for grant and loan making under G.S. 143B-472.127, which shall include, among other things, providing for (i) at least four grant application cycles during each fiscal year, (ii) the timely distribution of grants and loans so as to allow local government units to undertake infrastructure and other projects authorized under this Part without undue delay, and (iii) the use of federal funds first instead of General Fund appropriations where the project meets federal requirements or guidelines.

(4) To establish a threshold amount for emergency grants and loans that may be awarded by the Assistant Secretary without the prior approval of the Authority. Any emergency grants or loans awarded by the Assistant Secretary pursuant to this subdivision shall meet the requirements of G.S. 143B-472.127(a) or (b), and shall comply with policies and procedures adopted by the Authority. The Assistant Secretary shall, as soon as practicable, inform the Authority of any emergency grants or loans made under this subdivision, including the name of the local government unit to which the grant or loan was made, the amount of the grant or loan, and the project for which the grant or loan was requested.

(5) To determine ways in which the Rural Economic Development Division can aid local government units in meeting the costs for preliminary project planning needed for making an application for a grant or loan under G.S. 143B-472.127.

(6) To determine ways in which the Rural Economic Development Division can effectively disseminate information to local government units about the availability of grants or loans under G.S. 143B-472.127, the application and review process, and any other information that may be deemed useful to local government units in obtaining grants or loans.

(7) To review from time to time the effectiveness of the grant or loan programs under G.S. 143B-472.127 and to determine ways in which the programs may be improved to better serve local government units.

(8) No later than September 1 of each year, to submit a report to the Senate Appropriations Committee on Natural and Economic Resources, the House Appropriations Subcommittee on Natural and Economic Resources, and the Fiscal Research Division that details all of the following:

a. Total number of awards made in the previous fiscal year.

b. Geographic display of awards made.

c. Total number of jobs created in the previous fiscal year.

d. Recommended policy changes that would benefit economic development in rural areas of the State. (2013-360, s. 15.10(a); 2013-363, s. 5.13(b).)

§ 143B-472.129: Reserved for future codification purposes.

§ 143B-472.130: Reserved for future codification purposes.

§ 143B-472.131: Reserved for future codification purposes.

§ 143B-472.132: Reserved for future codification purposes.

§ 143B-472.133: Reserved for future codification purposes.

§ 143B-472.134: Reserved for future codification purposes.

Article 11.

Department of Crime Control and Public Safety.

Part 1. General Provisions.

§ 143B-473: Repealed by Session Laws 2011-145, s. 19.1(u), as amended by Session Laws 2011-391, s. 43(h), effective January 1, 2012.

§ 143B-474: Repealed by Session Laws 2011-145, s. 19.1(u), as amended by Session Laws 2011-391, s. 43(h), effective January 1, 2012.

§ 143B-475: Repealed by Session Laws 2011-145, s. 19.1(u), as amended by Session Laws 2011-391, s. 43(h), effective January 1, 2012.

§ 143B-475.1: Recodified as § 143B-262.4 by Session Laws 2001-487, s. 91(a).

§ 143B-475.2: Repealed by Session Laws 2010-31, s. 17.1(b), effective July 1, 2010.

§ 143B-476: Repealed by Session Laws 2011-145, s. 19.1(u), as amended by Session Laws 2011-391, s. 43(h), effective January 1, 2012.

Part 2. Crime Control Division.

§ 143B-477: Recodified as G.S. 143B-1103, effective January 1, 2012.

Part 3. Governor's Crime Commission.

§§ 143B-478 through 143B-480: Recodified as G.S. 143B-1100 through G.S. 143B-1102, effective January 1, 2012.

Part 3A. Assistance Program for Victims of Rape and Sex Offenses.

§ 143B-480.1: Recodified as G.S. 143B-1200, effective January 1, 2012.

§ 143B-480.2: Repealed by Session Laws 2009-354, s. 1(a), effective July 27, 2009.

§ 143B-480.3: Recodified as G.S. 143B-1201, effective January 1, 2012.

Part 4. State Fire Commission.

§§ 143B-481 through 143B-485. Recodified as §§ 58-27.30 to 58-27.34 by Session Laws 1985, c. 757, s. 167(b), effective July 15, 1985.

§§ 143B-486 through 143B-489. Reserved for future codification purposes.

Part 5. Civil Air Patrol.

§§ 143B-490 through 143B-492: Recodified as G.S. 143B-1030 through G.S. 143B-1032, effective January 1, 2012.

§§ 143B-493 through 143B-494. Reserved for future codification purposes.

Part 5A. North Carolina Center for Missing Persons.

§§ 143B-495 through 143B-499.8: Recodified as G.S. 143B-1010 through G.S. 143B-1022, effective January 1, 2012.

Part 6. Community Penalties Program.

§§ 143B-500 through 143B-507: Recodified as Article 61 of Subchapter XIII of Chapter 7A, §§ 7A-770 to 7A-777, by Session Laws 1991, c. 566, s. 2.

Part 7. Law Enforcement Support Services Division.

§ 143B-508: Repealed by Session Laws 2011-145, s. 19.1(u), as amended by Session Laws 2011-391, s. 43(h), effective January 1, 2012.

§ 143B-508.1: Repealed by Session Laws 2011-145, s. 19.1(u), as amended by Session Laws 2011-391, s. 43(h), effective January 1, 2012.

Part 8. Emergency Management Division.

§ 143B-509: Recodified as G.S. 143B-1000, effective January 1, 2012.

Part 9. State Capitol Police Division.

§ 143B-509.1: Recodified as G.S. 143B-900, effective January 1, 2012.

§ 143B-510: Reserved for future codification purposes.

Article 12.

Department of Juvenile Justice and Delinquency Prevention.

§§ 143B-511 through 143B-549: Recodified as G.S. 143B-800 through 143B-851 by Session Laws 2011-145, s. 19.1(t), effective January 1, 2012.

§ 143B-550: Recodified as G.S. 143B-1104 by Session Laws 2011-145, s. 19.1(s), effective January 1, 2012.

§§ 143B-551 through 143B-555. Reserved for future codification purposes.

Part 7. State Advisory Council on Juvenile Justice and Delinquency Prevention.

§ 143B-556: Repealed by Laws 2008-118, s. 3.12(a), effective July 1, 2008.

§ 143B-557: Repealed by Laws 2008-118, s. 3.12(a), effective July 1, 2008.

Article 13.

Department of Public Safety.

Part 1. General Provisions.

§ 143B-600. Organization.

(a) There is established the Department of Public Safety. The head of the Department of Public Safety is the Secretary of Public Safety, who shall be known as the Secretary.

(b) The powers and duties of the deputy secretaries, commissioners, directors, and the divisions of the Department shall be subject to the direction and control of the Secretary of Public Safety. (2011-145, s. 19.1(b); 2011-183, s. 127(c); 2011-195, s. 1(d); 2011-260, s. 6(c); 2011-391, s. 43(a); 2012-83, ss. 8, 64; 2012-168, s. 5(b); 2013-289, s. 2; 2013-360, s. 16D.7(a).)

§ 143B-601. Powers and duties of the Department of Public Safety.

It shall be the duty of the Department of Public Safety to do all of the following:

(1) Provide assigned law enforcement and emergency services to protect the public against crime and against natural and man-made disasters.

(2) To plan and direct a coordinated effort by the law enforcement agencies of State government and to ensure maximum cooperation between State and local law enforcement agencies in the fight against crime.

(3) To prepare annually, in consultation with the Judicial Department and the Department of Justice, a State plan for the State's criminal justice system.

(4) To serve as the State's chief coordinating agency to control crime, to ensure the safety of the public, and to ensure an effective and efficient State criminal justice system.

(5) To have charge of investigations of criminal matters particularly set forth in this Article and of such other crimes and areas of concern in the criminal justice system as the Governor may direct.

(6) To regularly patrol the highways of the State and enforce all laws and regulations respecting travel and the use of vehicles upon the highways of the State and all laws for the protection of the highways of the State.

(7) To provide North Carolina National Guard troops trained by the State to federal standards.

(8) To ensure the preparation, coordination, and currency of military and civil preparedness plans and the effective conduct of emergency operations by all participating agencies to sustain life and prevent, minimize, or remedy injury to persons and damage to property resulting from disasters caused by enemy attack or other hostile actions or from disasters due to natural or man-made causes.

(9) To develop a plan for a coordinated and integrated electronic communications system for State government and cooperating local agencies, including coordination and integration of existing electronic communications systems.

(10) To carry out the relevant provisions of Part 2 of this Article, Chapter 148 of the General Statutes, Chapter 15 of the General Statutes, Chapter 15A of the General Statutes, and other provisions of the General Statutes governing the provision of necessary custody, supervision, and treatment to control and rehabilitate criminal offenders and thereby reduce the rate and cost of crime and delinquency.

(11) To carry out the relevant provisions of Part 3 of this Article, Chapter 7B of the General Statutes, and other provisions of the General Statutes governing juvenile justice and the prevention of delinquent acts by juveniles.

(12) To provide central storage and management of evidence according to the provisions of Article 13 of Chapter 15A of the General Statutes and create

and maintain a databank of statewide storage locations of postconviction evidence or other similar programs.

(13) To provide central storage and management of rape kits according to the federal Violence Against Women and Department of Justice Reauthorization Act of 2005 with specific protections against release of names of victims providing anonymous or "Jane Doe" rape kits without victim consent.

(14) To provide for the storage and management of evidence. (2011-145, s. 19.1(b); 2011-183, s. 127(c); 2011-195, s. 1(d); 2011-391, s. 43(b); 2012-83, s. 65.)

§ 143B-602. Powers and duties of the Secretary of Public Safety.

The Secretary of Public Safety shall have the powers and duties as are conferred on the Secretary by this Article, delegated to the Secretary by the Governor, and conferred on the Secretary by the Constitution and laws of this State. These powers and duties include the following:

(1) Provision of assistance to other agencies. - The Secretary, through appropriate subunits of the Department, shall, at the request of the Governor, provide assistance to State and local law enforcement agencies, district attorneys, and judges when called upon by them and so directed.

(2) Coordination of government subunits emergencies. - In the event that the Governor, in the exercise of the Governor's constitutional and statutory responsibilities, shall deem it necessary to utilize the services of more than one subunit of State government to provide protection to the people from natural or man-made disasters or emergencies, including, but not limited to, wars, insurrections, riots, civil disturbances, or accidents, the Secretary, under the direction of the Governor, shall serve as the chief coordinating officer for the State between the respective subunits so utilized.

(3) Allocation of State resources during emergencies. - Whenever the Secretary exercises the authority provided in subdivision (2) of this section, the Secretary shall be authorized to utilize and allocate all available State resources as are reasonably necessary to cope with the emergency or disaster, including directing of personnel and functions of State agencies or units thereof for the purpose of performing or facilitating the initial response to the disaster or

emergency. Following the initial response, the Secretary, in consultation with the heads of the State agencies which have or appear to have the responsibility for dealing with the emergency or disaster, shall designate one or more lead agencies to be responsible for subsequent phases of the response to the emergency or disaster. Pending an opportunity to consult with the heads of such agencies, the Secretary may make interim lead agencies designations.

(4) Reporting of emergencies to the Secretary. - Every department of State government is required to report to the Secretary, by the fastest means practicable, all natural or man-made disasters or emergencies, including, but not limited to, wars, insurrections, riots, civil disturbances, or accidents which appear likely to require the utilization of the services of more than one subunit of State government.

(5) Rule making. - The Secretary is authorized to adopt rules and procedures for the implementation of this section.

(6) Powers of Governor and Council of State not superseded. - Nothing contained in this section shall be construed to supersede or modify those powers granted to the Governor or the Council of State to declare and react to a state of disaster as provided in Chapter 166A of the General Statutes, the Constitution, or elsewhere.

(7) Reporting required prior to grant awards. - Prior to any notification of proposed grant awards to State agencies for use in pursuing the objectives of the Governor's Crime Commission pursuant to sub-subdivisions a. through g. of subdivision (8) of this section, the Secretary shall report to the Senate and House of Representatives Appropriations Committees for review of the proposed grant awards.

(8) Other powers and duties. - The Secretary has the following additional powers and duties:

a. Accepting gifts, bequests, devises, grants, matching funds, and other considerations from private or governmental sources for use in promoting the work of the Governor's Crime Commission.

b. Making grants for use in pursuing the objectives of the Governor's Crime Commission.

c. Adopting rules as may be required by the federal government for federal grants-in-aid for criminal justice purposes and to implement and carry out the regulatory and enforcement duties assigned to the Department of Public Safety as provided by the various commercial vehicle, oversize/overweight, motor carrier safety, motor fuel, and mobile and manufactured home statutes.

d. Ascertaining the State's duties concerning grants to the State by the Law Enforcement Assistance Administration of the United States Department of Justice, and developing and administering a plan to ensure that the State fulfills its duties.

e. Administering the Assistance Program for Victims of Rape and Sex Offenses.

f. Appointing, with the Governor's approval, a special police officer to serve as Chief of the State Capitol Police Section of the Division of Law Enforcement.

g. Appointing an employee of the Division of Administration to be the central point of contact for any federal surplus property or purchasing programs.

h. Being responsible for federal and State liaison activities, victim services, the Victim Services Warehouse, and the storage and management of evidence and other contents housed in the warehouse, and public affairs. (2011-145, s. 19.1(b); 2013-289, s. 3.)

Part 2. Division of Adult Correction.

Subpart A. General Provisions

§ 143B-700. Division of Adult Correction of the Department of Public Safety - creation.

There is hereby created and established a division to be known as the Division of Adult Correction of the Department of Public Safety with the organization, powers, and duties hereafter defined in the Executive Organization Act of 1973. (1973, c. 1262, s. 2; 2011-145, s. 19.1(h), (s).)

§ 143B-701. Division of Adult Correction of the Department of Public Safety - duties.

It shall be the duty of the Division to provide the necessary custody, supervision, and treatment to control and rehabilitate criminal offenders and thereby to reduce the rate and cost of crime and delinquency. (1973, c. 1262, s. 3; 1999-423, s. 7; 2011-145, s. 19.1(h), (s).)

§ 143B-702. Division of Adult Correction of the Department of Public Safety - rules and regulations.

The Division of Adult Correction of the Department of Public Safety shall adopt rules and regulations related to the conduct, supervision, rights and privileges of persons in its custody or under its supervision. Such rules and regulations shall be filed with and published by the office of the Attorney General and shall be made available by the Division for public inspection. The rules and regulations shall include a description of the organization of the Division. A description or copy of all forms and instructions used by the Division, except those relating solely to matters of internal management, shall also be filed with the office of the Attorney General. (1975, c. 721, s. 2; 2011-145, s. 19.1(h), (s).)

§ 143B-703. Repair or replacement of personal property.

(a) The Secretary of Public Safety may adopt rules governing repair or replacement of personal property items excluding private passenger vehicles that belong to employees of State facilities within the Division of Adult Correction of the Department of Public Safety and that are damaged or stolen by inmates of the State facilities provided that the item is determined by the Secretary to be damaged or stolen on or off facility grounds during the performance of employment and necessary for the employee to have in his possession to perform his assigned duty.

(b) Reimbursement for items damaged or stolen shall not be granted in instances in which the employee is determined to be negligent or otherwise at fault for the damage or loss of the property. Negligence shall be determined by the superintendent of the facility.

(c) The superintendent of the facility shall determine if the person seeking reimbursement has made a good faith effort to recover the loss from all other non-State sources and has failed before reimbursement is granted.

(d) Reimbursement shall be limited to the amount specified in the rules and shall not exceed a maximum of two hundred dollars ($200.00) per incident. No employee shall receive more than five hundred dollars ($500.00) per year in reimbursement. Reimbursement is subject to the availability of funds.

(e) The Secretary of Public Safety shall establish by rule an appeals process consistent with Chapter 150B of the General Statutes. (1987, c. 639, s. 1; 1989, c. 189, s. 2; 2011-145, s. 19.1(h), (i), (s).)

§ 143B-704. Division of Adult Correction of the Department of Public Safety - functions.

(a) The functions of the Division of Adult Correction of the Department of Public Safety shall comprise, except as otherwise expressly provided by the Executive Organization Act of 1973 or by the Constitution of North Carolina, all functions of the executive branch of the State in relation to corrections and the rehabilitation of adult offenders, including detention, parole, and aftercare supervision, and further including those prescribed powers, duties, and functions enumerated in Article 14 of Chapter 143A of the General Statutes and other laws of this State.

(b) All such functions, powers, duties, and obligations heretofore vested in the Department of Social Rehabilitation and Control and any agency enumerated in Article 14 of Chapter 143A of the General Statutes and laws of this State are hereby transferred to and vested in the Division of Adult Correction of the Department of Public Safety except as otherwise provided by the Executive Organization Act of 1973. They shall include, by way of extension and not of limitation, the functions of:

(1) The State Department of Correction and Commission of Correction,

(2) Repealed by Session Laws 1999-423, s. 8, effective July 1, 1999.

(3) The State Probation Commission,

(4) The State Board of Paroles,

(5) The Interstate Agreement on Detainers, and

(6) The Uniform Act for Out-of-State Parolee Supervision.

(c) Repealed by Session Laws 2012-83, s. 9, effective June 26, 2012.

(d) The Division shall establish an alcoholism and chemical dependency treatment program. The program shall consist of a continuum of treatment and intervention services for male and female inmates, established in medium and minimum custody prison facilities, and for male and female probationers and parolees, established in community-based residential treatment facilities.

(e) The Department, in consultation with the Domestic Violence Commission, and in accordance with established best practices, shall establish a domestic violence treatment program for offenders sentenced to a term of imprisonment in the custody of the Department and whose official record includes a finding by the court that the offender committed acts of domestic violence.

The Department shall ensure that inmates, whose record includes a finding by the court that the offender committed acts of domestic violence, complete a domestic violence treatment program prior to the completion of the period of incarceration, unless other requirements, deemed critical by the Department, prevent program completion. In the event an inmate does not complete the program during the period of incarceration, the Department shall document, in the inmate's official record, specific reasons why that particular inmate did not or was not able to complete the program. (1973, c. 1262, s. 4; 1983, c. 682, s. 1; 1987, c. 479; c. 738, s. 111(a); 1989 (Reg. Sess., 1990), c. 994; 1997-57, s. 1; 1999-423, s. 8; 2001-487, s. 47(f); 2004-186, s. 1.2; 2009-372, s. 6; 2011-145, s. 19.1(h), (k), (s); 2012-83, s. 9.)

§ 143B-705. Division of Adult Correction of the Department of Public Safety - Alcoholism and Chemical Dependency Treatment Program.

(a) The Program established by G.S. 143B-704 shall be offered in correctional facilities, or a portion of correctional facilities that are self-contained, so that the residential and program space is separate from any other programs or inmate housing, and shall be operational by January 1, 1988, at those facilities as the Secretary or the Secretary's designee may designate.

(b)   A Section Chief for the Alcoholism and Chemical Dependency Treatment Program shall be employed and shall report directly to a deputy director for the Division of Adult Correction as designated by the Chief Deputy Secretary for the Division of Adult Correction. The duties of the Section Chief and staff shall include the following:

(1)   Administer and coordinate all substance abuse programs, grants, contracts, and related functions in the Division of Adult Correction of the Department of Public Safety.

(2)   Develop and maintain working relationships and agreements with agencies and organizations that will assist in developing and operating alcoholism and chemical dependency treatment and recovery programs in the Division of Adult Correction of the Department of Public Safety.

(3)   Develop and coordinate the use of volunteers in the Substance Abuse Program.

(4)   Develop and present training programs related to alcoholism and chemical dependency for employees and others at all levels in the agency.

(5)   Develop programs that provide effective treatment for inmates, probationers, and parolees with alcohol and chemical dependency problems.

(6)   Maintain contact with key leaders in the alcoholism and chemical dependency field, the service structure of various community recovery programs, and active supporters of the Correction Program.

(7)   Supervise directly the facility and district program managers, other specialized personnel, and programs that exist or may be developed in the Division of Adult Correction of the Department of Public Safety.

(8)   Repealed by Session Laws 2012-83, s. 10, effective June 26, 2012.

(c)   In each prison that houses an alcoholism and chemical dependency program, there shall be a unit superintendent under the Section of Prisons of the Division of Adult Correction and other custodial, administrative, and support staff as required to maintain the proper custody level at the facility. The unit superintendent shall be responsible for all matters pertaining to custody and administration of the unit. The Section Chief of the Alcoholism and Chemical Dependency Treatment Program shall designate and direct employees to manage treatment programs at each location. Duties of unit treatment program managers shall include program development and implementation, supervision of personnel assigned to treatment programs, adherence to all pertinent policy and procedural requirements of the Department, and other duties as assigned.

(d) Extensive use may be made of inmates working in the role of ancillary staff, treatment assistants, role models, or study group leaders as the program manager determines. Additional resource people who may be required for specialized treatment activities, presentations, or group work may be employed on a fee or contractual basis.

(e) Admission priorities shall be established as follows:

(1) Evaluation and referral from reception and diagnostic centers.

(2) General staff referral.

(3) Self-referral.

(f) The Program shall include extensive follow-up after the period of intensive treatment. There will be specific plans for each departing inmate for follow-up, including active involvement with Alcoholics Anonymous, community resources, and personal sponsorship. (1987, c. 738, s. 111(c); 1987 (Reg. Sess., 1988), c. 1086, s. 126.1(a); 2002-126, s. 17.7; 2003-141, s. 3; 2011-145, s. 19.1(h)-(j), (s); 2012-83, s. 10.)

§ 143B-706. Pilot program on sexual assault.

(a) The Division of Adult Correction of the Department of Public Safety shall establish pilot programs on sexual assault for inmates at three units of the State prison system. The Division shall select units with greater than average levels of inmate violence for participation in these pilot programs.

(b) Each pilot program shall operate as follows:

(1) The Division shall provide, as part of every inmate's orientation, a program on sexual assault, with a goal to complete that program within seven days of commitment to the Division of Adult Correction of the Department of Public Safety. The program shall provide inmates with at least the following information:

a. An accurate presentation pertaining to sexual assault violence;

b. Information on preventing and reducing the risk of sexual assault;

c. Information on available counseling for victims of sexual assault; and

d. The procedure for victims of sexual assault to request counseling.

(2) The division shall provide sexual assault counseling on-site at the prison unit to any prisoner requesting it. Counselors shall be granted reasonable access to Division of Adult Correction of the Department of Public Safety institutions and prisoners for the purpose of providing confidential sexual assault counseling.

(3) Unless the Director of the Section of Prisons of the Division of Adult Correction finds a particular item to be unsuitable, the Division shall allow the distribution of materials on sexual assault and rape trauma syndrome developed or sponsored by community rape crisis centers or nonprofit organizations with expertise in sexual assault. Any such material provided to a correctional institution shall be made available to inmates in places where they may make use of them privately and without attracting undue attention, such as in the library, law library, medical clinic, recreation hall, mental health offices, and educational lobby areas.

(4) The Division shall post notices of the availability of any community-based rape crisis counselors who are willing to provide confidential counseling. Communications between prisoners and rape crisis counselors are confidential. The Division shall cooperate with community rape crisis centers seeking to identify and provide counseling to former inmates who were the victims of sexual assault.

(5) The Division shall collect statistical data of all known, reported, or suspected incidents of sexual aggression or sexually motivated violence occurring at units participating in the pilot programs. The Division shall compile this data on a quarterly and annual basis.

(6) The Division shall develop and implement employee training on the identification and prevention of sexual assault among inmates, in coordination with the Division's employee basic training program. The training shall be provided to new employees at orientation and shall also be part of annual employee training.

(7) The Division shall evaluate and classify each prisoner with respect to the probable risk of sexual assault. When feasible, incoming inmates shall be handled separately until this classification is made. The classification shall be prominently displayed in the inmate's confidential file, and the Division shall consider the prisoner's classification when making housing assignments.

(8) The Division shall also rate prisoners as potential sexual assault offenders based upon (i) criminal history; (ii) incidents occurring during confinement; and (iii) reports of incidents that the Division determines to be credible. The Division shall take the prisoners' potential for sexual assault into consideration when making housing assignments.

(9) The Division shall ensure that prisoners rated vulnerable or highly vulnerable to sexual assault and prisoners rated as potential assaulters are not housed in the same cell or room holding four or fewer inmates or placed in the showers at the same time to the extent that it is practicable. Any exceptions to this policy shall be reported to the Secretary within three days. (1997-288, ss. 1, 2; 2011-145, s. 19.1(h), (j), (s).)

§ 143B-707. Reports to the General Assembly.

The Division of Adult Correction of the Department of Public Safety shall report by March 1 of each year to the Chairs of the Senate and House Appropriations Committees and the Chairs of the Senate and House Appropriations Subcommittees in Justice and Public Safety on their efforts to provide effective treatment to offenders with substance abuse problems. The report shall include:

(1) Details of any new initiatives and expansions or reduction of programs.

(2) Details on any treatment efforts conducted in conjunction with other departments.

(3) Utilization of the community-based programs at DART-Cherry and Black Mountain Substance Abuse Treatment Center for Women.

(4), (5) Repealed by Session Laws 2007-323, s. 17.3(a), effective July 1, 2007.

(6) Statistical information on the number of current inmates with substance abuse problems that require treatment, the number of treatment slots, the number who have completed treatment, and a comparison of available treatment slots to actual utilization rates. The report shall include this information for each DOC funded program.

(7) Evaluation of each substance abuse treatment program funded by the Division of Adult Correction of the Department of Public Safety. Evaluation measures shall include reduction in alcohol and drug dependency, improvements in disciplinary and infraction rates, recidivism (defined as return-to-prison rates), and other measures of the programs' success. (1998-212, s. 17.12(d); 2003-284, s. 16.19; 2007-323, s. 17.3(a); 2011-145, s. 19.1(h), (s); 2012-83, s. 51.)

§ 143B-707.1. Report on probation and parole caseloads.

(a) The Department of Public Safety shall report by March 1 of each year to the Chairs of the House of Representatives and Senate Appropriations Subcommittees on Justice and Public Safety and the Joint Legislative Oversight Committee on Justice and Public Safety on caseload averages for probation and parole officers. The report shall include:

(1) Data on current caseload averages and district averages for probation/parole officer positions.

(2) Data on current span of control for chief probation officers.

(3) An analysis of the optimal caseloads for these officer classifications.

(4) The number and role of paraprofessionals in supervising low-risk caseloads.

(5) The process of assigning offenders to an appropriate supervision level based on a riskeeds assessment.

(6) Data on cases supervised solely for the collection of court-ordered payments.

(b) The Department of Public Safety shall report by March 1 of each year to the Chairs of the House of Representatives and Senate Appropriations Subcommittees on Justice and Public Safety and the Joint Legislative Oversight Committee on Justice and Public Safety on the following:

(1) The number of sex offenders enrolled on active and passive GPS monitoring.

(2) The caseloads of probation officers assigned to GPS-monitored sex offenders.

(3) The number of violations.

(4) The number of absconders.

(5) The projected number of offenders to be enrolled by the end of the fiscal year. (2013-360, s. 16C.10.)

§ 143B-707.2. Mutual agreement parole program report; medical release program report.

(a) The Department of Public Safety and the Post-Release Supervision and Parole Commission shall report by March 1 of each year to the Chairs of the House of Representatives and Senate Appropriations Subcommittees on Justice and Public Safety and to the Chairs of the Joint Legislative Oversight Committee on Justice and Public Safety on the number of inmates enrolled in the mutual agreement parole program, the number completing the program and being paroled, and the number who enrolled but were terminated from the program. The information should be based on the previous calendar year.

(b) The Department of Public Safety and the Post-Release Supervision and Parole Commission shall report by March 1 of each year to the Chairs of the House of Representatives Appropriations Subcommittee on Justice and Public

Safety, to the Chairs of the Senate Appropriations Committee on Justice and Public Safety, and to the Chairs of the Joint Legislative Oversight Committee on Justice and Public Safety on the number of inmates proposed for release, considered for release, and granted release under Article 84B of Chapter 15A of the General Statutes, providing for the medical release of inmates who are either permanently and totally disabled, terminally ill, or geriatric. (2013-360, s. 16C.11(d); 2013-363, s. 6.5.)

§ 143B-708. Community service program.

(a) The Division of Adult Correction of the Department of Public Safety may conduct a community service program. The program shall provide oversight of offenders placed under the supervision of the Section of Community Corrections of the Division of Adult Correction and ordered to perform community service hours for criminal violations, including driving while impaired violations under G.S. 20-138.1. This program shall assign offenders, either on supervised or on unsupervised probation, to perform service to the local community in an effort to promote the offender's rehabilitation and to provide services that help restore or improve the community. The program shall provide appropriate work site placement for offenders ordered to perform community service hours. The Division may adopt rules to conduct the program. Each offender shall be required to comply with the rules adopted for the program.

(b) The Secretary of Public Safety may assign one or more employees to each district court district as defined in G.S. 7A-133 to assure and report to the Court the offender's compliance with the requirements of the program. Each county shall provide office space in the courthouse or other convenient place, for the use of the employees assigned to that county.

(c) A fee of two hundred fifty dollars ($250.00) shall be paid by all persons who participate in the program or receive services from the program staff. Only one fee may be assessed for each sentencing transaction, even if the person is assigned to the program on more than one occasion, or while on deferred prosecution, or while serving a sentence for the offense. A sentencing transaction shall include all offenses considered and adjudicated during the same term of court. Fees collected pursuant to this subsection shall be deposited in the General Fund. If the person is convicted in a court in this State, the fee shall be paid to the clerk of court in the county in which the person is convicted, regardless of whether the person is participating in the program as a condition of parole, of probation imposed by the court, or pursuant to the exercise of authority delegated to the probation officer pursuant to G.S. 15A-1343.2(e) or (f). If the person is participating in the program as a result of a deferred prosecution or similar program, the fee shall be paid to the clerk of court in the county in which the agreement is filed. Persons participating in the program for any other reason shall pay the fee to the clerk of court in the county in which the services are provided by the program staff. The fee shall be paid in full before the person may participate in the community service program, except that:

(1)   A person convicted in a court in this State may be given an extension of time or allowed to begin the community service before the person pays the fee by the court in which the person is convicted; or

(2)   A person performing community service pursuant to a deferred prosecution or similar agreement may be given an extension of time or allowed to begin community service before the fee is paid by the official or agency representing the State in the agreement.

(3)   A person performing community service as a condition of parole may be given an extension of time to pay the fee by the Post-Release Supervision and Parole Commission. No person shall be required to pay the fee before beginning the community service unless the Commission orders the person to do so in writing.

(4)   A person performing community service as ordered by a probation officer pursuant to authority delegated by G.S. 15A-1343.2 may be given an extension of time to pay the fee by the probation officer exercising the delegated authority.

(d)   A person is not liable for damages for any injury or loss sustained by an individual performing community or reparation service under this section unless the injury is caused by the person's gross negligence or intentional wrongdoing. As used in this subsection, "person" includes any governmental unit or agency, nonprofit corporation, or other nonprofit agency that is supervising the individual, or for whom the individual is performing community service work, as well as any person employed by the agency or corporation while acting in the scope and course of the person's employment. This subsection does not affect the immunity from civil liability in tort available to local governmental units or agencies. Notice of the provisions of this subsection shall be furnished to the individual at the time of assignment of community service work by the judicial service coordinator.

(e) The community service staff shall report to the court in which the community service was ordered, a significant violation of the terms of the probation, or deferred prosecution, related to community service, including a willful failure to pay any moneys due the State under any court order or payment schedule adopted by the Section of Community Corrections of the Division of Adult Correction. The community service staff shall give notice of the hearing to determine if there is a willful failure to comply to the person who was ordered to perform the community service. This notice shall be given by either personal delivery to the person to be notified or by depositing the notice in the United States mail in an envelope with postage prepaid, addressed to the person at the last known address available to the preparer of the notice and reasonably believed to provide actual notice to the person. The notice shall be mailed at least 10 days prior to any hearing and shall state the basis of the alleged willful failure to comply. The court shall then conduct a hearing, even if the person ordered to perform the community service fails to appear, to determine if there is a willful failure to complete the work as ordered by the community service staff within the applicable time limits. The hearing may be held in the county in which the probation judgment or deferred prosecution requiring the performance of community service was imposed, the county in which the violation occurred, or the county of residence of the person. If the court determines there is a willful failure to comply, it shall revoke any drivers license issued to the person and notify the Division of Motor Vehicles to revoke any drivers license issued to the person until the community service requirement has been met. In addition, if the person is present, the court may take any further action authorized by Article 82 of Chapter 15A of the General Statutes for violation of a condition of probation. (1983 (Reg. Sess., 1984), c. 1034, s. 102; 1985, c. 451; 1985 (Reg. Sess., 1986), c. 1012, s. 4; 1987 (Reg. Sess., 1988), c. 1037, s. 118; 1989, c. 752, s. 109; 1995, c. 330, s. 2; c. 507, s. 20(a); 1997-234, s. 2; 1998-217, s. 34; 2001-487, ss. 91(a), (b); 2002-126, s. 29A.1(c); 2009-372, s. 17; 2009-411, s. 2; 2009-451, s. 19.26(c), (e); 2009-575, s. 16A; 2010-31, s. 19.4(a); 2010-96, s. 28(c); 2010-123, s. 6.3; 2011-145, s. 19.1(h), (i), (k), (s).)

§ 143B-709. Security Staffing.

(a) The Division of Adult Correction of the Department of Public Safety shall conduct:

(1)   On-site postaudits of every prison at least once every three years;

(2)   Regular audits of postaudit charts through the automated postaudit system; and

(3)   Other staffing audits as necessary.

(b)   The Division of Adult Correction of the Department of Public Safety shall update the security staffing relief formula at least every three years. Each update shall include a review of all annual training requirements for security staff to determine which of these requirements should be mandatory and the appropriate frequency of the training. The Division shall survey other states to determine which states use a vacancy factor in their staffing relief formulas. (2002-126, s. 17.5(a), (b); 2005-276, s. 17.4(a); 2011-145, s. 19.1(h), (s).)

§ 143B-710: Repealed by Session Laws 2013-289, s. 4, effective July 18, 2013.

§ 143B-711. Division of Adult Correction of the Department of Public Safety - organization.

The Division of Adult Correction of the Department of Public Safety shall be organized initially to include the Post-Release Supervision and Parole Commission, the Board of Correction, the Section of Prisons of the Division of Adult Correction, the Section of Community Corrections, the Section of Alcoholism and Chemical Dependency Treatment Programs, and such other divisions as may be established under the provisions of the Executive Organization Act of 1973. (1973, c. 1262, s. 6; 1987, c. 738, s. 111(b); 1993, c. 538, s. 41; 1994, Ex. Sess., c. 24, s. 14(b); 2001-95, s. 7; 2011-145, s. 19.1(h), (j), (s); 2012-83, s. 52.)

§ 143B-712: Reserved for future codification purposes.

§ 143B-713: Reserved for future codification purposes.

§ 143B-714: Reserved for future codification purposes.

Subpart B. Board of Correction.

§ 143B-715. Board of Correction - duties and responsibilities; members; selection; compensation; meetings; quorum; services.

(a)   The Board of Correction shall consider and advise the Secretary of Public Safety upon any matter that the Secretary may refer to it. The Board shall assist the Secretary of Public Safety in the development of major programs and recommend priorities for the programs within the Division.

The Board of Correction shall have such other responsibilities and shall perform such other duties as may be specifically given to it by the Secretary of Public Safety.

(b)   The Board of Correction shall consist of one voting member from each of the 13 congressional districts, appointed by the Governor to serve at his pleasure. One member shall be a psychiatrist or a psychologist, one an attorney with experience in the criminal courts, one a judge in the General Court of Justice and nine members appointed at large. The Secretary of Public Safety shall be an additional nonvoting member and chairman ex officio. The terms of office of the nine members presently serving on the Board shall continue, but any vacancy occurring on or after July 1, 1983, shall be filled by the Governor in compliance with the requirement of membership from the various congressional districts.

(c)   Members of the Board shall receive per diem and necessary travel and subsistence expenses in accordance with the provisions of G.S. 138-5.

The Board of Correction shall meet at least quarterly and may hold special meetings at any time and place within the State at the call of its chairman.

A majority of the Board shall constitute a quorum for the transaction of business.

(d)   All clerical and other services required by the Board shall be supplied by the Secretary of Public Safety. (1973, c. 1262, s. 7; 1983, c. 709, s. 2; 1991 (Reg. Sess., 1992), c. 1038, s. 18; 2001-486, s. 2.15; 2011-145, s. 19.1(h), (i), (s); 2012-83, s. 53.)

§ 143B-716: Reserved for future codification purposes.

§ 143B-717: Reserved for future codification purposes.

§ 143B-718: Reserved for future codification purposes.

§ 143B-719: Reserved for future codification purposes.

Subpart C. Parole Commission.

§ 143B-720. Post-Release Supervision and Parole Commission - creation, powers and duties.

(a)   There is hereby created a Post-Release Supervision and Parole Commission of the Division of Adult Correction of the Department of Public Safety with the authority to grant paroles, including both regular and temporary paroles, to persons held by virtue of any final order or judgment of any court of this State as provided in Chapter 148 of the General Statutes and laws of the State of North Carolina, except that persons sentenced under Article 81B of Chapter 15A of the General Statutes are not eligible for parole but may be conditionally released into the custody and control of United States Immigration and Customs Enforcement pursuant to G.S. 148-64.1. The Commission shall also have authority to revoke, terminate, and suspend paroles of such persons (including persons placed on parole on or before the effective date of the Executive Organization Act of 1973) and to assist the Governor in exercising his authority in granting reprieves, commutations, and pardons, and shall perform such other services as may be required by the Governor in exercising his powers of executive clemency. The Commission shall also have authority to revoke and terminate persons on post-release supervision, as provided in Article 84A of Chapter 15A of the General Statutes. The Commission shall also have the authority to punish for criminal contempt for willful refusal to accept post-release supervision or to comply with the terms of post-release supervision by a prisoner whose offense requiring post-release supervision is a reportable conviction subject to the registration requirement of Article 27A of Chapter 14 of the General Statutes. Any contempt proceeding conducted by the Commission shall be in accordance with G.S. 5A-15 as if the Commission were a judicial official.

(b)   All releasing authority previously resting in the Commissioner and Commission of Correction with the exception of authority for extension of the limits of the place of confinement of a prisoner contained in G.S. 148-4 is hereby transferred to the Post-Release Supervision and Parole Commission. Specifically, such releasing authority includes work release (G.S. 148-33.1), indeterminate-sentence release (G.S. 148-42), and release of youthful offenders

(G.S. 148-49.8), provided the individual considered for work release or indeterminate-sentence release shall have been recommended for release by the Secretary of Public Safety or his designee. No recommendation for release is required for conditional release pursuant to G.S. 148-64.1.

(c) The Commission is authorized and empowered to adopt such rules and regulations, not inconsistent with the laws of this State, in accordance with which prisoners eligible for parole consideration may have their cases reviewed and investigated and by which such proceedings may be initiated and considered. All rules and regulations heretofore adopted by the Board of Paroles shall remain in full force and effect unless and until repealed or superseded by action of the Post-Release Supervision and Parole Commission. All rules and regulations adopted by the Commission shall be enforced by the Division of Adult Correction of the Department of Public Safety.

(d) The Commission is authorized and empowered to impose as a condition of parole or post-release supervision that restitution or reparation be made by the prisoner in accordance with the provisions of G.S. 148-57.1. The Commission is further authorized and empowered to make restitution or reparation a condition of work release in accordance with the provisions of G.S. 148-33.2.

(e) The Commission may accept and review requests from persons placed on probation, parole, or post-release supervision to terminate a mandatory condition of satellite-based monitoring as provided by G.S. 14-208.43. The Commission may grant or deny those requests in compliance with G.S. 14-208.43.

(f) The Commission may conduct the following proceedings by videoconference:

(1) All hearings regarding the revocation or termination of post-release supervision and all hearings regarding revocation, termination, or suspension of parole.

(2) All hearings regarding criminal contempt for willful refusal to accept post-release supervision or comply with the terms of post-release supervision by a prisoner whose offense requiring post-release supervision is a reportable conviction subject to the registration requirement of Article 27A of Chapter 14 of the General Statutes. (1973, c. 1262, s. 8; 1975, c. 220; 1977, c. 614, s. 5; c. 732, s. 5; 1993, c. 538, s. 42; 1994, Ex. Sess., c. 21, s. 6; c. 24, s. 14(b); 2006-

247, s. 15(i); 2007-213, s. 14; 2008-199, s. 2; 2011-145, s. 19.1(h), (i), (s); 2011-307, s. 7; 2012-188, s. 7.)

§ 143B-721. Post-Release Supervision and Parole Commission - members; selection; removal; chair; compensation; quorum; services.

(a) Effective August 1, 2005, the Post-Release Supervision and Parole Commission shall consist of one full-time member and two half-time members. The three members shall be appointed by the Governor from persons whose recognized ability, training, experience, and character qualify them for service on the Commission. The terms of office of any members serving on the Commission on June 30, 2005, shall expire on that date. The terms of office of persons appointed by the Governor as members of the Commission shall be for four years or until their successors are appointed and qualify. Any appointment to fill a vacancy on the Commission created by the resignation, removal, death or disability of a member shall be for the balance of the unexpired term only.

(a1) Effective August 1, 2012, both half-time commissioners shall begin serving as full-time members of the Commission, and the Post-Release Supervision and Parole Commission shall consist of three full-time members.

(a2) Effective February 1, 2013, an additional member shall be appointed by the Governor to the Commission, and the Post-Release Supervision and Parole Commission shall consist of four full-time members.

(b) All members of the Post-Release Supervision and Parole Commission appointed by the Governor shall possess the recognized ability, training, experience, and character to qualify each person to serve ably on the Commission.

(c) The Governor shall have the authority to remove any member of the Commission from office for misfeasance, malfeasance or nonfeasance, pursuant to the provisions of G.S. 143B-13. The Governor shall designate a member of the Commission to serve as chair of the Commission at the pleasure of the Governor.

(d) The granting, denying, revoking, or rescinding of parole, the authorization of work-release privileges to a prisoner, or any other matters of business coming before the Commission for consideration and action shall be decided by majority vote of the full Commission, except that a three-member panel of the Commission may set the terms and conditions for a post-release supervisee under G.S. 15A-1368.4 and may decide questions of violations thereunder, including the issuance of warrants. In the event of a tie in a vote by the full Commission, the chair shall break the tie with an additional vote.

(e) The members of the Commission shall receive the salary fixed by the General Assembly in the Current Operations Appropriations Act and shall receive necessary travel and subsistence expenses in accordance with the provisions of G.S. 138-6. Notwithstanding any other provision of law, the half-time members of the Commission shall not be subject to the provisions of G.S. 135-3(8)(c).

(f) All clerical and other services required by the Commission shall be supplied by the Secretary of the Department of Public Safety. (1973, c. 1262, s. 9; 1977, c. 704, s. 1; 1979, c. 2; 1983, c. 709, s. 3; c. 717, s. 80; 1983 (Reg. Sess., 1984), c. 1034, s. 164; 1993, c. 337, s. 1; c. 538, s. 43; 1994, Ex. Sess., c. 14, s. 63; c. 24, s. 14(b); 1999-237, s. 18.2; 2005-276, s. 17.25(a); 2006-264, s. 89(a); 2011-145, s. 19.1(i), (s); 2012-142, s. 25.1(g); 2013-196, s. 2; 2013-410, s. 12.1.)

§ 143B-722: Reserved for future codification purposes.

§ 143B-723: Reserved for future codification purposes.

§ 143B-724: Reserved for future codification purposes.

§ 143B-725: Reserved for future codification purposes.

§ 143B-726: Reserved for future codification purposes.

§ 143B-727: Reserved for future codification purposes.

§ 143B-728: Reserved for future codification purposes.

§ 143B-729: Reserved for future codification purposes.

§ 143B-730: Reserved for future codification purposes.

§ 143B-731: Reserved for future codification purposes.

§ 143B-732: Reserved for future codification purposes.

§ 143B-733: Reserved for future codification purposes.

§ 143B-734: Reserved for future codification purposes.

§ 143B-735: Reserved for future codification purposes.

§ 143B-736: Reserved for future codification purposes.

§ 143B-737: Reserved for future codification purposes.

§ 143B-738: Reserved for future codification purposes.

§ 143B-739: Reserved for future codification purposes.

§ 143B-740: Reserved for future codification purposes.

§ 143B-741: Reserved for future codification purposes.

§ 143B-742: Reserved for future codification purposes.

§ 143B-743: Reserved for future codification purposes.

§ 143B-744: Reserved for future codification purposes.

§ 143B-745: Reserved for future codification purposes.

§ 143B-746: Reserved for future codification purposes.

§ 143B-747: Reserved for future codification purposes.

§ 143B-748: Reserved for future codification purposes.

§ 143B-749: Reserved for future codification purposes.

§ 143B-750: Reserved for future codification purposes.

§ 143B-751: Reserved for future codification purposes.

§ 143B-752: Reserved for future codification purposes.

§ 143B-753: Reserved for future codification purposes.

§ 143B-754: Reserved for future codification purposes.

§ 143B-755: Reserved for future codification purposes.

§ 143B-756: Reserved for future codification purposes.

§ 143B-757: Reserved for future codification purposes.

§ 143B-758: Reserved for future codification purposes.

§ 143B-759: Reserved for future codification purposes.

§ 143B-760: Reserved for future codification purposes.

§ 143B-761: Reserved for future codification purposes.

§ 143B-762: Reserved for future codification purposes.

§ 143B-763: Reserved for future codification purposes.

§ 143B-764: Reserved for future codification purposes.

§ 143B-765: Reserved for future codification purposes.

§ 143B-766: Reserved for future codification purposes.

§ 143B-767: Reserved for future codification purposes.

§ 143B-768: Reserved for future codification purposes.

§ 143B-769: Reserved for future codification purposes.

§ 143B-770: Reserved for future codification purposes.

§ 143B-771: Reserved for future codification purposes.

§ 143B-772: Reserved for future codification purposes.

§ 143B-773: Reserved for future codification purposes.

§ 143B-774: Reserved for future codification purposes.

§ 143B-775: Reserved for future codification purposes.

§ 143B-776: Reserved for future codification purposes.

§ 143B-777: Reserved for future codification purposes.

§ 143B-778: Reserved for future codification purposes.

§ 143B-779: Reserved for future codification purposes.

Part 3. Division of Juvenile Justice.

Subpart A. Creation of Division.

§ 143B-800. Creation of the Division of Juvenile Justice of the Department of Public Safety.

There is hereby created and constituted a division to be known as the "Division of Juvenile Justice of the Department of Public Safety", with the organization, powers, and duties defined in Article 1 of this Chapter, except as modified in this Part. (1998-202, s. 1(b); 2000-137, s. 1(b); 2011-145, s. 19.1(l), (t).)

§ 143B-801. Transfer of Office of Juvenile Justice authority to the Division of Juvenile Justice of the Department of Public Safety.

(a) All (i) statutory authority, powers, duties, and functions, including directives of S.L. 1998-202, rule making, budgeting, and purchasing, (ii) records, (iii) personnel, personnel positions, and salaries, (iv) property, and (v) unexpended balances of appropriations, allocations, reserves, support costs, and other funds of the Office of Juvenile Justice under the Office of the Governor are transferred to and vested in the Division of Juvenile Justice of the Department of Public Safety. This transfer has all of the elements of a Type I transfer as defined in G.S. 143A-6.

(b) The Division shall be considered a continuation of the Office of Juvenile Justice for the purpose of succession to all rights, powers, duties, and obligations of the Office and of those rights, powers, duties, and obligations exercised by the Office of the Governor on behalf of the Office of Juvenile Justice. Where the Office of Juvenile Justice is referred to by law, contract, or other document, that reference shall apply to the Division. Where the Office of the Governor is referred to by contract or other document, where the Office of the Governor is acting on behalf of the Office of Juvenile Justice, that reference shall apply to the Division.

(c) All institutions previously operated by the Office of Juvenile Justice and the present central office of the Office of Juvenile Justice, including land, buildings, equipment, supplies, personnel, or other properties rented or controlled by the Office or by the Office of the Governor for the Office of Juvenile Justice, shall be administered by the Division of Juvenile Justice of the Department of Public Safety. (1998-202, s. 1(b); 2000-137, s. 1(b); 2011-145, s. 19.1(l), (t).)

§ 143B-802: Reserved for future codification purposes.

§ 143B-803: Reserved for future codification purposes.

§ 143B-804: Reserved for future codification purposes.

Subpart B. General Provisions.

§ 143B-805. Definitions.

In this Part, unless the context clearly requires otherwise, the following words have the listed meanings:

(1) Chief court counselor. - The person responsible for administration and supervision of juvenile intake, probation, and post-release supervision in each judicial district, operating under the supervision of the Division of Juvenile Justice of the Department of Public Safety.

(2) Community-based program. - A program providing nonresidential or residential treatment to a juvenile under the jurisdiction of the juvenile court in the community where the juvenile's family lives. A community-based program

may include specialized foster care, family counseling, shelter care, and other appropriate treatment.

(3) County Councils. - Juvenile Crime Prevention Councils created under G.S. 143B-846.

(4) Court. - The district court division of the General Court of Justice.

(5) Custodian. - The person or agency that has been awarded legal custody of a juvenile by a court.

(6) Delinquent juvenile. - Any juvenile who, while less than 16 years of age but at least 6 years of age, commits a crime or infraction under State law or under an ordinance of local government, including violation of the motor vehicle laws.

(7) Detention. - The secure confinement of a juvenile under a court order.

(8) Detention facility. - A facility approved to provide secure confinement and care for juveniles. Detention facilities include both State and locally administered detention homes, centers, and facilities.

(9) District. - Any district court district as established by G.S. 7A-133.

(10) Division. - The Division of Juvenile Justice of the Department of Public Safety.

(11) Judge. - Any district court judge.

(12) Judicial district. - Any district court district as established by G.S. 7A-133.

(13) Juvenile. - Except as provided in subdivisions (6) and (20) of this section, any person who has not reached the person's eighteenth birthday and is not married, emancipated, or a member of the Armed Forces of the United States. Wherever the term "juvenile" is used with reference to rights and privileges, that term encompasses the attorney for the juvenile as well.

(14) Juvenile court. - Any district court exercising jurisdiction under this Chapter.

(15) Juvenile court counselor. - A person responsible for intake services and court supervision services to juveniles under the supervision of the chief court counselor.

(16) Post-release supervision. - The supervision of a juvenile who has been returned to the community after having been committed to the Division for placement in a training school.

(17) Probation. - The status of a juvenile who has been adjudicated delinquent, is subject to specified conditions under the supervision of a juvenile court counselor, and may be returned to the court for violation of those conditions during the period of probation.

(18) Protective supervision. - The status of a juvenile who has been adjudicated undisciplined and is under the supervision of a juvenile court counselor.

(19) Secretary. - The Secretary of Public Safety.

(20) Undisciplined juvenile. -

a. A juvenile who, while less than 16 years of age but at least 6 years of age, is unlawfully absent from school; or is regularly disobedient to and beyond the disciplinary control of the juvenile's parent, guardian, or custodian; or is regularly found in places where it is unlawful for a juvenile to be; or has run away from home for a period of more than 24 hours; or

b. A juvenile who is 16 or 17 years of age and who is regularly disobedient to and beyond the disciplinary control of the juvenile's parent, guardian, or custodian; or is regularly found in places where it is unlawful for a juvenile to be; or has run away from home for a period of more than 24 hours.

(21) Youth development center. - A secure residential facility authorized to provide long-term treatment, education, and rehabilitative services for delinquent juveniles committed by the court to the Division. (1998-202, ss. 1(b), 2(a); 2000-137, s. 1(b); 2001-95, ss. 3, 4; 2001-490, s. 2.39; 2008-118, s. 3.12(b); 2011-145, s. 19.1(l), (m), (t), (ccc); 2011-183, s. 105.)

§ 143B-806. Duties and powers of the Division of Juvenile Justice of the Department of Public Safety.

(a)   Repealed by Session Laws 2013-289, s. 5, effective July 18, 2013.

(b)   The Secretary shall have the following powers and duties and may delegate those powers and duties to the appropriate deputy secretary, commissioner, or director within the Department of Public Safety:

(1)   Give leadership to the implementation as appropriate of State policy that requires that youth development centers be phased out as populations diminish.

(2)   Close a State youth development center when its operation is no longer justified and transfer State funds appropriated for the operation of that youth development center to fund community-based programs, to purchase care or services for predelinquents, delinquents, or status offenders in community-based or other appropriate programs, or to improve the efficiency of existing youth development centers, after consultation with the Joint Legislative Commission on Governmental Operations.

(3)   Administer a sound admission or intake program for juvenile facilities, including the requirement of a careful evaluation of the needs of each juvenile prior to acceptance and placement.

(4)   Operate juvenile facilities and implement programs that meet the needs of juveniles receiving services and that assist them to become productive, responsible citizens.

(5)   Adopt rules to implement this Part and the responsibilities of the Secretary and the Division under Chapter 7B of the General Statutes. The Secretary may adopt rules applicable to local human services agencies providing juvenile court and delinquency prevention services for the purpose of program evaluation, fiscal audits, and collection of third-party payments.

(6)   Ensure a statewide and uniform system of juvenile intake, protective supervision, probation, and post-release supervision services in all district court districts of the State. The system shall provide appropriate, adequate, and uniform services to all juveniles who are alleged or found to be undisciplined or delinquent.

(7) Establish procedures for substance abuse testing for juveniles adjudicated delinquent for substance abuse offenses.

(8) Plan, develop, and coordinate comprehensive multidisciplinary services and programs statewide for the prevention of juvenile delinquency, early intervention, and rehabilitation of juveniles.

(9) Develop standards, approve yearly program evaluations, and make recommendations based on the evaluations to the General Assembly concerning continuation funding.

(10) Collect expense data for every program operated and contracted by the Division.

(11) Develop a formula for funding, on a matching basis, juvenile court and delinquency prevention services as provided for in this Part. This formula shall be based upon the county's or counties' relative ability to fund community-based programs for juveniles.

Local governments receiving State matching funds for programs under this Part must maintain the same overall level of effort that existed at the time of the filing of the county assessment of juvenile needs with the Division.

(12) Assist local governments and private service agencies in the development of juvenile court services and delinquency prevention services and provide information on the availability of potential funding sources and assistance in making application for needed funding.

(13) Develop and administer a comprehensive juvenile justice information system to collect data and information about delinquent juveniles for the purpose of developing treatment and intervention plans and allowing reliable assessment and evaluation of the effectiveness of rehabilitative and preventive services provided to delinquent juveniles.

(14) Coordinate State-level services in relation to delinquency prevention and juvenile court services so that any citizen may go to one place in State government to receive information about available juvenile services.

(15) Appoint the chief court counselor in each district.

(16) Develop a statewide plan for training and professional development of chief court counselors, court counselors, and other personnel responsible for the care, supervision, and treatment of juveniles. The plan shall include attendance at appropriate professional meetings and opportunities for educational leave for academic study.

(17) Study issues related to qualifications, salary ranges, appointment of personnel on a merit basis, including chief court counselors, court counselors, secretaries, and other appropriate personnel, at the State and district levels in order to adopt appropriate policies and procedures governing personnel.

(18) Set, in consultation with the Office of State Human Resources, the salary supplement paid to teachers, instructional support personnel, and school-based administrators who are employed at juvenile facilities and are licensed by the State Board of Education. The salary supplement shall be at least five percent (5%), but not more than the percentage supplement they would receive if they were employed in the local school administrative unit where the job site is located. These salary supplements shall not be paid to central office staff. Nothing in this subdivision shall be construed to include "merit pay" under the term "salary supplement".

(19) Designate persons, as necessary, as State juvenile justice officers, to provide for the care and supervision of juveniles placed in the physical custody of the Division.

(c) Except as otherwise specifically provided in this Part and in Article 1 of this Chapter, the Secretary of Public Safety shall prescribe the functions, powers, duties, and obligations of every agency or section in the Division.

(d) Where Division statistics indicate the presence of minority youth in juvenile facilities disproportionate to their presence in the general population, the Division shall develop and recommend appropriate strategies designed to ensure fair and equal treatment in the juvenile justice system.

(e) The Division may provide consulting services and technical assistance to courts, law enforcement agencies, and other agencies, local governments, and public and private organizations. The Division may develop or assist Juvenile Crime Prevention Councils in developing community needs, assessments, and programs relating to the prevention and treatment of delinquent and undisciplined behavior.

(f) The Division shall develop a cost-benefit model for each State-funded program. Program commitment and recidivism rates shall be components of the model. (1998-202, ss. 1(b), 2(b), 2(f); 1998-217, ss. 57(2), 57(3); 2000-137, s. 1(b); 2001-95, s. 5; 2001-490, s. 2.40; 2003-284, s. 17.2(a); 2005-276, s. 29.19(b); 2006-203, s. 111; 2008-118, s. 3.12(c); 2011-145, s. 19.1(l), (t); 2012-83, s. 12; 2013-289, s. 5; 2013-360, s. 16D.7(b); 2013-382, s. 9.1(c).)

§ 143B-807. Authority to contract with other entities.

(a) The Division may contract with any governmental agency, person, or association for the accomplishment of its duties and responsibilities. The expenditure of funds under these contracts shall be for the purposes for which the funds were appropriated and not otherwise prohibited by law.

(b) The Division may enter into contracts with, and act as intermediary between, any federal government agency and any county of this State for the purpose of assisting the county to recover monies expended by a county-funded financial assistance program. As a condition of assistance, the county shall agree to hold and save harmless the Division against any claims, loss, or expense which the Division might incur under the contracts by reason of any erroneous, unlawful, or tortious act or omission of the county or its officials, agents, or employees.

(c) The Division and any other appropriate State or local agency may purchase services from public or private agencies providing delinquency prevention programs or juvenile court services, including parenting responsibility classes. The programs shall meet State standards. As institutional populations are reduced, the Division may divert State funds appropriated for institutional programs to purchase the services under the Executive Budget Act.

(d) Each programmatic, residential, and service contract or agreement entered into by the Division shall include a cooperation clause to ensure compliance with the Division's quality assurance requirements and cost-accounting requirements. (1998-202, s. 1(b); 2000-137, s. 1(b); 2011-145, s. 19.1(l), (t).)

§ 143B-808. Authority to assist private nonprofit foundations.

The Division may provide appropriate services or allow employees of the Division to assist any private nonprofit foundation that works directly with the Division's services or programs and whose sole purpose is to support these services and programs. A Division employee shall be allowed to work with a foundation no more than 20 hours in any one month. These services are not subject to Chapter 150B of the General Statutes.

The board of directors of each private, nonprofit foundation shall secure and pay for the services of the Department of State Auditor or employ a certified public accountant to conduct an annual audit of the financial accounts of the foundation. The board of directors shall transmit to the Division a copy of the annual financial audit report of the private nonprofit foundation. (1998-202, s. 1(b); 2000-137, s. 1(b); 2011-145, s. 19.1(l), (t).)

§ 143B-809. Teen court programs.

(a) All teen court programs administered by the Division of Juvenile Justice of the Department of Public Safety shall operate as community resources for the diversion of juveniles pursuant to G.S. 7B-1706(c). A juvenile diverted to a teen court program shall be tried by a jury of other juveniles, and, if the jury finds the juvenile has committed the delinquent act, the jury may assign the juvenile to a rehabilitative measure or sanction, including counseling, restitution, curfews, and community service.

Teen court programs may also operate as resources to the local school administrative units to handle problems that develop at school but that have not been turned over to the juvenile authorities.

(b) Every teen court program that receives funds from Juvenile Crime Prevention Councils shall comply with rules and reporting requirements of the Division of Juvenile Justice of the Department of Public Safety. (2001-424, s. 24.8; 2002-126, s. 16.2(b); 2011-145, s. 19.1(l), (t).)

§ 143B-810. Youth Development Center annual report.

The Department of Public Safety shall report by October 1 of each year to the Chairs of the House of Representatives and Senate Appropriations

Subcommittees on Justice and Public Safety, the Chairs of the Joint Legislative Oversight Committee on Justice and Public Safety, and the Fiscal Research Division of the Legislative Services Commission on the Youth Development Center (YDC) population, staffing, and capacity in the preceding fiscal year. Specifically, the report shall include all of the following:

(1) The on-campus population of each YDC, including the county the juveniles are from.

(2) The housing capacity of each YDC.

(3) A breakdown of staffing for each YDC, including number, type of position, position title, and position description.

(4) The per-bed and average daily population cost for each facility.

(5) The operating cost for each facility, including personnel and nonpersonnel items.

(6) A brief summary of the treatment model, education, services, and plans for reintegration into the community offered at each facility.

(7) The average length of stay in the YDCs.

(8) The number of incidents of assaults and attacks on staff at each facility. (2013-360, s. 16D.3.)

§ 143B-811. Annual evaluation of community programs and multiple purpose group homes.

The Department of Public Safety shall conduct an annual evaluation of the community programs and of multipurpose group homes. In conducting the evaluation of each of these, the Department shall consider whether participation in each program results in a reduction of court involvement among juveniles. The Department shall also determine whether the programs are achieving the goals and objectives of the Juvenile Justice Reform Act, S.L. 1998-202.

The Department shall report the results of the evaluation to the Chairs of the Joint Legislative Oversight Committee on Justice and Public Safety and the

Chairs of the Senate and House of Representatives Appropriations Subcommittees on Justice and Public Safety by March 1 of each year. (2013-360, s. 16D.1.)

§ 143B-812: Reserved for future codification purposes.

§ 143B-813: Reserved for future codification purposes.

§ 143B-814: Reserved for future codification purposes.

Subpart C. Juvenile Facilities.

§ 143B-815. Juvenile facilities.

In order to provide any juvenile in a juvenile facility with appropriate treatment according to that juvenile's need, the Division shall be responsible for the administration of statewide educational, clinical, psychological, psychiatric, social, medical, vocational, and recreational services or programs. (1998-202, s. 1(b); 2000-137, s. 1(b); 2011-145, s. 19.1(l), (t).)

§ 143B-816. Authority to provide necessary medical or surgical care.

The Division may provide any medical and surgical treatment necessary to preserve the life and health of juveniles committed to the custody of the Division; however, no surgical operation may be performed except as authorized in G.S. 148-22.2. (1998-202, s. 1(b); 2000-137, s. 1(b); 2011-145, s. 19.1(l), (t).)

§ 143B-817. Compensation to juveniles in care.

A juvenile who has been committed to the Division may be compensated for work or participation in training programs at rates approved by the Secretary within available funds. The Secretary may provide for a reasonable allowance to the juvenile for incidental personal expenses, and any balance of the juvenile's earnings remaining at the time the juvenile is released shall be paid to the juvenile or the juvenile's parent or guardian. The Division may accept grants or funds from any source to compensate juveniles under this section. (1998-202, s. 1(b); 2000-137, s. 1(b); 2011-145, s. 19.1(l), (t).)

§ 143B-818. Visits and community activities.

(a) The Division shall encourage visits by parents or guardians and responsible relatives of juveniles committed to the custody of the Division.

(b) The Division shall develop a program of home visits for juveniles in the custody of the Division. The visits shall begin after the juvenile has been in the custody of the Division for a period of at least six months. In developing the program, the Division shall adopt criteria that promote the protection of the public and the best interests of the juvenile. (1998-202, ss. 1(b), (2)c; 2000-137, s. 1(b); 2011-145, s. 19.1(l), (t).)

§ 143B-819. Regional detention services.

The Division is responsible for juvenile detention services, including the development of a statewide plan for regional juvenile detention services that offer juvenile detention care of sufficient quality to meet State standards to any juvenile requiring juvenile detention care within the State in a detention facility as follows:

(1) The Division shall plan with the counties operating a county detention facility to provide regional juvenile detention services to surrounding counties. The Division has discretion in defining the geographical boundaries of the regions based on negotiations with affected counties, distances, availability of juvenile detention care that meets State standards, and other appropriate factors.

(2) The Division may plan with any county that has space within its county jail system to use the existing space for a county detention facility when needed, if the space meets the State standards for a detention facility and meets all of the requirements of G.S. 153A-221. The use of space within the county jail system shall be constructed to ensure that juveniles are not able to converse with, see, or be seen by the adult population, and juveniles housed in a space within a county jail shall be supervised closely.

(3) The Division shall plan for and administer regional detention facilities. The Division shall carefully plan the location, architectural design, construction, and administration of a program to meet the needs of juveniles in juvenile detention care. The physical facility of a regional detention facility shall comply with all applicable State and federal standards. The programs of a regional detention facility shall comply with the standards established by the Division. (1998-202, ss. 1(b), 2(f); 1998-217, s. 57(3); 2000-137, s. 1(b); 2011-145, s. 19.1(l), (t).)

§ 143B-820. State subsidy to county detention facilities.

The Division shall administer a State subsidy program to pay a county that provides juvenile detention services and meets State standards a certain per diem per juvenile. In general, this per diem should be fifty percent (50%) of the total cost of caring for a juvenile from within the county and one hundred percent (100%) of the total cost of caring for a juvenile from another county. Any county placing a juvenile in a detention facility in another county shall pay fifty percent (50%) of the total cost of caring for the juvenile to the Division. The Division may vary the exact funding formulas to operate within existing State appropriations or other funds that may be available to pay for juvenile detention care. (1998-202, ss. 1(b), 2(f); 1998-217, s. 57(3); 2000-137, s. 1(b); 2011-145, s. 19.1(l), (t).)

§ 143B-821. Authority for implementation.

In order to allow for effective implementation of a statewide regional approach to juvenile detention, the Division may:

(1) Release or transfer a juvenile from one detention facility to another when necessary to administer the juvenile's detention appropriately.

(2) Plan with counties that operate county detention facilities to provide regional services and to upgrade physical facilities to contract with counties for services and care, and to pay State subsidies to counties providing regional juvenile detention services that meet State standards.

(3) Allow the State to reimburse law enforcement officers or other appropriate employees of local government for the costs of transportation of a juvenile to and from any juvenile detention facility.

(4) Seek funding for juvenile detention services from federal sources, and accept gifts of funds from public or private sources. (1998-202, ss. 1(b), 2(f); 1998-217, s. 57(3); 2000-137, s. 1(b); 2011-145, s. 19.1(l), (t).)

§ 143B-822. Juvenile facility monthly commitment report.

The Department of Public Safety shall report electronically on the first day of each month to the Fiscal Research Division regarding each juvenile correctional facility and the average daily population for the previous month. The report shall include (i) the average daily population for each detention center and (ii) the monthly summary of the Committed Youth Report. (2013-360, s. 16D.4.)

§ 143B-823: Reserved for future codification purposes.

§ 143B-824: Reserved for future codification purposes.

§ 143B-825: Reserved for future codification purposes.

§ 143B-826: Reserved for future codification purposes.

§ 143B-827: Reserved for future codification purposes.

§ 143B-828: Reserved for future codification purposes.

§ 143B-829: Reserved for future codification purposes.

Subpart D. Juvenile Court Services.

§ 143B-830. Duties and powers of chief court counselors.

The chief court counselor in each district appointed under G.S. 143B-806(b)(15) may:

(1) Appoint juvenile court counselors, secretaries, and other personnel authorized by the Division in accordance with the personnel policies adopted by the Division.

(2) Supervise and direct the program of juvenile intake, protective supervision, probation, and post-release supervision within the district.

(3) Provide in-service training for staff as required by the Division.

(4) Keep any records and make any reports requested by the Secretary in order to provide statewide data and information about juvenile needs and services.

(5) Delegate to a juvenile court counselor or supervisor the authority to carry out specified responsibilities of the chief court counselor to facilitate the effective operation of the district.

(6) Designate a juvenile court counselor in the district as acting chief court counselor, to act during the absence or disability of the chief court counselor. (1998-202, ss. 1(b), 2(f); 1998-217, s. 57(3); 2000-137, s. 1(b); 2009-320, s. 1; 2011-145, s. 19.1(l), (t), (ddd).)

§ 143B-831. Duties and powers of juvenile court counselors.

As the court or the chief court counselor may direct or require, all juvenile court counselors shall have the following powers and duties:

(1) Secure or arrange for any information concerning a case that the court may require before, during, or after the hearing.

(2) Prepare written reports for the use of the court.

(3) Appear and testify at court hearings.

(4) Assume custody of a juvenile as authorized by G.S. 7B-1900, or when directed by court order.

(5) Furnish each juvenile on probation or protective supervision and that juvenile's parents, guardian, or custodian with a written statement of the

juvenile's conditions of probation or protective supervision, and consult with the juvenile's parents, guardian, or custodian so that they may help the juvenile comply with the conditions.

(6)   Keep informed concerning the conduct and progress of any juvenile on probation or under protective supervision through home visits or conferences with the parents or guardian and in other ways.

(7)   See that the juvenile complies with the conditions of probation or bring to the attention of the court any juvenile who violates the juvenile's probation.

(8)   Make periodic reports to the court concerning the adjustment of any juvenile on probation or under court supervision.

(9)   Keep any records of the juvenile's work as the court may require.

(10)   Account for all funds collected from juveniles.

(11)   Serve necessary court documents pertaining to delinquent and undisciplined juvenile matters.

(12)   Assume custody of juveniles under the jurisdiction of the court when necessary for the protection of the public or the juvenile, and when necessary to carry out the responsibilities of juvenile court counselors under this section and under Chapter 7B of the General Statutes.

(13)   Use reasonable force and restraint necessary to secure custody assumed under subdivision (12) of this section.

(14)   Provide supervision for a juvenile transferred to the counselor's supervision from another court or another state, and provide supervision for any juvenile released from an institution operated by the Division when requested by the Division to do so.

(15)   Assist in the implementation of any order entered pursuant to G.S. 5A-32 as directed by a judicial official exercising jurisdiction under that section.

(16)   Assist in the development of post-release supervision and the supervision of juveniles.

(17) Screen and evaluate a complaint alleging that a juvenile is delinquent or undisciplined to determine whether the complaint should be filed as a petition.

(18) Have any other duties as the court may direct.

(19) Have any other duties as the Division may direct. (1998-202, ss. 1(b), 2(d), 2(e), 2(f); 1998-217, s. 57(3); 2000-137, s. 1(b); 2001-490, s. 2.41; 2007-168, s. 7; 2011-145, s. 19.1(l), (t).)

§ 143B-832: Reserved for future codification purposes.

§ 143B-833: Reserved for future codification purposes.

§ 143B-834: Reserved for future codification purposes.

§ 143B-835: Reserved for future codification purposes.

§ 143B-836: Reserved for future codification purposes.

§ 143B-837: Reserved for future codification purposes.

§ 143B-838: Reserved for future codification purposes.

§ 143B-839: Reserved for future codification purposes.

Subpart E. Comprehensive Juvenile Delinquency and Substance Abuse Prevention Plan.

§ 143B-840. Comprehensive Juvenile Delinquency and Substance Abuse Prevention Plan.

(a) The Division shall develop and implement a comprehensive juvenile delinquency and substance abuse prevention plan and shall coordinate with County Councils for implementation of a continuum of services and programs at the community level.

The Division shall ensure that localities are informed about best practices in juvenile delinquency and substance abuse prevention.

(b) The plan shall contain the following:

(1) Identification of the risk factors at the developmental stages of a juvenile's life that may result in delinquent behavior.

(2) Identification of the protective factors that families, schools, communities, and the State must support to reduce the risk of juvenile delinquency.

(3) Programmatic concepts that are effective in preventing juvenile delinquency and substance abuse and that should be made available as basic services in the communities, including:

a. Early intervention programs and services.

b. In-home training and community-based family counseling and parent training.

c. Adolescent and family substance abuse prevention services, including alcohol abuse prevention services, and substance abuse education.

d. Programs and activities offered before and after school hours.

e. Life and social skills training programs.

f. Classes or seminars that teach conflict resolution, problem solving, and anger management.

g. Services that provide personal advocacy, including mentoring relationships, tutors, or other caring adult programs.

(c) The Division shall cooperate with all other affected State agencies and entities in implementing this section. (1998-202, s. 1(b); 2000-137, s. 1(b); 2011-145, s. 19.1(l), (t); 2012-83, s. 13.)

§ 143B-841: Reserved for future codification purposes.

§ 143B-842: Reserved for future codification purposes.

§ 143B-843: Reserved for future codification purposes.

§ 143B-844: Reserved for future codification purposes.

Subpart F. Juvenile Crime Prevention Councils.

§ 143B-845. Legislative intent.

It is the intent of the General Assembly to prevent juveniles who are at risk from becoming delinquent. The primary intent of this Subpart is to develop community-based alternatives to youth development centers and to provide community-based delinquency, substance abuse, and gang prevention strategies and programs. Additionally, it is the intent of the General Assembly to provide noninstitutional dispositional alternatives that will protect the community and the juveniles.

These programs and services shall be planned and organized at the community level and developed in partnership with the State. These planning efforts shall include appropriate representation from local government, local public and private agencies serving juveniles and their families, local business leaders, citizens with an interest in youth problems, youth representatives, and others as may be appropriate in a particular community. The planning bodies at the local level shall be the Juvenile Crime Prevention Councils. (1998-202, s. 1(b); 2000-137, s. 1(b); 2001-95, s. 5; 2008-56, s. 2; 2011-145, s. 19.1(t), (eee).)

§ 143B-846. Creation; method of appointment; membership; chair and vice-chair.

(a)   As a prerequisite for a county receiving funding for juvenile court services and delinquency prevention programs, the board of commissioners of a county shall appoint a Juvenile Crime Prevention Council. Each County Council is a continuation of the corresponding Council created under G.S. 147-33.61. The County Council shall consist of not more than 26 members and should include, if possible, the following:

(1)   The local school superintendent, or that person's designee;

(2)   A chief of police in the county;

(3)   The local sheriff, or that person's designee;

(4) The district attorney, or that person's designee;

(5) The chief court counselor, or that person's designee;

(6) The director of the area mental health, developmental disabilities, and substance abuse authority, or that person's designee;

(7) The director of the county department of social services, or consolidated human services agency, or that person's designee;

(8) The county manager, or that person's designee;

(9) A substance abuse professional;

(10) A member of the faith community;

(11) A county commissioner;

(12) Two persons under the age of 18 years, one of whom is a member of the State Youth Council;

(13) A juvenile defense attorney;

(14) The chief district court judge, or a judge designated by the chief district court judge;

(15) A member of the business community;

(16) The local health director, or that person's designee;

(17) A representative from the United Way or other nonprofit agency;

(18) A representative of a local parks and recreation program; and

(19) Up to seven members of the public to be appointed by the board of commissioners of a county.

The board of commissioners of a county shall modify the County Council's membership as necessary to ensure that the members reflect the racial and socioeconomic diversity of the community and to minimize potential conflicts of interest by members.

(b) Two or more counties may establish a multicounty Juvenile Crime Prevention Council under subsection (a) of this section. The membership shall be representative of each participating county.

(c) The members of the County Council shall elect annually the chair and vice-chair. (1998-202, s. 1(b); 2000-137, s. 1(b); 2001-199, s. 1; 2011-145, s. 19.1(t).)

§ 143B-847. Terms of appointment.

Each member of a County Council shall serve for a term of two years, except for initial terms as provided in this section. Each member's term is a continuation of that member's term under G.S. 147-33.62. Members may be reappointed. The initial terms of appointment began January 1, 1999. In order to provide for staggered terms, persons appointed for the positions designated in subdivisions (9), (10), (12), (15), (17), and (18) of G.S. 143B-846(a) were appointed for an initial term ending on June 30, 2000. The initial term of the second member added to each County Council pursuant to G.S. 143B-846(a)(12) shall begin on July 1, 2001, and end on June 30, 2002. After the initial terms, persons appointed for the positions designated in subdivisions (9), (10), (12), (15), (17), and (18) of G.S. 143B-846(a) shall be appointed for two-year terms, beginning on July 1. All other persons appointed to the Council were appointed for an initial term ending on June 30, 2001, and, after those initial terms, persons shall be appointed for two-year terms beginning on July 1. (1998-202, s. 1(b); 1999-423, s. 15; 2000-137, s. 1(b); 2001-199, s. 2; 2011-145, s. 19.1(t), (fff).)

§ 143B-848. Vacancies; removal.

Appointments to fill vacancies shall be for the remainder of the former member's term.

Members shall be removed only for malfeasance or nonfeasance as determined by the board of county commissioners. (1998-202, s. 1(b); 2000-137, s. 1(b); 2011-145, s. 19.1(t).)

§ 143B-849. Meetings; quorum.

County Councils shall meet at least bimonthly, or more often if a meeting is called by the chair.

A majority of members constitutes a quorum. (1998-202, s. 1(b); 1999-423, s. 16; 2000-137, s. 1(b); 2011-145, s. 19.1(t).)

§ 143B-850. Compensation of members.

Members of County Councils shall receive no compensation but may receive a per diem in an amount established by the board of county commissioners. (1998-202, s. 1(b); 2000-137, s. 1(b); 2011-145, s. 19.1(t).)

§ 143B-851. Powers and duties.

(a) Each County Council shall review annually the needs of juveniles in the county who are at risk of delinquency or who have been adjudicated undisciplined or delinquent and the resources available to address those needs. In particular, each County Council shall assess the needs of juveniles in the county who are at risk or who have been associated with gangs or gang activity, and the local resources that are established to address those needs. The Council shall develop and advertise a request for proposal process and submit a written plan of action for the expenditure of juvenile sanction and prevention funds to the board of county commissioners for its approval. Upon the county's authorization, the plan shall be submitted to the Division for final approval and subsequent implementation.

(b) Each County Council shall ensure that appropriate intermediate dispositional options are available and shall prioritize funding for dispositions of intermediate and community-level sanctions for court-adjudicated juveniles under minimum standards adopted by the Division.

(c) On an ongoing basis, each County Council shall:

(1) Assess the needs of juveniles in the community, evaluate the adequacy of resources available to meet those needs, and develop or propose ways to address unmet needs.

(2) Evaluate the performance of juvenile services and programs in the community. The Council shall evaluate each funded program as a condition of continued funding.

(3) Increase public awareness of the causes of delinquency and of strategies to reduce the problem.

(4) Develop strategies to intervene and appropriately respond to and treat the needs of juveniles at risk of delinquency through appropriate risk assessment instruments.

(5) Provide funds for services for treatment, counseling, or rehabilitation for juveniles and their families. These services may include court-ordered parenting responsibility classes.

(6) Plan for the establishment of a permanent funding stream for delinquency prevention services.

(7) Develop strategies to intervene and appropriately respond to the needs of juveniles who have been associated with gang activity or who are at risk of becoming associated with gang activity.

(d) The Councils may examine the benefits of joint program development between counties within the same judicial district. (1998-202, s. 1(b); 2000-137, s. 1(b); 2008-56, s. 3; 2011-145, s. 19.1(l), (t).)

§ 143B-852. Department of Public Safety to report on Juvenile Crime Prevention Council grants.

(a) On or before February 1 of each year, the Department of Public Safety shall submit to the Chairs of the Joint Legislative Commission on Governmental Operations and the Chairs of the Senate and House of Representatives Appropriations Subcommittees on Justice and Public Safety a list of the recipients of the grants awarded, or preapproved for award, from funds appropriated to the Department for local Juvenile Crime Prevention Council (JCPC) grants, including the following information:

(1) The amount of the grant awarded.

(2) The membership of the local committee or council administering the award funds on the local level.

(3) The type of program funded.

(4) A short description of the local services, programs, or projects that will receive funds.

(5) Identification of any programs that received grant funds at one time but for which funding has been eliminated by the Department.

(6) The number of at-risk, diverted, and adjudicated juveniles served by each county.

(7) The Department's actions to ensure that county JCPCs prioritize funding for dispositions of intermediate and community-level sanctions for court-adjudicated juveniles under minimum standards adopted by the Department.

(8) The total cost for each funded program, including the cost per juvenile and the essential elements of the program.

(b) On or before February 1 of each year, the Department of Public Safety shall send to the Fiscal Research Division of the Legislative Services Commission an electronic copy of the list and information required under subsection (a) of this section. (2013-360, s. 16D.2(a).)

§ 143B-853: Reserved for future codification purposes.

§ 143B-854: Reserved for future codification purposes.

§ 143B-855: Reserved for future codification purposes.

§ 143B-856: Reserved for future codification purposes.

§ 143B-857: Reserved for future codification purposes.

§ 143B-858: Reserved for future codification purposes.

§ 143B-859: Reserved for future codification purposes.

§ 143B-860: Reserved for future codification purposes.

§ 143B-861: Reserved for future codification purposes.

§ 143B-862: Reserved for future codification purposes.

§ 143B-863: Reserved for future codification purposes.

§ 143B-864: Reserved for future codification purposes.

§ 143B-865: Reserved for future codification purposes.

§ 143B-866: Reserved for future codification purposes.

§ 143B-867: Reserved for future codification purposes.

§ 143B-868: Reserved for future codification purposes.

§ 143B-869: Reserved for future codification purposes.

§ 143B-870: Reserved for future codification purposes.

§ 143B-871: Reserved for future codification purposes.

§ 143B-872: Reserved for future codification purposes.

§ 143B-873: Reserved for future codification purposes.

§ 143B-874: Reserved for future codification purposes.

§ 143B-875: Reserved for future codification purposes.

§ 143B-876: Reserved for future codification purposes.

§ 143B-877: Reserved for future codification purposes.

§ 143B-878: Reserved for future codification purposes.

§ 143B-879: Reserved for future codification purposes.

§ 143B-880: Reserved for future codification purposes.

§ 143B-881: Reserved for future codification purposes.

§ 143B-882: Reserved for future codification purposes.

§ 143B-883: Reserved for future codification purposes.

§ 143B-884: Reserved for future codification purposes.

§ 143B-885: Reserved for future codification purposes.

§ 143B-886: Reserved for future codification purposes.

§ 143B-887: Reserved for future codification purposes.

§ 143B-888: Reserved for future codification purposes.

§ 143B-889: Reserved for future codification purposes.

§ 143B-890: Reserved for future codification purposes.

§ 143B-891: Reserved for future codification purposes.

§ 143B-892: Reserved for future codification purposes.

§ 143B-893: Reserved for future codification purposes.

§ 143B-894: Reserved for future codification purposes.

§ 143B-895: Reserved for future codification purposes.

§ 143B-896: Reserved for future codification purposes.

§ 143B-897: Reserved for future codification purposes.

§ 143B-898: Reserved for future codification purposes.

§ 143B-899: Reserved for future codification purposes.

Part 4. Division of Law Enforcement.

§ 143B-900. State Capitol Police Section - powers and duties.
(a) Section Established. - There is hereby established, within the Law Enforcement Division of the Department of Public Safety, the State Capitol Police Section, which shall be organized and staffed in accordance with applicable laws and regulations and within the limits of authorized appropriations.

(b) Purpose. - The State Capitol Police Section shall serve as a special police agency of the Department of Public Safety. The Chief of the State Capitol Police, appointed by the Secretary pursuant to G.S. 143B-602, with the approval of the Governor, may appoint as special police officers such reliable persons as he may deem necessary.

(c) Appointment of Officers. - Special police officers appointed pursuant to this section may not exercise the power of arrest until they shall take an oath, to be administered by any person authorized to administer oaths, as required by law.

(d) Jurisdiction of Officers. - Each special police officer of the State Capitol Police shall have the same power of arrest as the police officers of the City of Raleigh. Such authority may be exercised within the same territorial jurisdiction as exercised by the police officers of the City of Raleigh, and in addition thereto the authority of a deputy sheriff may be exercised on property owned, leased, or maintained by the State located in the County of Wake.

(e) Reserved for future codification purposes.

(f) Public Safety. - The Chief of the State Capitol Police, or the Chief's designee, shall exercise at all times those means that, in the opinion of the Chief or the designee, may be effective in protecting all State buildings and grounds, except for the State legislative buildings and grounds as defined in G.S. 120-32.1(d), and the persons within those buildings and grounds from fire, bombs, bomb threats, or any other emergency or potentially hazardous conditions, including both the ordering and control of the evacuation of those buildings and grounds. The Chief, or the Chief's designee, may employ the assistance of other available law enforcement agencies and emergency agencies to aid and assist in evacuations of those buildings and grounds. (2009-451, s. 17.3(f); 2011-145, s. 19.1(g), (u), (y).)

§§ 143B-901 through 143B-999: Reserved for future codification purposes.

Part 5. Division of Emergency Management.

Subpart A. Emergency Management Division.

§ 143B-1000. Division of Emergency Management of the Department of Public Safety.

(a)   There is established, within the Department of Public Safety, the Division of Emergency Management, which shall be organized and staffed in accordance with applicable laws and regulations and within the limits of authorized appropriations.

(b)   The Division of Emergency Management shall have the following powers and duties:

(1)   Repealed by Session Laws 2011-145, s. 19.1(aa), effective January 1, 2012.

(2)   To exercise the powers and duties conferred on it by Chapter 166A of the General Statutes.

(3)   To exercise any other powers vested by law. (2009-397, s. 3; 2011-145, s. 19.1(g), (w), (aa).)

§ 143B-1001: Reserved for future codification purposes.

§ 143B-1002: Reserved for future codification purposes.

§ 143B-1003: Reserved for future codification purposes.

§ 143B-1004: Reserved for future codification purposes.

§ 143B-1005: Reserved for future codification purposes.

§ 143B-1006: Reserved for future codification purposes.

§ 143B-1007: Reserved for future codification purposes.

§ 143B-1008: Reserved for future codification purposes.

§ 143B-1009: Reserved for future codification purposes.

Subpart B. North Carolina Center for Missing Persons.

§ 143B-1010. North Carolina Center for Missing Persons established.

There is established within the Department of Public Safety the North Carolina Center for Missing Persons, which shall be organized and staffed in accordance with applicable laws. The purpose of the Center is to serve as a central repository for information regarding missing persons and missing children, with special emphasis on missing children. The Center may utilize the Federal Bureau of Investigation/National Crime Information Center's missing person computerized file (hereinafter referred to as FBI/NCIC) through the use of the Police Information Network in the North Carolina Department of Justice. (1985, c. 765, s. 1; 1985 (Reg. Sess., 1986), c. 1000, s. 1; 2011-145, s. 19.1(g), (w).)

§ 143B-1011. Definitions.

For the purpose of this Part:

(1) "Missing child" means a juvenile as defined in G.S. 7B-101 whose location has not been determined, who has been reported as missing to a law-enforcement agency, and whose parent's, spouse's, guardian's or legal custodian's temporary or permanent residence is in North Carolina or is believed to be in North Carolina.

(2) "Missing person" means any individual who is 18 years of age or older, whose temporary or permanent residence is in North Carolina, or is believed to be in North Carolina, whose location has not been determined, and who has been reported as missing to a law-enforcement agency.

(3) "Missing person report" is a report prepared on a prescribed form for transmitting information about a missing person or a missing child to an appropriate law-enforcement agency. (1985 (Reg. Sess., 1986), c. 1000, s. 1; 1998-202, s. 13(mm); 2011-145, s. 19.1(w).)

§ 143B-1012. Control of the Center.

The Center is under the direction of the Secretary of the Department of Public Safety and may be organized and structured in a manner as the Secretary deems appropriate to ensure that the objectives of the Center are achieved. The Secretary may employ those Center personnel as the General Assembly may authorize and provide funding for. (1985 (Reg. Sess., 1986), c. 1000, s. 1; 2011-145, s. 19.1(g), (w).)

§ 143B-1013. Secretary to adopt rules.

The Secretary shall adopt rules prescribing:

(1)   procedures for accepting and disseminating information maintained at the Center;

(2)   the confidentiality of the data and information, including the missing person report, maintained by the Center;

(3)   the proper disposition of all obsolete data, including the missing person report; provided, data for an individual who has reached the age of 18 and remains missing must be preserved;

(4)   procedures allowing a communication link with the Police Information Network and the FBI/NCIC's missing person file to ensure compliance with FBI/NCIC policies; and

(5)   forms, including but not limited to a missing person report, considered necessary for the efficient and proper operation of the Center. (1985 (Reg. Sess., 1986), c. 1000, s. 1; 2011-145, s. 19.1(w).)

§ 143B-1014. Submission of missing person reports to the Center.

Any parent, spouse, guardian, legal custodian, or person responsible for the supervision of the missing individual may submit a missing person report to the Center of any missing child or missing person, regardless of the circumstances, after having first submitted a missing person report on the individual to the law-enforcement agency having jurisdiction of the area in which the individual became or is believed to have become missing, regardless of the circumstances. (1985 (Reg. Sess., 1986), c. 1000, s. 1; 2007-469, s. 1; 2011-145, s. 19.1(w).)

§ 143B-1015. Dissemination of missing persons data by law-enforcement agencies.

A law-enforcement agency, upon receipt of a missing person report by a parent, spouse, guardian, legal custodian, or person responsible for the supervision of the missing individual shall immediately make arrangements for the entry of data about the missing person or missing child into the national missing persons file in accordance with criteria set forth by the FBI/NCIC, immediately inform all of its on-duty law-enforcement officers of the missing person report, initiate a statewide broadcast to all appropriate law-enforcement agencies to be on the lookout for the individual, and transmit a copy of the report to the Center. No law enforcement agency shall establish or maintain any policy which requires the observance of any waiting period before accepting a missing person report.

If the report involves a missing child and the report meets the criteria established in G.S. 143B-1021(b), as soon as practicable after receipt of the report, the law enforcement agency shall notify the Center and the National Center for Missing and Exploited Children of the relevant data about the missing child. (1985 (Reg. Sess., 1986), c. 1000, s. 1; 2002-126, s. 18.7(a); 2003-191, s. 1; 2007-469, s. 2; 2011-145, s. 19.1(w), (yy).)

§ 143B-1016. Responsibilities of Center.

The Center shall:

(1) Assist local law-enforcement agencies with entering data about missing persons or missing children into the national missing persons file, ensure that proper entry criteria have been met as set forth by the FBI/NCIC, and confirm entry of the data about the missing persons or missing children;

(2) Gather and distribute information and data on missing children and missing persons;

(3) Encourage research and study of missing children and missing persons, including the prevention of child abduction and the prevention of the exploitation of missing children;

(4) Serve as a statewide resource center to assist local communities in programs and initiatives to prevent child abduction and the exploitation of missing children;

(5) Continue increasing public awareness of the reasons why children are missing and vulnerability of missing children;

(6) Achieve maximum cooperation with other agencies of the State, with agencies of other states and the federal government and with the National Center for Missing and Exploited Children in rendering assistance to missing children and missing persons and their parents, guardians, spouses, or legal custodians; and cooperate with interstate and federal efforts to identify deceased individuals;

(7) Develop and maintain the AMBER Alert System as created by G.S. 143B-1021.

(8) Forward the appropriate information to the Police Information Network to assist it in maintaining and publishing a bulletin of currently missing children and missing persons;

(9) Maintain a directory of existing public and private agencies, groups, and individuals that provide effective assistance to families in the areas of prevention of child abduction, location of missing children and missing persons, and follow-up services to the child or person and family, as determined by the Secretary of Public Safety;

(10) Annually compile and publish reports on the actual number of children and persons missing each year, listing the categories and causes, when known, for the disappearances;

(11) Provide follow-up referrals for services to missing children or persons and their families;

(12) Maintain a toll-free 1-800 telephone service that will be in service at all times; and

(13) Perform such other activities that the Secretary of Public Safety considers necessary to carry out the intent of its mandate. (1985 (Reg. Sess., 1986), c. 1000, s. 1; 2002-126, s. 18.7(b); 2003-191, s. 2; 2011-145, s. 19.1(g), (w), (zz).)

§ 143B-1017. Duty of individuals to notify Center and law-enforcement agency when missing person has been located.

Any parent, spouse, guardian, legal custodian, or person responsible for the supervision of the missing individual who submits a missing person report to a law-enforcement agency or to the Center, shall immediately notify the law-enforcement agency and the Center of any individual whose location has been determined. The Center shall confirm the deletion of the individual's records from the FBI/NCIC's missing person file, as long as there are no grounds for criminal prosecution, and follow up with the local law-enforcement agency having jurisdiction of the records. (1985 (Reg. Sess., 1986), c. 1000, s. 1; 2007-469, s. 3; 2011-145, s. 19.1(w).)

§ 143B-1018. Release of information by Center.

The following may make inquiries of, and receive data or information from, the Center:

(1) Any police, law-enforcement, or criminal justice agency investigating a report of a missing or unidentified person or child, whether living or deceased.

(2) A court, upon a finding by the court that access to the data, information, or records of the Center may be necessary for the determination of an issue before the court.

(3) Any district attorney of a prosecutorial district as defined in G.S. 7A-60 in this State or the district attorney's designee or representative.

(4) Any person engaged in bona fide research when approved by the Secretary; provided, no names or addresses may be supplied to this person.

(5) Any other person authorized by the Secretary of the Department of Public Safety pursuant to G.S. 143B-1013. (1985 (Reg. Sess., 1986), c. 1000, s. 1; 1987, c. 282, s. 28; 1987 (Reg. Sess., 1988), c. 1037, s. 119; 2011-145, s. 19.1(g), (w), (aaa).)

§ 143B-1019. Provision of toll-free service; instructions to callers; communication with law-enforcement agencies.

The Center shall provide a toll-free telephone line for anyone to report the disappearance of any individual or the sighting of any missing child or missing person. The Center personnel shall instruct the caller, in the case of a report concerning the disappearance of an individual, of the requirements contained in G.S. 143B-1014 of first having to submit a missing person report on the individual to the law-enforcement agency having jurisdiction of the area in which the individual became or is believed to have become missing. Any law-enforcement agency may retrieve information imparted to the Center by means of this phone line. The Center shall directly communicate any report of a sighting of a missing person or a missing child to the law-enforcement agency having jurisdiction in the area of disappearance or sighting. (1985 (Reg. Sess., 1986), c. 1000, s. 1; 2007-469, s. 4; 2011-145, s. 19.1(w), (bbb).)

§ 143B-1020. Improper release of information; penalty.

Any person working under the supervision of the Director of Victims and Justice Services who knowingly and willfully releases, or authorizes the release of, any data, information, or records maintained or possessed by the Center to any agency, entity, or person other than as specifically permitted by Subpart B or in violation of any rule adopted by the Secretary is guilty of a Class 2 misdemeanor. (1985 (Reg. Sess., 1986), c. 1000, s. 1; 1993, c. 539, s. 1050; 1994, Ex. Sess., c. 24, s. 14(c); 2011-145, s. 19.1(w).)

§ 143B-1021. North Carolina AMBER Alert System established.

(a) There is established within the North Carolina Center for Missing Persons the AMBER Alert System. The purpose of AMBER Alert is to provide a statewide system for the rapid dissemination of information regarding abducted children.

(b)   The AMBER Alert System shall make every effort to disseminate information on missing children as quickly as possible when the following criteria are met:

(1)   The child is 17 years of age or younger;

(2)   The abduction is not known or suspected to be by a parent of the child, unless the child's life is suspected to be in danger of injury or death;

(3)   The child is believed:

a.   To have been abducted, or

b.   To be in danger of injury or death;

(4)   The child is not a runaway or voluntarily missing; and

(5)   The abduction has been reported to and investigated by a law enforcement agency.

If the abduction of the child is known or suspected to be by a parent of the child, the Center, in its discretion, may disseminate information through the AMBER Alert System if the child is believed to be in danger of injury or death.

(c)   The Center shall adopt guidelines and develop procedures for the statewide implementation of the AMBER Alert System and shall provide education and training to encourage radio and television broadcasters to participate in the System. The Center shall work with the Department of Justice in developing training material regarding the AMBER Alert System for law enforcement, broadcasters, and community interest groups.

(d)   The Center shall consult with the Department of Transportation and develop a procedure for the use of overhead permanent changeable message signs to provide information on the abduction of a child meeting the criteria established in subsection (b) of this section, when information is available that would enable motorists to assist law enforcement in the recovery of the missing child. The Center and the Department of Transportation shall develop guidelines for the content, length, and frequency of any message to be placed on an overhead permanent changeable message sign.

(e)   The Center shall consult with the Division of Emergency Management, in the Department of Public Safety, to develop a procedure for the use of the Emergency Alert System to provide information on the abduction of a child meeting the criteria established in subsection (b) of this section.

(f)   The Department of Public Safety, on behalf of the Center, may accept grants, contributions, devises, and gifts, which shall be kept in a separate fund, which shall be nonreverting, and shall be used to fund the operations of the Center and the AMBER Alert System. (2002-126, s. 18.7(c); 2003-191, s. 3; 2011-145, s. 19.1(g), (w); 2011-284, s. 103.)

§ 143B-1022. North Carolina Silver Alert System established.

(a)   There is established within the North Carolina Center for Missing Persons the Silver Alert System. The purpose of the Silver Alert System is to provide a statewide system for the rapid dissemination of information regarding a missing person or missing child who is believed to be suffering from dementia or other cognitive impairment.

(b)   If the Center receives a report that involves a missing person or missing child who is believed to be suffering from dementia or other cognitive impairment, for the protection of the missing person or missing child from potential abuse or other physical harm, neglect, or exploitation, the Center shall issue an alert providing for rapid dissemination of information statewide regarding the missing person or missing child. The Center shall make every effort to disseminate the information as quickly as possible when the person's or child's status as missing has been reported to a law enforcement agency.

(c)   The Center shall adopt guidelines and develop procedures for issuing an alert for missing persons and missing children believed to be suffering from dementia or other cognitive impairment and shall provide education and training to encourage radio and television broadcasters to participate in the alert. The guidelines and procedures shall ensure that specific health information about the missing person or missing child is not made public through the alert or otherwise.

(d) The Center shall consult with the Department of Transportation and develop a procedure for the use of overhead permanent changeable message signs to provide information on the missing person or missing child meeting the criteria of this section when information is available that would enable motorists to assist in the recovery of the missing person or missing child. The Center and the Department of Transportation shall develop guidelines for the content, length, and frequency of any message to be placed on an overhead permanent changeable message sign. (2007-469, s. 5; 2008-83, s. 1; 2009-143, s. 1; 2010-96, s. 16; 2011-145, s. 19.1(w).)

§ 143B-1023: Reserved for future codification purposes.

§ 143B-1024: Reserved for future codification purposes.

§ 143B-1025: Reserved for future codification purposes.

§ 143B-1026: Reserved for future codification purposes.

§ 143B-1027: Reserved for future codification purposes.

§ 143B-1028: Reserved for future codification purposes.

§ 143B-1029: Reserved for future codification purposes.

Subpart C. Civil Air Patrol

§ 143B-1030. Civil Air Patrol Section - powers and duties.

(a) There is hereby established, within the Department of Public Safety the Civil Air Patrol Section, which shall be organized and staffed in accordance with this Subpart and within the limits of authorized appropriations.

(b) The Civil Air Patrol Section shall:

(1) Receive and supervise the expenditure of State funds provided by the General Assembly or otherwise secured by the State of North Carolina for the use and benefit of the North Carolina Wing-Civil Air Patrol;

(2) Supervise the maintenance and use of State provided facilities and equipment by the North Carolina Wing-Civil Air Patrol;

(3) Receive, from State and local governments, their agencies, and private citizens, requests for State approval for assistance by the North Carolina Wing-Civil Air Patrol in natural or man-made disasters or other emergency situations. Such State requested and approved missions shall be approved or denied by the Secretary of Public Safety or his designee under such rules, terms and conditions as are adopted by the Department. (1979, c. 516, s. 1; 2011-145, s. 19.1(g), (w), (bb2); 2011-391, s. 43(k).)

§ 143B-1031. Personnel and benefits.

(a) The Wing Commander of the North Carolina Wing-Civil Air Patrol shall certify to the Secretary or his designee those members who are in good standing as members eligible for benefits. The Wing Commander shall provide the Secretary with two copies of the certification. The Secretary shall acknowledge receipt of, sign, and date both copies and return one to the Wing Commander. The Wing Commander shall, in the form and manner provided above, notify the Secretary of any changes in personnel within 30 days thereof. Upon the Secretary's signature, those members listed on the certification shall be eligible for the benefits listed below.

(b) Those members of the North Carolina Wing-Civil Air Patrol certified under subsection (a) of this section shall be deemed and considered employees of the Department of Public Safety for workers' compensation purposes, and for no other purposes, while performing duties incident to a State approved mission. Such period of employment shall not extend to said members wile performing duties incident to a United States Air Force authorized mission or any other Wing activities. (1979, c. 516, s. 1; c. 714, s. 2; 1993, c. 389, s. 2; 2011-145, s. 19.1(g), (w).)

§ 143B-1032. State liability.

Unless otherwise specifically provided, the members of the North Carolina Wing-Civil Air Patrol shall serve without compensation and shall not be entitled to the benefits of the retirement system for teachers and State employees as set forth in Chapter 135 of the General Statutes. The provisions of Article 31 of Chapter 143 of the General Statutes, with respect to tort claims against State departments and agencies, shall not be applicable to the activities of the North Carolina Wing-Civil Air Patrol, unless those activities are State-approved issions which are not covered by the Federal Tort Claims Act. The State shall not in any manner be liable for any of the contracts, debts, or obligations of the said organization. (1979, c. 516, s. 1; 1993, c. 389, s. 1; 2011-145, s. 19.1(w).)

§ 143B-1033: Reserved for future codification purposes.

§ 143B-1034: Reserved for future codification purposes.

§ 143B-1035: Reserved for future codification purposes.

§ 143B-1036: Reserved for future codification purposes.

§ 143B-1037: Reserved for future codification purposes.

§ 143B-1038: Reserved for future codification purposes.

§ 143B-1039: Reserved for future codification purposes.

§ 143B-1040: Reserved for future codification purposes.

§ 143B-1041: Reserved for future codification purposes.

§ 143B-1042: Reserved for future codification purposes.

§ 143B-1043: Reserved for future codification purposes.

§ 143B-1044: Reserved for future codification purposes.

§ 143B-1045: Reserved for future codification purposes.

§ 143B-1046: Reserved for future codification purposes.

§ 143B-1047: Reserved for future codification purposes.

§ 143B-1048: Reserved for future codification purposes.

§ 143B-1049: Reserved for future codification purposes.

§ 143B-1050: Reserved for future codification purposes.

§ 143B-1051: Reserved for future codification purposes.

§ 143B-1052: Reserved for future codification purposes.

§ 143B-1053: Reserved for future codification purposes.

§ 143B-1054: Reserved for future codification purposes.

§ 143B-1055: Reserved for future codification purposes.

§ 143B-1056: Reserved for future codification purposes.

§ 143B-1057: Reserved for future codification purposes.

§ 143B-1058: Reserved for future codification purposes.

§ 143B-1059: Reserved for future codification purposes.

§ 143B-1060: Reserved for future codification purposes.

§ 143B-1061: Reserved for future codification purposes.

§ 143B-1062: Reserved for future codification purposes.

§ 143B-1063: Reserved for future codification purposes.

§ 143B-1064: Reserved for future codification purposes.

§ 143B-1065: Reserved for future codification purposes.

§ 143B-1066: Reserved for future codification purposes.

§ 143B-1067: Reserved for future codification purposes.

§ 143B-1068: Reserved for future codification purposes.

§ 143B-1069: Reserved for future codification purposes.

§ 143B-1070: Reserved for future codification purposes.

§ 143B-1071: Reserved for future codification purposes.

§ 143B-1072: Reserved for future codification purposes.

§ 143B-1073: Reserved for future codification purposes.

§ 143B-1074: Reserved for future codification purposes.

§ 143B-1075: Reserved for future codification purposes.

§ 143B-1076: Reserved for future codification purposes.

§ 143B-1077: Reserved for future codification purposes.

§ 143B-1078: Reserved for future codification purposes.

§ 143B-1079: Reserved for future codification purposes.

§ 143B-1080: Reserved for future codification purposes.

§ 143B-1081: Reserved for future codification purposes.

§ 143B-1082: Reserved for future codification purposes.

§ 143B-1083: Reserved for future codification purposes.

§ 143B-1084: Reserved for future codification purposes.

§ 143B-1085: Reserved for future codification purposes.

§ 143B-1086: Reserved for future codification purposes.

§ 143B-1087: Reserved for future codification purposes.

§ 143B-1088: Reserved for future codification purposes.

§ 143B-1089: Reserved for future codification purposes.

§ 143B-1090: Reserved for future codification purposes.

§ 143B-1091: Reserved for future codification purposes.

§ 143B-1092: Reserved for future codification purposes.

§ 143B-1093: Reserved for future codification purposes.

§ 143B-1094: Reserved for future codification purposes.

§ 143B-1095: Reserved for future codification purposes.

§ 143B-1096: Reserved for future codification purposes.

§ 143B-1097: Reserved for future codification purposes.

§ 143B-1098: Reserved for future codification purposes.

§ 143B-1099: Reserved for future codification purposes.

Part 6. Division of Administration.

Subpart A. Governor's Crime Commission.

§ 143B-1100. Governor's Crime Commission - creation; composition; terms; meetings, etc.

(a)   There is hereby created the Governor's Crime Commission of the Department of Public Safety. The Commission shall consist of 37 voting members and five nonvoting members. The composition of the Commission shall be as follows:

(1)   The voting members shall be:

a.   The Governor, the Chief Justice of the Supreme Court of North Carolina (or the Chief Justice's designee), the Attorney General, the Director of the Administrative Office of the Courts, the Secretary of the Department of Health and Human Services, the Secretary of Public Safety (or the Secretary's designee), and the Superintendent of Public Instruction;

b. A judge of superior court, a judge of district court specializing in juvenile matters, a chief district court judge, a clerk of superior court, and a district attorney;

c. A defense attorney, three sheriffs (one of whom shall be from a "high crime area"), three police executives (one of whom shall be from a "high crime area"), eight citizens (two with knowledge of juvenile delinquency and the public school system, two of whom shall be under the age of 21 at the time of their appointment, one advocate for victims of all crimes, one representative from a domestic violence or sexual assault program, one representative of a "private juvenile delinquency program," and one in the discretion of the Governor), three county commissioners or county officials, and three mayors or municipal officials;

d. Two members of the North Carolina House of Representatives and two members of the North Carolina Senate.

(2) The nonvoting members shall be the Director of the State Bureau of Investigation, the Deputy Director of the Division of Juvenile Justice of the Department of Public Safety who is responsible for Intervention/Prevention programs, the Deputy Director of the Division of Juvenile Justice of the Department of Public Safety who is responsible for Youth Development programs, the Section Chief of the Section of Prisons of the Division of Adult Correction and the Section Chief of the Section of Community Corrections of the Division of Adult Correction.

(b) The membership of the Commission shall be selected as follows:

(1) The following members shall serve by virtue of their office: the Governor, the Chief Justice of the Supreme Court, the Attorney General, the Director of the Administrative Office of the Courts, the Secretary of the Department of Health and Human Services, the Secretary of Public Safety, the Director of the State Bureau of Investigation, the Section Chief of the Section of Prisons of the Division of Adult Correction, the Section Chief of the Section of Community Corrections of the Division of Adult Correction, the Deputy Director who is responsible for Intervention/Prevention of the Division of Juvenile Justice of the Department of Public Safety, the Deputy Director who is responsible for Youth Development of the Division of Juvenile Justice of the Department of Public Safety, and the Superintendent of Public Instruction. Should the Chief Justice of the Supreme Court choose not to serve, his alternate shall be selected by the Governor from a list submitted by the Chief Justice which list

must contain no less than three nominees from the membership of the Supreme Court.

(2) The following members shall be appointed by the Governor: the district attorney, the defense attorney, the three sheriffs, the three police executives, the eight citizens, the three county commissioners or county officials, the three mayors or municipal officials.

(3) The following members shall be appointed by the Governor from a list submitted by the Chief Justice of the Supreme Court, which list shall contain no less than three nominees for each position and which list must be submitted within 30 days after the occurrence of any vacancy in the judicial membership: the judge of superior court, the clerk of superior court, the judge of district court specializing in juvenile matters, and the chief district court judge.

(4) The two members of the House of Representatives provided by subdivision (a)(1)d. of this section shall be appointed by the Speaker of the House of Representatives and the two members of the Senate provided by subdivision (a)(1)d. of this section shall be appointed by the President Pro Tempore of the Senate. These members shall perform the advisory review of the State plan for the General Assembly as permitted by section 206 of the Crime Control Act of 1976 (Public Law 94-503).

(5) The Governor may serve as chairman, designating a vice-chairman to serve at his pleasure, or he may designate a chairman and vice-chairman both of whom shall serve at his pleasure.

(c) The initial members of the Commission shall be those appointed under subsection (b) above, which appointments shall be made by March 1, 1977. The terms of the present members of the Governor's Commission on Law and Order shall expire on February 28, 1977. Effective March 1, 1977, the Governor shall appoint members, other than those serving by virtue of their office, to serve staggered terms; seven shall be appointed for one-year terms, seven for two-year terms, and seven for three-year terms. At the end of their respective terms of office their successors shall be appointed for terms of three years and until their successors are appointed and qualified. The Commission members from the House and Senate shall serve two-year terms effective March 1, of each odd-numbered year; and they shall not be disqualified from Commission membership because of failure to seek or attain reelection to the General Assembly, but resignation or removal from office as a member of the General Assembly shall constitute resignation or removal from the Commission. Any other Commission member no longer serving in the office from which he qualified for appointment shall be disqualified from membership on the Commission. Any appointment to fill a vacancy on the Commission created by the resignation, dismissal, death, disability, or disqualification of a member shall be for the balance of the unexpired term.

(d) The Governor shall have the power to remove any member from the Commission for misfeasance, malfeasance or nonfeasance.

(e) The Commission shall meet quarterly and at other times at the call of the chairman or upon written request of at least eight of the members. A majority of the voting members shall constitute a quorum for the transaction of business.

(f) The Commission shall be treated as a board for purposes of Chapter 138A of the General Statutes. (1965, c. 663; 1977, c. 11, s. 1; 1981, c. 467, ss. 1-5; 1981 (Reg. Sess., 1982), c. 1189, s. 4; 1991, c. 739, s. 32; 1997-443, s. 11A.118(a); 1998-170, s. 3; 1998-202, s. 4(aa); 1999-423, s. 11; 2000-137, s. 4(ee); 2001-95, s. 6; 2001-487, s. 47(g); 2007-454, s. 1; 2010-169, s. 11; 2011-145, s. 19.1(g), (i)-(l), (x); 2012-83, s. 54; 2013-410, s. 13.)

§ 143B-1101. Governor's Crime Commission - powers and duties.

(a) The Governor's Crime Commission shall have the following powers and duties:

(1) To serve, along with its adjunct committees, as the chief advisory board to the Governor and to the Secretary of the Department of Public Safety on matters pertaining to the criminal justice system.

(2) To recommend a comprehensive statewide plan for the improvement of criminal justice throughout the State which is consistent with and serves to foster the following established goals of the criminal justice system:

a. To reduce crime,

b. To protect individual rights,

c. To achieve justice,

d. To increase efficiency in the criminal justice system,

e. To promote public safety,

f. To provide for the administration of a fair and humane system which offers reasonable opportunities for adjudicated offenders to develop progressively responsible behavior, and

g. To increase professional skills of criminal justice officers.

(3) To advise State and local law-enforcement agencies in improving law enforcement and the administration of criminal justice;

(4) To make studies and recommendations for the improvement of law enforcement and the administration of criminal justice;

(5) To encourage public support and respect for the criminal justice system in North Carolina;

(6) To seek ways to continue to make North Carolina a safe and secure State for its citizens;

(7) To recommend objectives and priorities for the improvement of law enforcement and criminal justice throughout the State;

(8) To recommend recipients of grants for use in pursuing its objectives, under such conditions as are deemed to be necessary;

(9) To serve as a coordinating committee and forum for discussion of recommendations from its adjunct committees formed pursuant to G.S. 143B-1102; and

(10) To serve as the primary channel through which local law-enforcement departments and citizens can lend their advice, and state their needs, to the Department of Public Safety.

(b) The Governor's Crime Commission shall review the level of gang activity throughout the State and assess the progress and accomplishments of the State, and of local governments, in preventing the proliferation of gangs and addressing the needs of juveniles who have been identified as being associated with gang activity.

The Governor's Crime Commission shall develop recommendations concerning the establishment of priorities and needed improvements with respect to gang prevention to the General Assembly on or before March 1 of each year.

(c) All directives of the Governor's Crime Commission shall be administered by the Director, Crime Control Division of the Department of Public Safety. (1975, c. 663; 1977, c. 11, s. 2; 1979, c. 107, s. 11; 1981, c. 931, s. 3; 1981 (Reg. Sess., 1982), c. 1191, s. 15; 2008-56, s.7; 2008-187, s. 44.5(b); 2011-145, s. 19.1(g), (x), (xx).)

§ 143B-1102. Adjunct committees of the Governor's Crime Commission - creation; purpose; powers and duties.

(a) There are hereby created by way of extension and not limitation, the following adjunct committees of the Governor's Crime Commission: the Judicial Planning Committee, the Juvenile Justice Planning Committee, the Law Enforcement Planning Committee, the Corrections Planning Committee, and the Juvenile Code Revision Committee.

(b) The composition of the adjunct committees shall be as designated by the Governor by executive order, except for the Judicial Planning Committee, the composition of which shall be designated by the Supreme Court. The Governor's appointees shall serve two-year terms beginning March 1, of each odd-numbered year, and members of the Judicial Planning Committee shall serve at the pleasure of the Supreme Court.

(c) The adjunct committees created herein shall report directly to the Governor's Crime Commission and shall have the following powers and duties:

(1) The Law Enforcement Planning Committee shall advise the Governor's Crime Commission on all matters which are referred to it relevant to law enforcement, including detention; shall participate in the development of the law-enforcement component of the State's comprehensive plan; shall consider and recommend priorities for the improvement of law-enforcement services; and shall offer technical assistance to State and local agencies in the planning and implementation of programs contemplated by the comprehensive plan for the improvement of law-enforcement services.

The Law Enforcement Planning Committee shall maintain contact with the National Commission on Accreditation for Law Enforcement Agencies, assist the National Commission in the furtherance of its efforts, adapt the work of the National Commission by an analysis of law-enforcement agencies in North Carolina, develop standards for the accreditation of law-enforcement agencies in North Carolina, make these standards available to those law-enforcement agencies which desire to participate voluntarily in the accreditation program, and assist participants to achieve voluntary compliance with the standards.

(2) The Judicial Planning Committee (which shall be appointed by the Supreme Court) shall establish court improvement priorities, define court improvement programs and projects, and develop an annual judicial plan in accordance with the Crime Control Act of 1976 (Public Law 94-503); shall advise the Governor's Crime Commission on all matters which are referred to it relevant to the courts; shall consider and recommend priorities for the improvement of judicial services; and shall offer technical assistance to State agencies in the planning and implementation of programs contemplated by the comprehensive plan for the improvement of judicial services.

(3) The Corrections Planning Committee shall advise the Governor's Crime Commission on all matters which are referred to it relevant to corrections; shall participate in the development of the adult corrections component of the State's comprehensive plan; shall consider and recommend priorities for the improvement of correction services; and shall offer technical assistance to State agencies in the planning and implementation of programs contemplated by the comprehensive plan for the improvement of corrections.

(4) The Juvenile Justice Planning Committee shall advise the Governor's Crime Commission on all matters which are referred to it relevant to juvenile justice; shall participate in the development of the juvenile justice component of the State's comprehensive plan; shall consider and recommend priorities for the improvement of juvenile justice services; and shall offer technical assistance to State and local agencies in the planning and implementation of programs contemplated by the comprehensive plan for the improvement of juvenile justice.

(5) The Juvenile Code Revision Committee shall study problems relating to young people who come within the juvenile jurisdiction of the district court as defined by Article 23 of Chapter 7A of the General Statutes and develop a legislative plan which will best serve the needs of young people and protect the interests of the State; shall study the existing laws, services, agencies and

commissions and recommend whether they should be continued, amended, abolished or merged; and shall take steps to insure that all agencies, organizations, and private citizens in the State of North Carolina have an opportunity to lend advice and suggestions to the development of a revised juvenile code. If practical, the Committee shall submit a preliminary report to the General Assembly prior to its adjournment in 1977. It shall make a full and complete report to the General Assembly by March 1, 1979. This adjunct committee shall terminate on February 28, 1979.

(d)   The Governor shall have the power to remove any member of any adjunct committee from the Committee for misfeasance, malfeasance or nonfeasance. Each Committee shall meet at the call of the chairman or upon written request of one third of its membership. A majority of a committee shall constitute a quorum for the transaction of business.

(e)   The actions and recommendations of each adjunct committee shall be subject to the final approval of the Governor's Crime Commission. (1975, c. 663; 1977, c. 11, s. 3; 1981, c. 605, s. 1; 1983 (Reg. Sess., 1984), c. 995, s. 8; 2011-145, s. 19.1(x).)

§ 143B-1103. Additional duties of the Grants Management Section.

(a)   Repealed by Session Laws 2011-145, s. 19.1(ww), effective January 1, 2012.

(b)   The Grants Management Section shall administer the State Law Enforcement Assistance Program and such additional related programs as may be established by or assigned to the Section. It shall serve as the single State planning agency for purposes of the Crime Control Act of 1976 (Public Laws 94-503). Administrative responsibilities shall include, but are not limited to, the following:

(1)   Compiling data, establishing needs and setting priorities for funding and policy recommendations for the Governor's Crime Commission;

(2)   Preparing and revising statewide plans for adoption by the Governor's Crime Commission which are designed to improve the administration of criminal justice and to reduce crime in North Carolina;

(3) Advising State and local interests of opportunities for securing federal assistance for crime reduction and for improving criminal justice administration and planning within the State of North Carolina;

(4) Stimulating and seeking financial support from federal, State, and local government and private sources for programs and projects which implement adopted criminal justice administration improvement and crime reduction plans;

(5) Assisting State agencies and units of general local government and combinations thereof in the preparation and processing of applications for financial aid to support improved criminal justice administration, planning and crime reduction;

(6) Encouraging and assisting coordination at the federal, State, and local government levels in the preparation and implementation of criminal justice administration improvements and crime reduction plans;

(7) Applying for, receiving, disbursing, and auditing the use of funds received for the program from any public and private agencies and instrumentalities for criminal justice administration, planning, and crime reduction purposes;

(8) Entering into, monitoring, and evaluating the results of contracts and agreements necessary or incidental to the discharge of its assigned responsibilities;

(9) Providing technical assistance to State and local law-enforcement agencies in developing programs for improvement of the law-enforcement and criminal justice system; and

(10) Taking such other actions as may be deemed necessary or appropriate to carry out its assigned duties and responsibilities.

(c) Repealed by Session Laws 2011-145, s. 19.1(ww), effective January 1, 2012. (1977, c. 11, s. 4; 2011-145, s. 19.1(x), (ww).)

§ 143B-1104. Funding for programs.

(a) Annually, the Division of Administration shall develop and implement a funding mechanism for programs that meet the standards developed under Subpart F of Part 3 of Article 13 of Chapter 143B of the General Statutes. The Division shall ensure that the guidelines for the State and local partnership's funding process include the following requirements:

(1) Fund effective programs. - The Division shall fund programs that it determines to be effective in preventing delinquency and recidivism. Programs that have proven to be ineffective shall not be funded.

(2) Use a formula for the distribution of funds. - A funding formula shall be developed that ensures that even the smallest counties will be able to provide the basic prevention and alternative services to juveniles in their communities.

(3) Allow and encourage local flexibility. - A vital component of the State and local partnership established by this section is local flexibility to determine how best to allocate prevention and alternative funds.

(4) Combine resources. - Counties shall be allowed and encouraged to combine resources and services.

(b) The Division shall adopt rules to implement this section. The Division shall provide technical assistance to County Councils and shall require them to evaluate all State-funded programs and services on an ongoing and regular basis.

(c) The Division of Juvenile Justice of the Department of Public Safety shall report to the Senate and House of Representatives Appropriations Subcommittees on Justice and Public Safety no later than March 1, 2006, and annually thereafter, on the results of the alternatives to commitment demonstration programs funded by Section 16.7 of S.L. 2004-124. The 2007 report and all annual reports thereafter shall also include projects funded by Section 16.11 of S.L. 2005-276 for the 2005-2006 fiscal year. Specifically, the report shall provide a detailed description of each of the demonstration programs, including the numbers of juveniles served, their adjudication status at the time of service, the services/treatments provided, the length of service, the total cost per juvenile, and the six- and 12-month recidivism rates for the juveniles after the termination of program services. (1998-202, s. 1(b); 2000-137, s. 1(b); 2005-276, s. 16.11(c); 2011-145, s. 19.1(l), (x), (ggg).)

§ 143B-1105: Reserved for future codification purposes.

§ 143B-1106: Reserved for future codification purposes.

§ 143B-1107: Reserved for future codification purposes.

§ 143B-1108: Reserved for future codification purposes.

§ 143B-1109: Reserved for future codification purposes.

§ 143B-1110: Reserved for future codification purposes.

§ 143B-1111: Reserved for future codification purposes.

§ 143B-1112: Reserved for future codification purposes.

§ 143B-1113: Reserved for future codification purposes.

§ 143B-1114: Reserved for future codification purposes.

§ 143B-1115: Reserved for future codification purposes.

§ 143B-1116: Reserved for future codification purposes.

§ 143B-1117: Reserved for future codification purposes.

§ 143B-1118: Reserved for future codification purposes.

§ 143B-1119: Reserved for future codification purposes.

§ 143B-1120: Reserved for future codification purposes.

§ 143B-1121: Reserved for future codification purposes.

§ 143B-1122: Reserved for future codification purposes.

§ 143B-1123: Reserved for future codification purposes.

§ 143B-1124: Reserved for future codification purposes.

§ 143B-1125: Reserved for future codification purposes.

§ 143B-1126: Reserved for future codification purposes.

§ 143B-1127: Reserved for future codification purposes.

§ 143B-1128: Reserved for future codification purposes.

§ 143B-1129: Reserved for future codification purposes.

§ 143B-1130: Reserved for future codification purposes.

§ 143B-1131: Reserved for future codification purposes.

§ 143B-1132: Reserved for future codification purposes.

§ 143B-1133: Reserved for future codification purposes.

§ 143B-1134: Reserved for future codification purposes.

§ 143B-1135: Reserved for future codification purposes.

§ 143B-1136: Reserved for future codification purposes.

§ 143B-1137: Reserved for future codification purposes.

§ 143B-1138: Reserved for future codification purposes.

§ 143B-1139: Reserved for future codification purposes.

§ 143B-1140: Reserved for future codification purposes.

§ 143B-1141: Reserved for future codification purposes.

§ 143B-1142: Reserved for future codification purposes.

§ 143B-1143: Reserved for future codification purposes.

§ 143B-1144: Reserved for future codification purposes.

§ 143B-1145: Reserved for future codification purposes.

§ 143B-1146: Reserved for future codification purposes.

§ 143B-1147: Reserved for future codification purposes.

§ 143B-1148: Reserved for future codification purposes.

§ 143B-1149: Reserved for future codification purposes.

Subpart B. Treatment for Effective Community Supervision Program.

§ 143B-1150. Short title.

This Subpart is the "Treatment for Effective Community Supervision Act of 2011" and may be cited by that name. (2011-192, s. 6(b).)

§ 143B-1151. Legislative policy.

The policy of the General Assembly with respect to the Treatment for Effective Community Supervision Program is to support the use of evidence-based practices to reduce recidivism and to promote coordination between State and community-based corrections programs. (2011-192, s. 6(b).)

§ 143B-1152. Definitions.

The following definitions apply in this Subpart:

(1) Certified and licensed. - North Carolina Substance Abuse Professional Practice Board certified or licensed substance abuse professionals or Department of Health and Human Services licensed agencies.

(2) Division. - The Division of Adult Correction.

(3) Repealed by Session Laws 2012-83, s. 55, effective June 26, 2012.

(4) Eligible entity. - A local or regional government, a nongovernmental entity, or collaborative partnership that demonstrates capacity to provide services that address the criminogenic needs of offenders.

(5) Program. - A community-based corrections program.

(6) Secretary. - The Secretary of Public Safety.

(6a) Section. - The Section of Community Corrections of the Division of Adult Correction.

(7) State Board. - The State Community Corrections Advisory Board. (2011-145, s. 19.1(h), (k); 2011-192, s. 6(b); 2012-83, s. 55.)

§ 143B-1153. Goals of community-based corrections programs funded under this Subpart.

The goals of community-based programs funded under this Subpart are to reduce recidivism and to reduce the rate of probation and post-release supervision revocations from the rate in the 2009-2010 fiscal year. (2011-192, s. 6(b).)

§ 143B-1154. Eligible population.

(a) An eligible offender is an adult offender who was convicted of a misdemeanor or a felony offense or is sentenced under the conditional discharge program as defined in G.S. 90-96 and meets any one of the following criteria:

(1) Received a nonincarcerative sentence of a community punishment.

(2) Received a nonincarcerative sentence of an intermediate punishment.

(3) Is serving a term of parole or post-release supervision after serving an active sentence of imprisonment.

(b) The priority populations for programs funded under this Subpart shall be as follows:

(1) Offenders convicted of a felony or offenders sentenced under G.S. 90-96 conditional discharge for a felony offense.

(2) Offenders identified by the Division of Adult Correction using a validated risk assessment instrument to have a high likelihood of reoffending and a moderate to high need for substance abuse treatment. (2011-145, s. 19.1(h); 2011-192, s. 6(b).)

§ 143B-1155. Duties of Division of Adult Correction.

(a) In addition to those otherwise provided by law, the Division of Adult Correction shall have the following duties:

(1) To enter into contractual agreements with eligible entities for the operation of community-based corrections programs and monitor compliance with those agreements.

(2) To develop the minimum program standards, policies, and rules for community-based corrections programs and to consult with the Department of Health and Human Services on those standards, policies, and rules that are applicable to licensed and credentialed substance abuse services.

(3) To monitor, oversee, and evaluate contracted service providers.

(4) To act as an information clearinghouse regarding community-based corrections programs.

(5) To collaborate with the Department of Health and Human Services on focusing treatment resources on high-risk and moderate to high need offenders on probation, parole, and post-release supervision.

(b) The Section of Community Corrections of the Division of Adult Correction shall develop and publish a recidivism reduction plan for the State that accomplishes the following:

(1) Articulates a goal of reducing revocations among people on probation and post-release supervision by twenty percent (20%) from the rate in the 2009-2010 fiscal year.

(2) Identifies the number of people on probation and post-release supervision in each county that are in the priority population and have a likely

need for substance abuse and/or mental health treatment, employment, education, and/or housing.

(3)   Identifies the program models that research has shown to be effective at reducing recidivism for the target population and ranks those programs based on their cost-effectiveness.

(4)   Propose a plan to fund the provision of the most cost-effective programs and services across the State. The plan shall describe the number and types of programs and/or services to be funded in each region of the State and how that program capacity compares with the needs of the target population in that region.

(c)   The Division of Adult Correction shall report by March 1 of each year to the Chairs of the Senate and House of Representatives Appropriations Committees, the Senate and House of Representatives Appropriations Subcommittees on Justice and Public Safety, and the Joint Legislative Oversight Committee on Justice and Public Safety on the status of the Treatment for Effective Community Supervision Program. The report shall include the following information:

(1)   The dollar amount and purpose of funds provided on a contractual basis to service providers for the previous fiscal year.

(2)   An analysis of offender participation data received, including the following:

a.   The number of people on probation and post-release supervision that are in the priority population that received services.

b.   The number of people on probation and post-release supervision that are in the priority population that did not receive services.

c.   The number of people on probation and post-release supervision outside of the priority population that received services.

d.   The type of services provided to these populations.

e.   The rate of revocations and successful completions for people who received services.

f. Other measures as determined appropriate.

(3) The dollar amount needed to provide additional services to meet the needs of the priority population in the upcoming budget year.

(4) Details of personnel, travel, contractual, operating, and equipment expenditures for each program type. (2011-145, s. 19.1(h), (k); 2011-192, s. 6(b); 2012-83, s. 56.)

§ 143B-1156. Contract for services.

(a) The Division of Adult Correction shall contract with service providers through a competitive procurement process to provide community-based services to offenders on probation, parole, or post-release supervision.

(b) Contracts for substance abuse treatment services shall be awarded to certified or licensed substance abuse professionals and appropriately licensed agencies to provide services and use practices that have a demonstrated evidence base.

(c) The Division of Adult Correction, in partnership with the Department of Health and Human Services, shall develop standard service definitions and performance measures for substance abuse and aftercare support services for inclusion in the contracts.

(d) The percentage of funds received by a service provider that may be used for administrative purposes is up to fifteen percent (15%). (2011-145, s. 19.1(h); 2011-192, s. 6(b).)

§ 143B-1157. State Community Corrections Advisory Board.

(a) The State Board shall act as an advisory body to the Secretary with regard to this Subpart. The State Board shall consist of 23 members as follows, to be appointed as provided in subsection (b) of this section:

(1) A member of the Senate.

(2) A member of the House of Representatives.

(3) A judge of the superior court.

(4) A judge of the district court.

(5) A district attorney.

(6) A criminal defense attorney.

(7) A county sheriff.

(8) A chief of a city police department.

(9) Two county commissioners, one from a predominantly urban county and one from a predominantly rural county.

(10) A representative of an existing community-based corrections program.

(11) A member of the public who has been the victim of a crime.

(12) Two rehabilitated ex-offenders.

(13) A member of the business community.

(14) Three members of the general public, one of whom is a person recovering from chemical dependency or who is a previous consumer of substance abuse treatment services.

(15) A victim service provider.

(16) A member selected from each of the following service areas: mental health, substance abuse, and employment and training.

(17) A clerk of superior court.

(b) The membership of the State Board shall be selected as follows:

(1) The Governor shall appoint the following members: the county sheriff, the chief of a city police department, the member of the public who has been the

victim of a crime, a rehabilitated ex-offender, and the members selected from each of the service areas.

(2) The Lieutenant Governor shall appoint the following members: the member of the business community, one member of the general public who is a person recovering from chemical dependency or who is a previous consumer of substance abuse treatment services, and the victim service provider.

(3) The Chief Justice of the North Carolina Supreme Court shall appoint the following members: the superior court judge, the district court judge, the district attorney, the clerk of superior court, the criminal defense attorney, and the representative of an existing community-based corrections program.

(4) The President Pro Tempore of the Senate shall appoint the following members: the member of the Senate, the county commissioner from a predominantly urban county, and one member of the general public.

(5) The Speaker of the House of Representatives shall appoint the following members: the member of the House of Representatives, the county commissioner from a predominantly rural county, and one member of the general public.

In appointing the members of the State Board, the appointing authorities shall make every effort to ensure fair geographic representation of the State Board membership and to ensure that minority persons and women are fairly represented.

(c) The initial members shall serve staggered terms; one-third shall be appointed for a term of one year, one-third shall be appointed for a term of two years, and one-third shall be appointed for a term of three years. The members identified in subdivisions (1) through (7) of subsection (a) of this section shall be appointed initially for a term of one year. The members identified in subdivisions (8) through (13) in subsection (a) of this section shall be appointed initially for a term of two years. The members identified in subdivisions (14) through (16) of subsection (a) of this section shall each be appointed for a term of three years. The additional member identified in subdivision (17) in subsection (a) of this section shall be appointed initially for a term of three years.

At the end of their respective terms of office their successors shall be appointed for terms of three years. A vacancy occurring before the expiration of the term of office shall be filled in the same manner as original appointments for the remainder of the term. Members may be reappointed without limitation.

(d)   Each appointing authority shall have the power to remove a member it appointed from the State Board for misfeasance, malfeasance, or nonfeasance.

(e)   The members of the State Board shall, within 30 days after the last initial appointment is made, meet and elect one member as Chair and one member as Vice-Chair.

(f)   The State Board shall meet at least quarterly and may also hold special meetings at the call of the Chair. For purposes of transacting business, a majority of the membership shall constitute a quorum.

(g)   Any member who has an interest in a governmental agency or unit or private nonprofit agency which is applying for a Treatment for Effective Community Supervision Program contract or which has received a contract and which is the subject of an inquiry or vote by a contract oversight committee, shall publicly disclose that interest on the record and shall take no part in discussion or have any vote in regard to any matter directly affecting that particular grant applicant or grantee. "Interest" in a grant applicant or grantee means a formal and direct connection to the entity, including, but not limited to, employment, partnership, serving as an elected official, board member, director, officer, or trustee, or being an immediate family member of someone who has such a connection to the grant applicant or grantee.

(h)   The members of the State Board shall serve without compensation but shall be reimbursed for necessary travel and subsistence expenses. (2011-192, s. 6(b).)

§ 143B-1158. State Community Corrections Advisory Board; powers and duties.

The State Community Corrections Advisory Board, as defined under this Subpart, has the following duties and responsibilities:

(1)   To review the criteria for monitoring and evaluating community-based corrections programs.

(2) To recommend community-based corrections program priorities.

(3) To review the minimum program standards, policies, and rules for community-based corrections programs.

(4) To review the evaluation of programs funded by this Subpart. (2011-192, s. 6(b).)

§ 143B-1159: Repealed by Session Laws 2013-101, s. 5, effective June 12, 2013.

§ 143B-1160. Program types eligible for funding; community-based corrections programs.

Based on the prioritized populations in G.S. 143B-1154(b), program types eligible for funding may include, but are not limited to, the following:

(1) Substance abuse treatment services, to include co-occurring substance abuse and mental health disorder services, residential, intensive outpatient, outpatient, peer support, and relapse prevention.

(2) Cognitive behavioral programming and other evidence-based programming deemed to be the most cost-effective method to reduce criminogenic needs identified by the risk/needs assessment. (2011-192, s. 6(b).)

§ 143B-1161: Reserved for future codification purposes.

§ 143B-1162: Reserved for future codification purposes.

§ 143B-1163: Reserved for future codification purposes.

§ 143B-1164: Reserved for future codification purposes.

§ 143B-1165: Reserved for future codification purposes.

§ 143B-1166: Reserved for future codification purposes.

§ 143B-1167: Reserved for future codification purposes.

§ 143B-1168: Reserved for future codification purposes.

§ 143B-1169: Reserved for future codification purposes.

§ 143B-1170: Reserved for future codification purposes.

§ 143B-1171: Reserved for future codification purposes.

§ 143B-1172: Reserved for future codification purposes.

§ 143B-1173: Reserved for future codification purposes.

§ 143B-1174: Reserved for future codification purposes.

§ 143B-1175: Reserved for future codification purposes.

§ 143B-1176: Reserved for future codification purposes.

§ 143B-1177: Reserved for future codification purposes.

§ 143B-1178: Reserved for future codification purposes.

§ 143B-1179: Reserved for future codification purposes.

§ 143B-1180: Reserved for future codification purposes.

§ 143B-1181: Reserved for future codification purposes.

§ 143B-1182: Reserved for future codification purposes.

§ 143B-1183: Reserved for future codification purposes.

§ 143B-1184: Reserved for future codification purposes.

§ 143B-1185: Reserved for future codification purposes.

§ 143B-1186: Reserved for future codification purposes.

§ 143B-1187: Reserved for future codification purposes.

§ 143B-1188: Reserved for future codification purposes.

§ 143B-1189: Reserved for future codification purposes.

§ 143B-1190: Reserved for future codification purposes.

§ 143B-1191: Reserved for future codification purposes.

§ 143B-1192: Reserved for future codification purposes.

§ 143B-1193: Reserved for future codification purposes.

§ 143B-1194: Reserved for future codification purposes.

§ 143B-1195: Reserved for future codification purposes.

§ 143B-1196: Reserved for future codification purposes.

§ 143B-1197: Reserved for future codification purposes.

§ 143B-1198: Reserved for future codification purposes.

§ 143B-1199: Reserved for future codification purposes.

Part 7. Office of External Affairs.

§ 143B-1200. Assistance Program for Victims of Rape and Sex Offenses.

(a) Establishment of Program. - There is established an Assistance Program for Victims of Rape and Sex Offenses, hereinafter referred to as the "Program." The Secretary shall administer and implement the Program and shall have authority over all assistance awarded through the Program. The Secretary shall promulgate rules and guidelines for the Program.

(b) Victims to Be Provided Free Forensic Medical Examinations. - It is the policy of this State to arrange for victims to obtain forensic medical examinations free of charge. Whenever a forensic medical examination is conducted as a result of a sexual assault or an attempted sexual assault that occurred in this State, the Program shall pay for the cost of the examination. A medical facility or medical professional that performs a forensic medical examination on the victim of a sexual assault or attempted sexual assault shall not seek payment for the examination except from the Program.

(c) No Billing of Victim. - A medical facility or medical professional that performs a forensic medical examination shall accept payment made under this section as payment in full of the amount owed for the cost of the examination and other eligible expenses and shall not bill victims, their personal insurance, Medicaid, Medicare, or any other collateral source for the examination. Furthermore, a medical facility or medical professional shall not seek reimbursement from the Program after one year from the date of the examination.

(d) Eligible Expenses. - Medical facilities and medical professionals who perform forensic medical examinations shall do so using a Sexual Assault Evidence Collection Kit. Payments by the Program for the forensic medical examination shall be limited to the following:

Service	Maximum Amount Paid by Program
Physician or SANE Nurse	$350.00
Hospital/Facility Fee	$250.00
Other Expenses Deemed Eligible by the Program	$200.00
Total:	$800.00

(e) Payment Directly to Provider. - The Program shall make payment directly to the medical facility or medical professional. Bills submitted to the Program for payment shall specify under which categories of expense set forth in subsection (d) of this section the billed services fall.

(f) Additional Victim Notification Requirements. - A medical facility or medical professional who performs a forensic medical examination shall encourage victims to submit an application for reimbursement of medical expenses beyond the forensic examination to the Crime Victims Compensation Commission for consideration of those expenses. Medical facilities and medical professionals shall not seek reimbursement from the Program after one year from the date of the exam.

(g) Judicial Review. - Upon an adverse determination by the Secretary on a claim for assistance under this Part, a victim is entitled to judicial review of that decision. The person seeking review shall file a petition in the Superior Court of Wake County.

(h) The Secretary shall adopt rules to encourage, whenever practical, the use of licensed registered nurses trained under G.S. 90-171.38(b) to conduct medical examinations and procedures.

(i) Definitions. - The following definitions apply in this section:

(1) Forensic medical examination. - An examination provided to a sexual assault victim by medical personnel trained to gather evidence of a sexual assault in a manner suitable for use in a court of law. The examination should include at a minimum an examination of physical trauma, a patient interview, a determination of penetration or force, and a collection and evaluation of evidence. This definition shall be interpreted consistently with 28 C.F.R. § 90.2(b) and other relevant federal law.

(2) SANE nurse. - A Sexual Assault Nurse Examiner that is a licensed registered nurse trained pursuant to G.S. 90-171.38(b) who obtains preliminary histories, conducts in-depth interviews, and conducts medical examinations of rape victims or victims of related sexual offenses.

(3) Sexual assault. - Any of the following crimes:

a. First-degree rape as defined in G.S. 14-27.2.

b. Second degree rape as defined in G.S. 14-27.3.

c. First-degree sexual offense as defined in G.S. 14-27.4.

d. Second degree sexual offense as defined in G.S. 14-27.5.

e. Statutory rape as defined in G.S. 14-27.7A.

(4) Sexual Assault Evidence Collection Kit. - The kit assembled and paid for by the Program and used to conduct forensic medical examinations in this State. (1981, c. 931, s. 2; 1981 (Reg. Sess., 1982), c. 1191, s. 16; 2009-354, s. 1(b); 2011-145, s. 19.1(x1); 2011-391, s. 43(i).)

§ 143B-1201. Restitution; actions.

(a)   The Program shall be an eligible recipient for restitution or reparation under G.S. 15A-1021, 15A-1343, 148-33.1, 148-33.2, 148-57.1, and any other applicable statutes.

(b)   When any victim who:

(1)   Has received assistance under this Part;

(2)   Brings an action for damages arising out of the rape, attempted rape, sexual offense, or attempted sexual offense for which she received that assistance; and

(3)   Recovers damages including the expenses for which she was awarded assistance, the court shall make as part of its judgment an order for reimbursement to the Program of the amount of any assistance awarded less reasonable expenses allocated by the court to that recovery.

(c)   Funds appropriated to the Department of Public Safety for this program may be used to purchase and distribute rape evidence collection kits approved by the State Bureau of Investigation. (1981, c. 931, s. 2; 1983, c. 715, s. 3; 2008-107, s. 18.2(b); 2009-354, s. 2; 2011-145, s. 19.1(g), (x1).)

Vision Books Order Form

Fax Orders: 1-980-299-5965

Phone Orders: 1-704-898-0770

E-mail Orders: www.visionbooks.org

Mail Orders: Vision Books, LLC
P.O. Box 42406
Charlotte, NC 28215

Shipp To:
Name_____
Address_____
City_____State_____Zip_____
Phone_____Fax_____
Email_____@_____

Bill To: We can bill a third party on your behalf.
Name_____
Address_____
City_____State_____Zip_____
Phone____(_____)_____Fax_____
Email_____@_____

Pamphlet Number ($15.00 Each)	Qty	Total Cost
_____	_____	_____
_____	_____	_____
_____	_____	_____
_____	_____	_____
_____	_____	_____
_____	_____	_____
_____	_____	_____
_____	_____	_____
<u>Full Volume Set 1-92</u>	<u>92 Pamphlets</u>	<u>1,380.00</u>

Free Shipping & Handling on Full Volume Orders
Add $1.00 Shipping & Handling Per Pamphlet $_____

Total Cost $_____

Thank you for your support. Management!

DID YOU ENJOY THIS BOOK?

Vision Books, LLC would like to hear from you! If you or someone you know has been fasely imprisoned, we would like to hear your story. If the 'North Carolina Criminal Law and Procedure' has had an effect in your life or if you have suggestions, we would like to hear from you. Send your letters to:

Vision Books, LLC
Attn: Staff Writers
P.O. Box 42406
Charlotte, NC 28215
Email: staff@visionbooks.org

Order Additional Copies:

Fax Orders: 1-980-299-5965

Phone Orders: 1-704-898-0770

E-mail Orders: www.visionbooks.org

Mail Orders: Vision Books, LLC
                    P.O. Box 42406
                    Charlotte, NC 28215

www.ingramcontent.com/pod-product-compliance
Lightning Source LLC
Chambersburg PA
CBHW051626170526
45167CB00001B/77